GW01605661

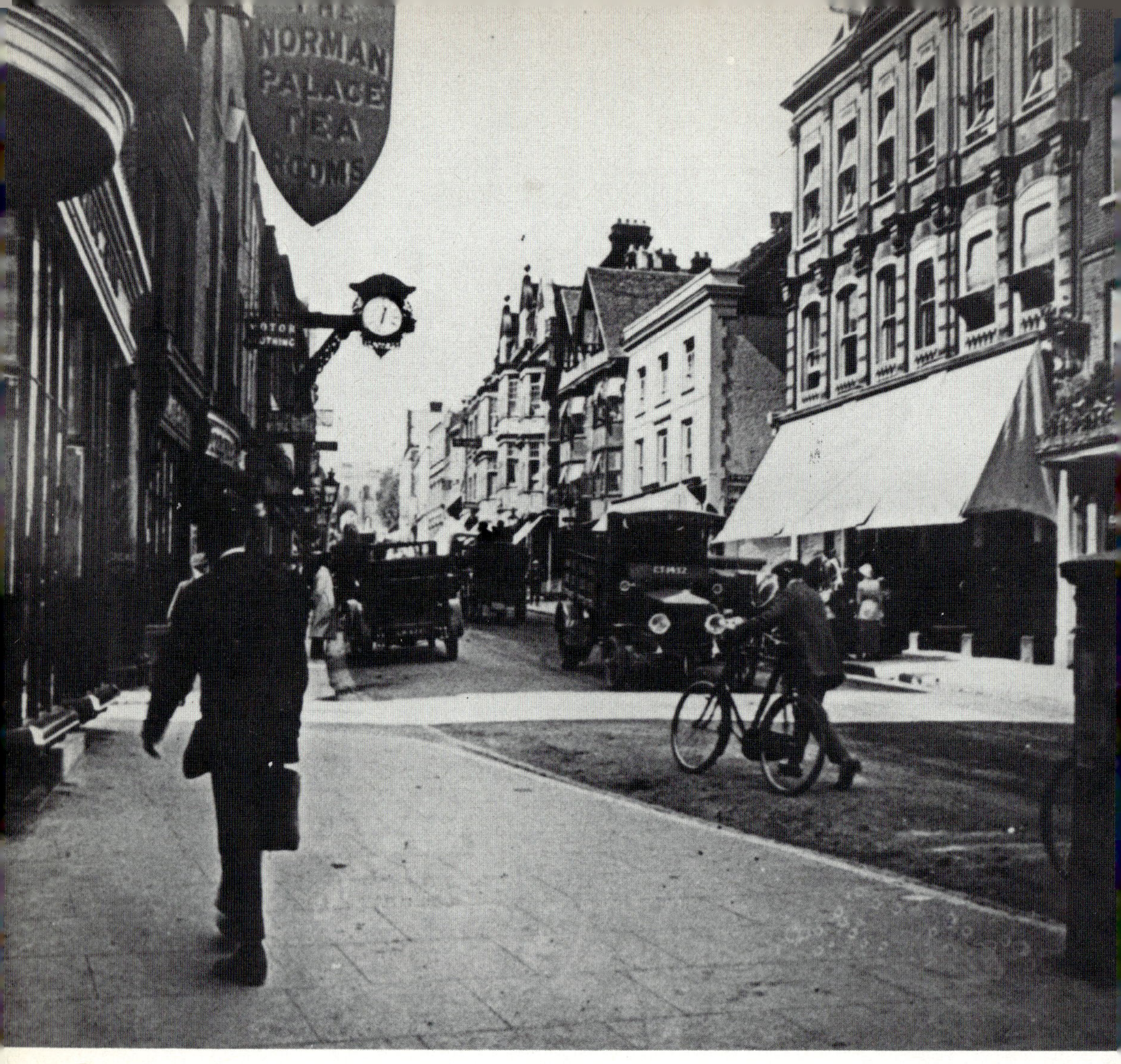

Winchester High St. looking towards the Westgate from the Butter Cross, about 1911.

IN AND AROUND WINCHESTER

in old photographs

collected and written by

EDWARD ROBERTS

General Editor Laurence Oxley

LAURENCE OXLEY

Broad Street. Alresford. Hampshire

1977

ISBN 0 9504096 1 8

Printed in Great Britain by
The Scolar Press Limited, Ilkley, Yorkshire.

Contents

Acknowledgements

The author and publisher are happy to have an opportunity to thank the following people and institutions who kindly lent photographs to be copied. In the case of Winchester City Museum, the plate number is followed by the museum catalogue number in brackets.

Mr. R. A. Baverstock (frontispiece, 19.): Miss Best (103, 105, 113.): Mr. Bunney (106, 118, 119.): Mrs. Chandler (137.): Capt. M. Dann (139, 140.): Mr. P. A. Finch (125, 126, 130.): Mrs. Griffin (143.): Miss Galbraith (96, 135, 136.): Hants. County Library (29, 62, 73, 76, 77.): Hants. County Museum Service (19, 94.): Hants. Record Office (3, 8, 11, 22, 38, 68.): Mr. and Mrs. E. Harfield (120 – 122.): Mr. M. Hewin (43.): Mr. J. Holdaway (51.): Miss G. Houghton (150, 151.): Mr. H. Jewell (45.): Mr. H. Jones (27, 124.): Capt. Kitchin (89, 147.): Mr. D. Long (13, 23, 72, 75, 78, 80, 85, 97, 133, 142.): Mrs. Macleod (46, 47): Mr. C. Martin (7.): Mrs. New (94.): Mr. H. E. North (49.): Mr. L. Oxley (55.): Prof. A. Phillips (145.): Royal Hants. County Hospital (54.): The Misses Smith (10, 26, 65, 72.): Mrs. L. Stockwell (81.): Sparsholt Women's Institute (127–129, 131.): Miss. F. Tanner (141.): Twyford Women's Institute (39, 102, 104, 107, 109–112.): Mr. A. Unsworth (146.): Mr. Warren (9, 17, 25, 32, 34, 35, 37, 44, 59, 100, 138.): Mr. G. Watson (20, 84.): Mr. W. Webb (148.): Mr. K. Walker (67.): Miss I. Whatmore (101.): Mr. S. C. Whitcher (98, 99.): Mr. and Mrs. J. Wilmot (95, 144.): Winchester City Museum (1 [3570], 2 [3569]. 4 [3714], 5 [1187], 6 [3815], 12 [6063], 14 [7599], 15 [5410], 16 [3563], 18 [7822], 21 [6402], 24 [5609], 28 [5606], 30 [7380], 31 [3736], 36 [3793], 38 [5975], 40 [2737], 41 [3599], 42 [7492], 48 [6362], 50 [5375], 52 [2949], 53 [3311], 56 [2706], 57 [6043], 58 [3368], 60 [3185], 61 [3758], 63 [3831], 64 [7352], 66 [3147], 69 [2799], 70 [3099], 71 [3910], 74 [1062], 79 [6562], 83 [3059], 86 [3918], 87 [3909], 88 [7582], 91 [3173], 92 [3199], 93 [3200], 108 [2721], 114 [3250], 115 [3219], 116 [3023], 117 [2898A], 123 [4447], 132 [3938], 149 [4151].): Mr. L. A. Lampard (82).

Many people have kindly lent photographs which have not been included in this book. The author and publisher would like to thank them for their co-operation.

Mr. Peter Jacobs undertook the copying of most of these photographs, many calling for considerable skill.

Introduction

This book is the result of hours of fascinating conversation with people who remember the Winchester area as it was many years ago. I would like to thank them all for generously giving their time to me. Regrettably, it is impossible to mention them all by name, but I hope that they will feel that the publication of this book, which makes permanent some of their cherished memories, will be some repayment for their kindness.

Edward Roberts.

Brandy Mount,
Cheriton.
1977.

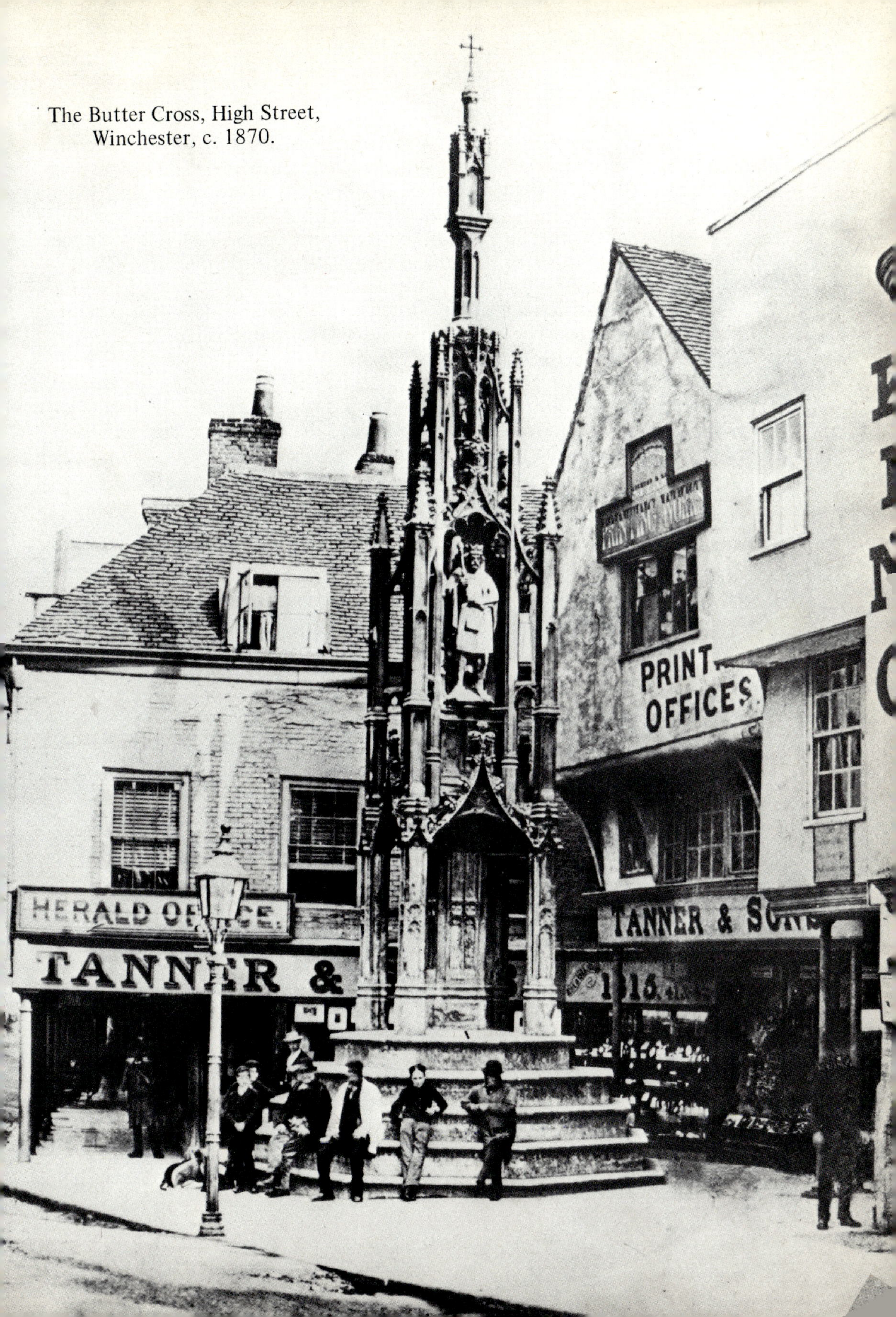

The Butter Cross, High Street, Winchester, c. 1870.

2 (Below) The courtyard of the George Hotel in about 1870. The George, which had been one of Winchester's principal inns since the Middle Ages was demolished in 1956 for road widening. It stood on the corner of Jewry St. and High St., where Barclays Bank now stands. This picture was taken from the High St. entrance. On the far side of the courtyard on the first floor was the ballroom and beneath it can be seen the gateway leading into St. George's St.

3 (Above right) Outside the George Hotel c. 1910, looking down the High St. towards the Butter Cross. The shop adjoining the George in this picture belonged to Mr. Edwin Hillier, the florist and nurseryman.

4 (Below right) c. 1895. The shop of Mr. Edwin Hillier (the forerunner of the present well-known nursery business) adjoined the old George Inn. This shop was demolished at the same time as the George.

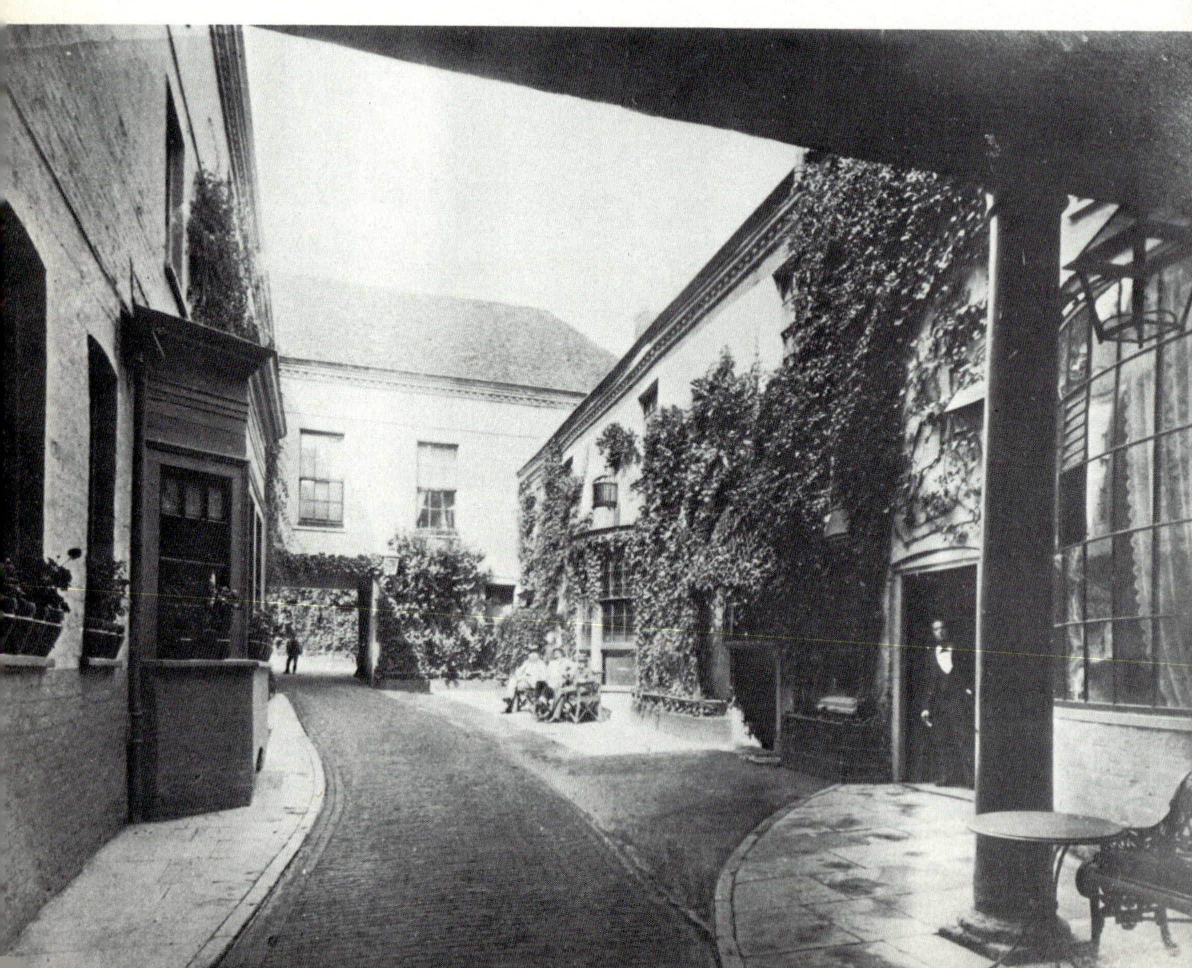

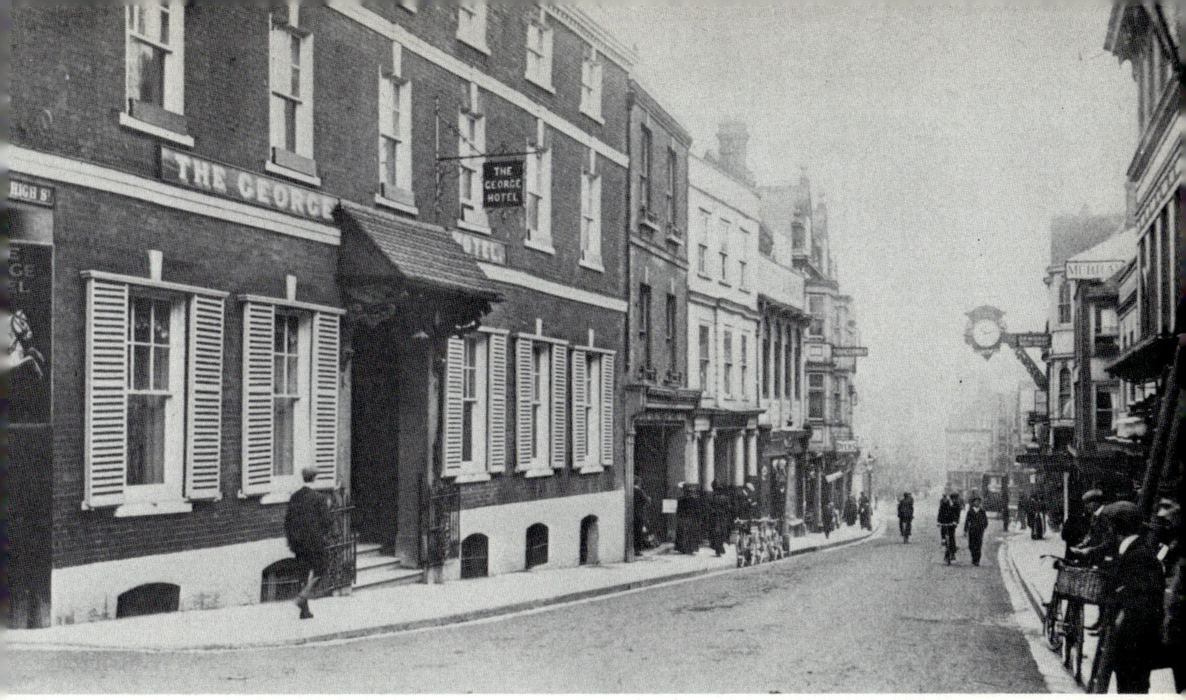

THE GEORGE
THE GEORGE HOTEL

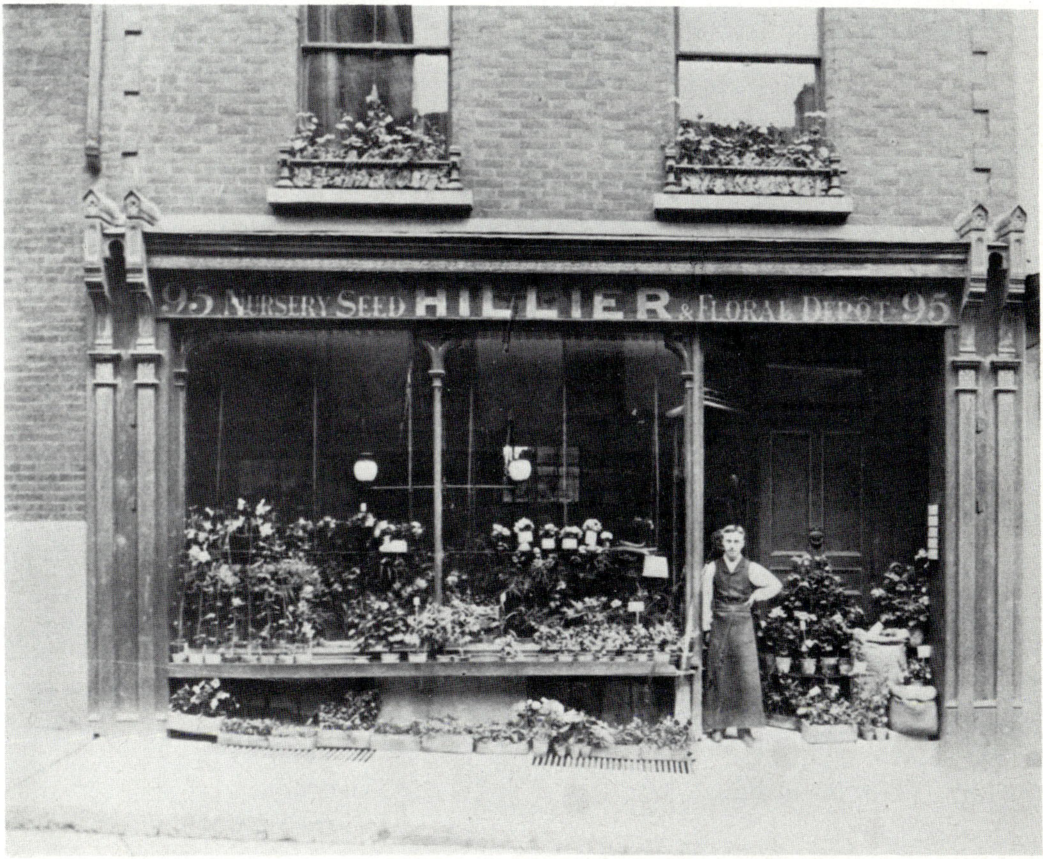

95 NURSERY SEED HILLIER & FLORAL DEPÔT 95

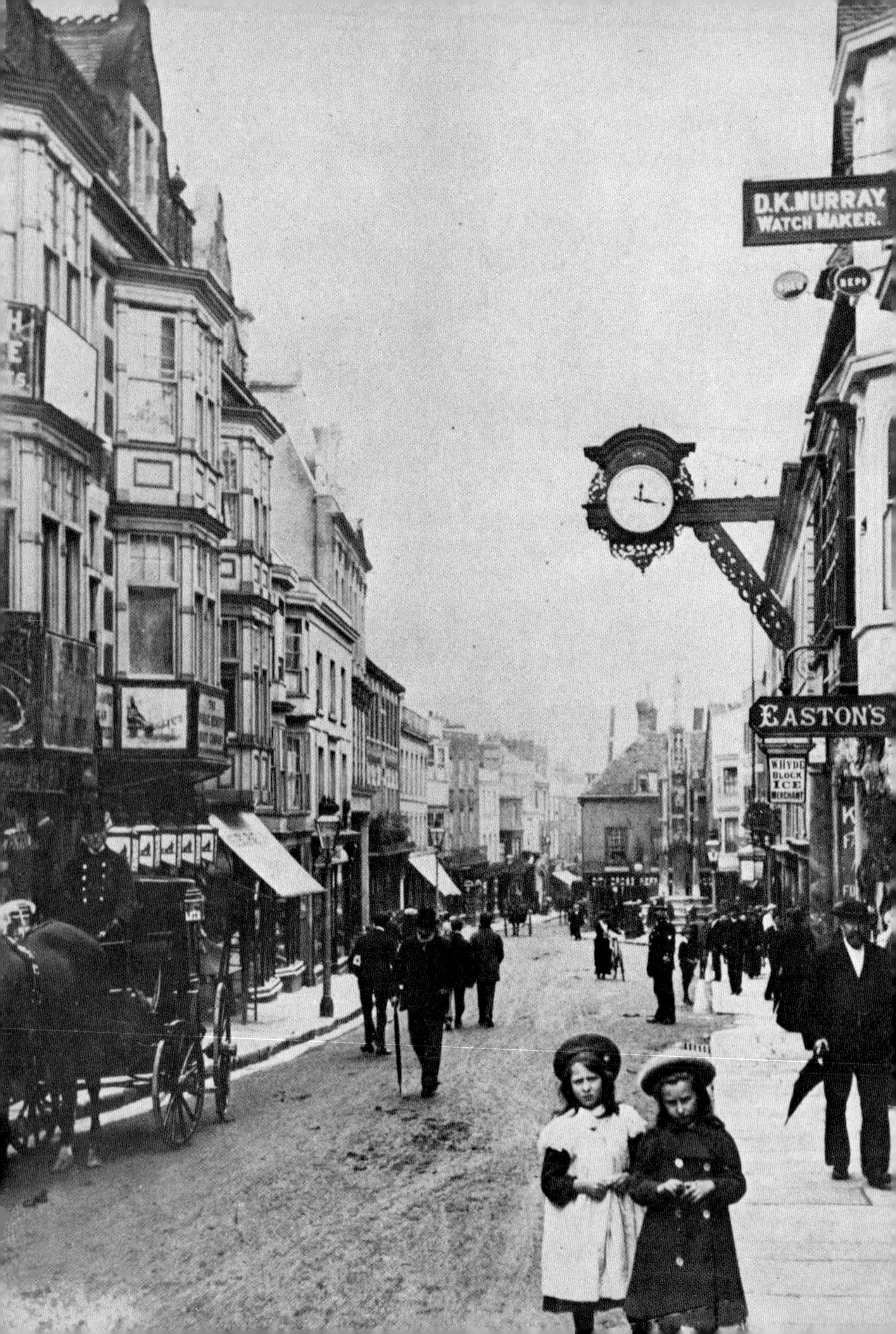
D.K.MURRAY
WATCH MAKER.
EASTON'S
W HYDE
BLOCK
ICE
MERCHANT

5 (Left) High St. looking down towards the Butter Cross. c. 1900.

6 (Below) The Black Swan Hotel on the corner of High St. and Southgate St., c. 1875. The Black Swan was demolished between the wars, but the Black Swan sign, which can be seen on the right of the building in this picture, has been placed above the modern shops which occupy this site. On the left of the picture, the shop of Edward Corfe, tailor and woollen draper, may be seen (now an optician's).

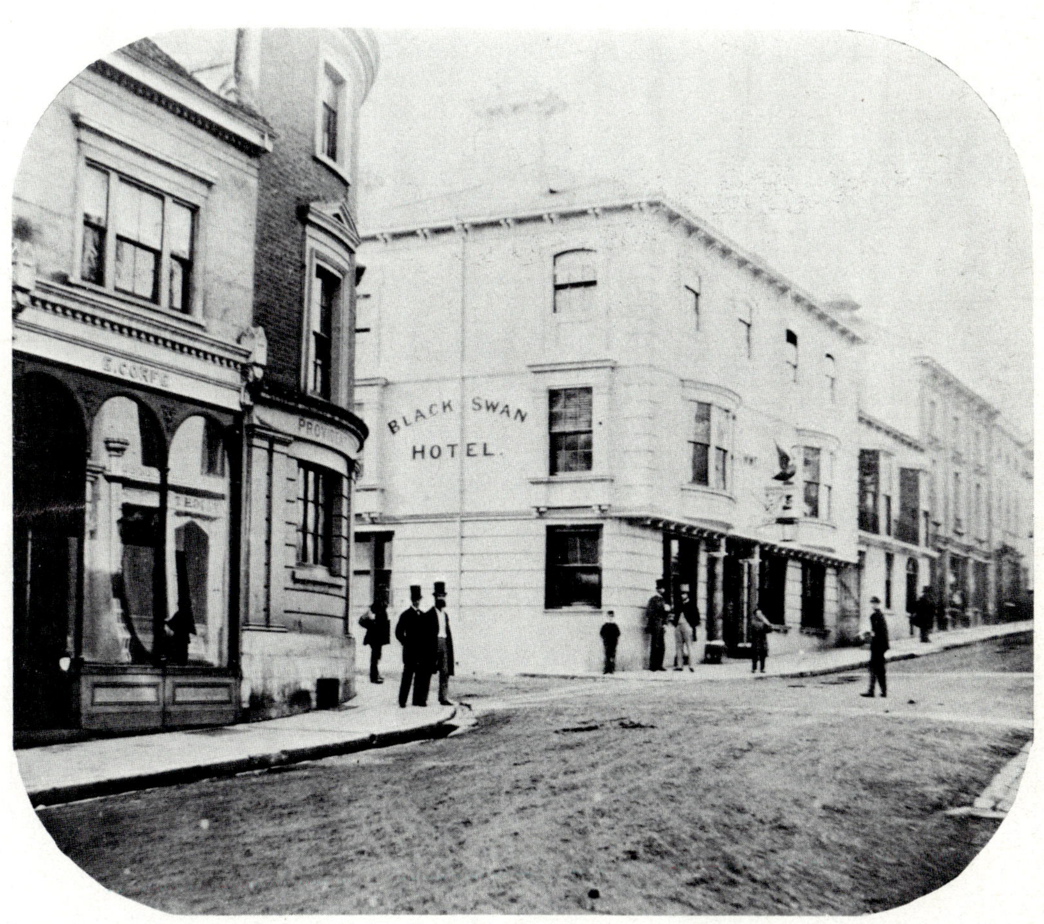

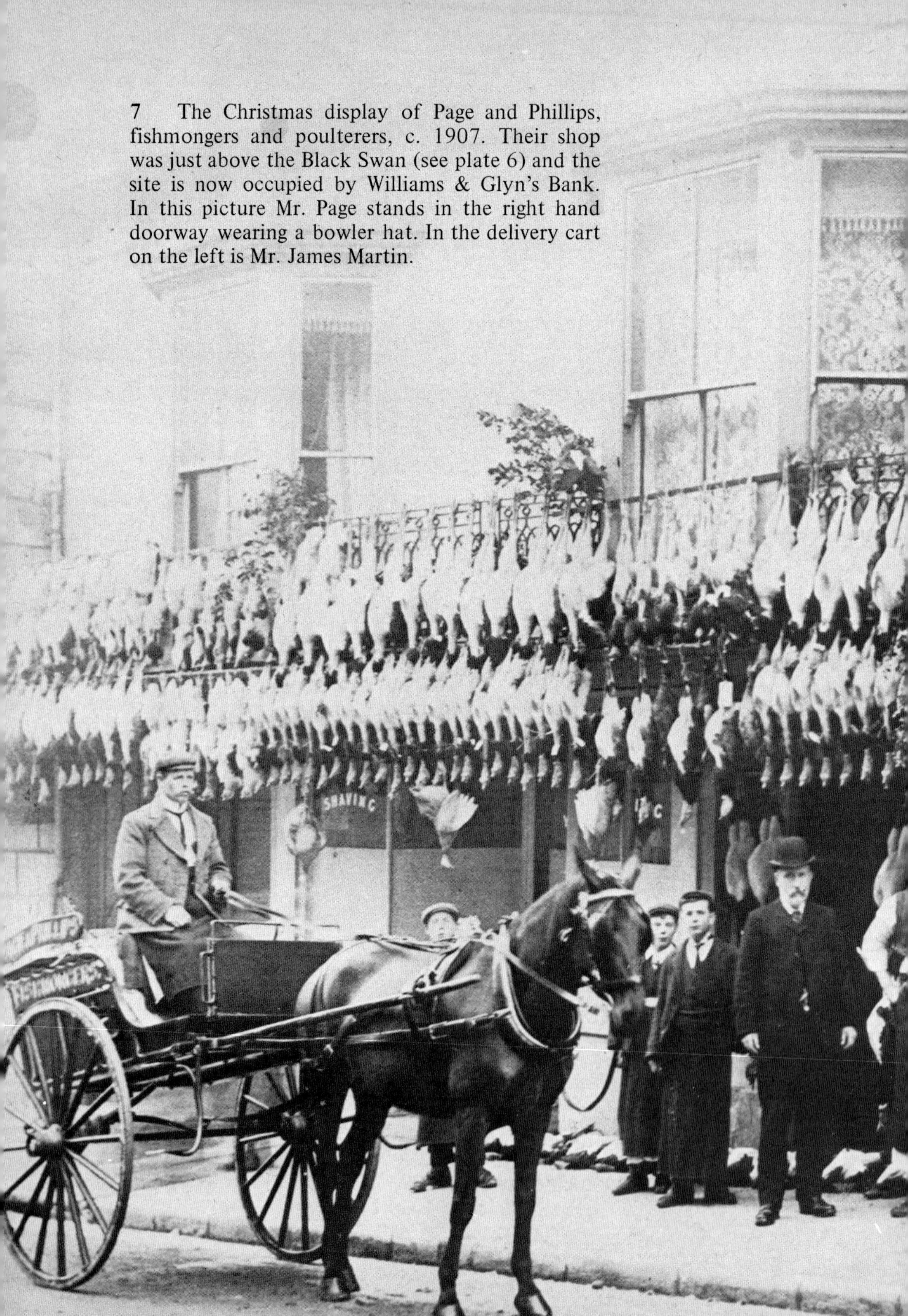

7 The Christmas display of Page and Phillips, fishmongers and poulterers, c. 1907. Their shop was just above the Black Swan (see plate 6) and the site is now occupied by Williams & Glyn's Bank. In this picture Mr. Page stands in the right hand doorway wearing a bowler hat. In the delivery cart on the left is Mr. James Martin.

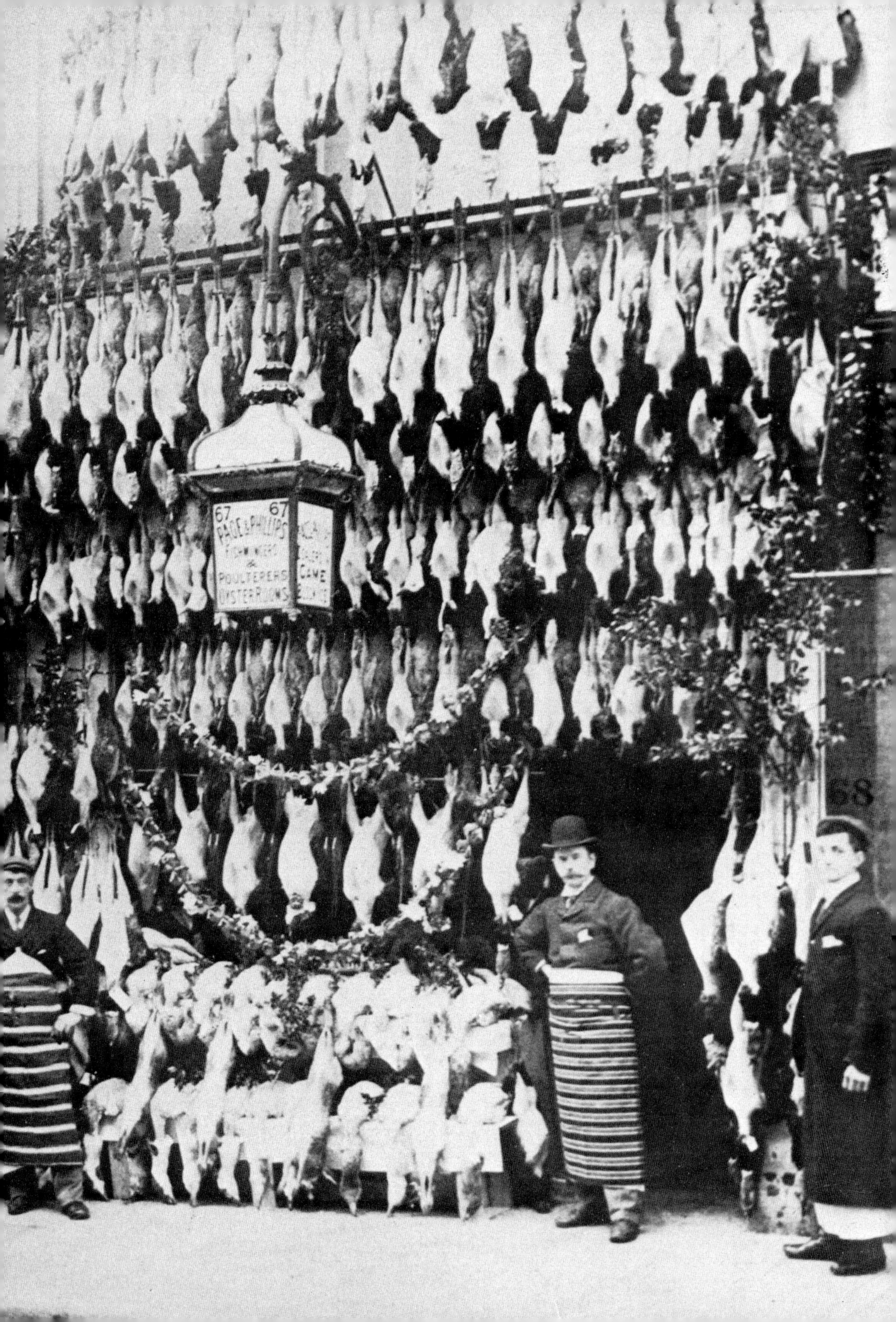
67 67
PAGE & PHILLIPS
POULTERERS
OYSTER ROOMS
GAME
68

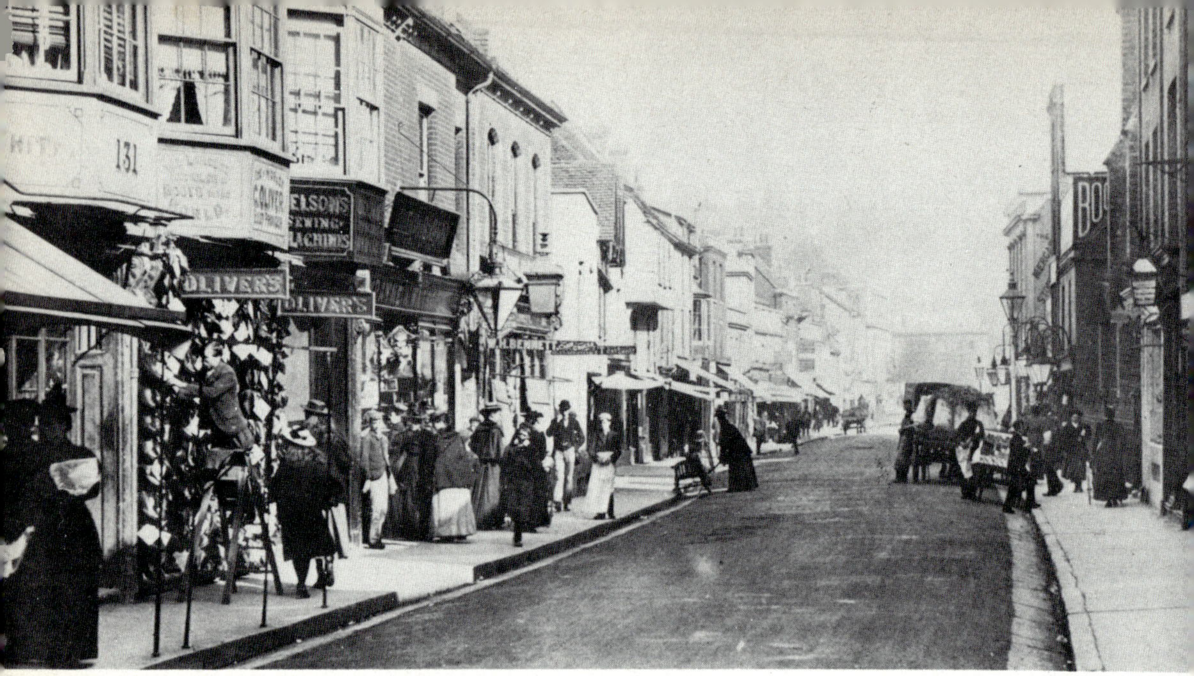

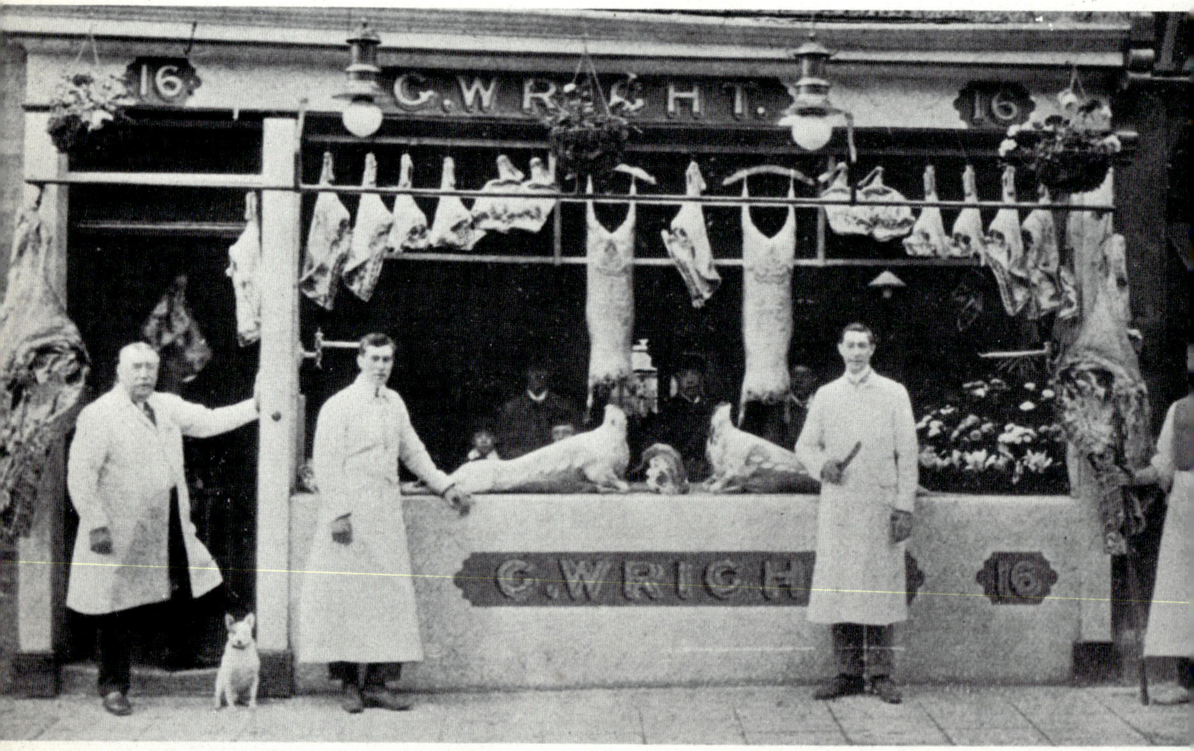

8 (Above left) The High St. below the Pentice and looking towards St. Giles's Hill, c. 1903. On the left of the picture is Mr. G. Oliver's bootshop. Oliver's shop is still there today. Some way down on the right may be seen a multitude of newly-installed lamps outside Sherriff and Ward, the drapers. Such brilliant lighting had not been seen in Winchester before and people exclaimed that they could now see a pin in the road at night.

9 (Below left) About 1908, Mr. George Wright's shop at 16 High St. (opposite what is now Marks and Spencer). Mr. Wright, who was a kindly and jovial man, stands in the shop doorway.

10 Mr. George Smith's sweet shop at 156 High St. (now Read's sewing machine shop). This picture, taken in about 1920, shows a window display for a Trade Festival competition. Miss Nora Southwell, an assistant, stands in the doorway.

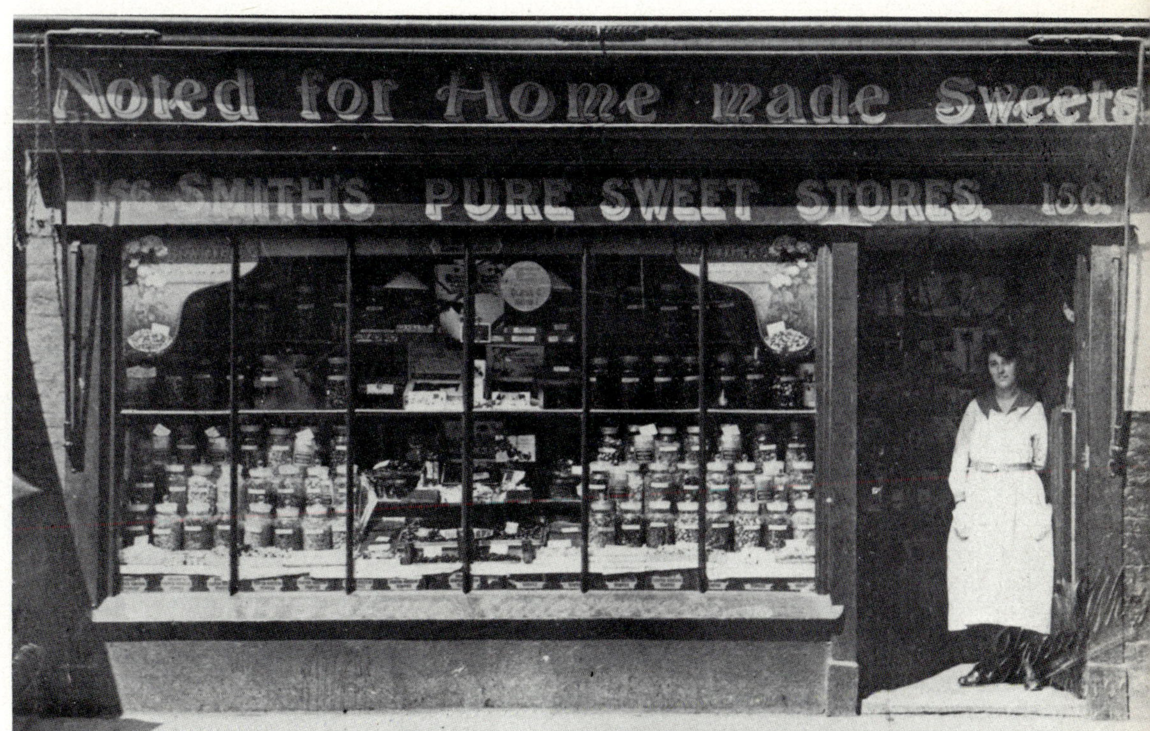

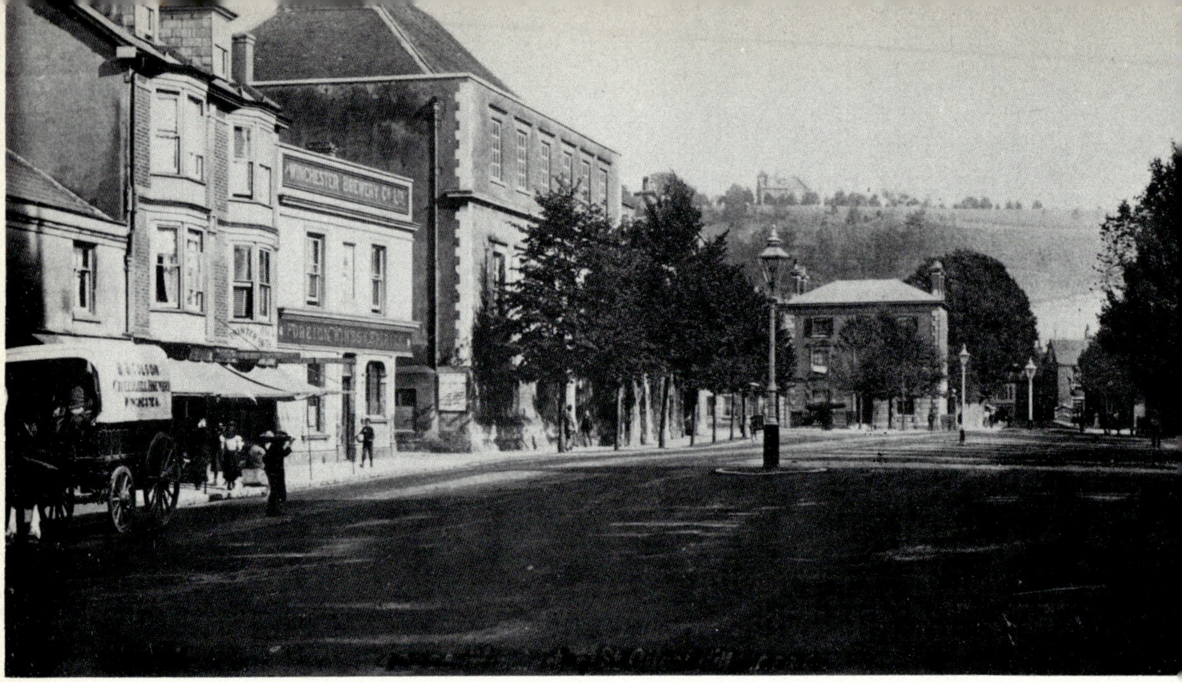

WINCHESTER BREWERY Co Ltd

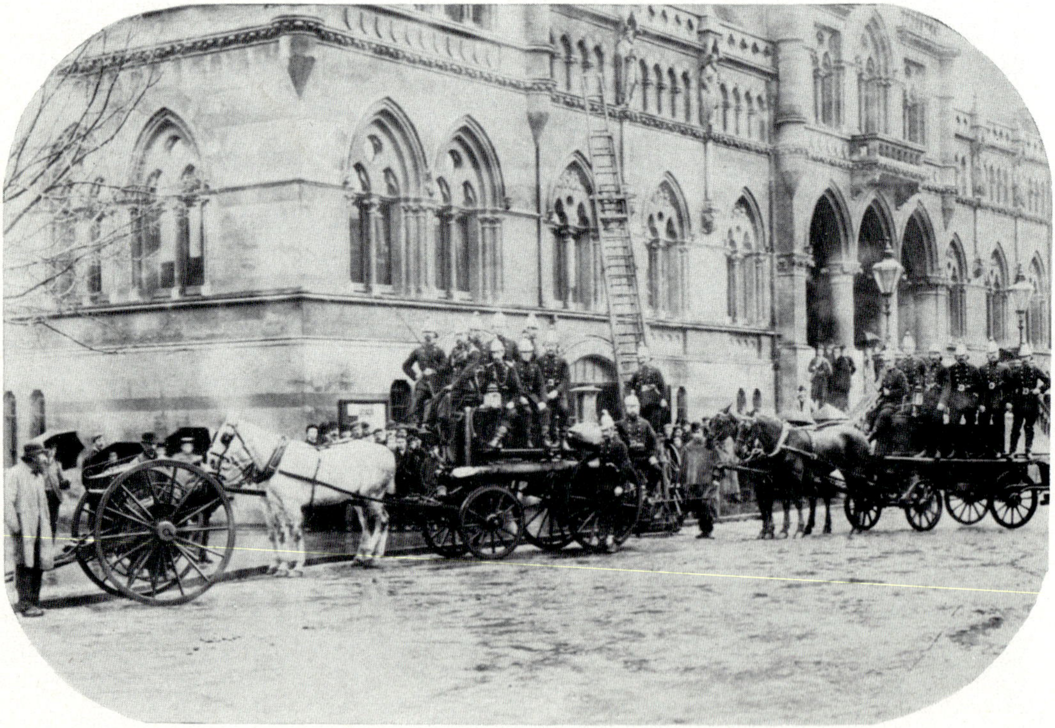

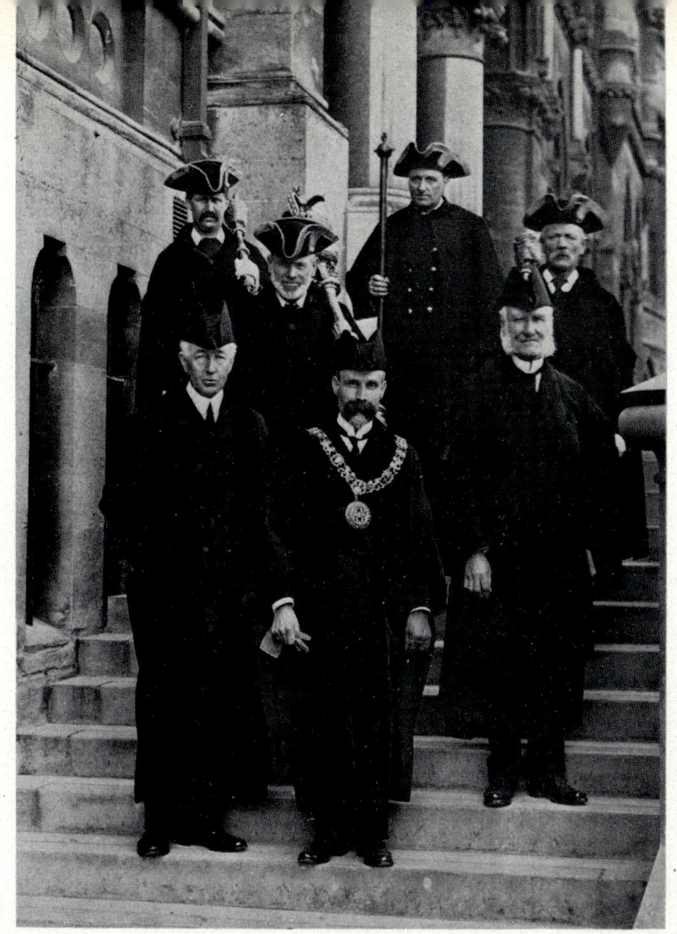

11 (Above left) The Broadway opposite the Guildhall c. 1895, before the statue of King Alfred was erected. Through the trees, a glimpse can be caught of the chalk cutting for the Great Western Railway made in 1885 (see plate 17). The chalk still seems to be quite freshly cut.

12 (Below left) Winchester City Fire Brigade in 1894. W. Gamon, the captain, holds the reins of the leading pair. The fire station was then in the Guildhall and behind the funnel of the fire engine may just be seen the archway which led to the space where it was stored. Inconveniently, the horses were stabled at Station Hill.

13 (Above) The Mayor of Winchester in 1909 stands on the Guildhall steps. He was Councillor F. W. King of Teague & King, the music shop in the High St. In the right foreground is Mr. W. Bailey, the Town Clerk, and on the left, Mr. Fort, the second master at Winchester College.

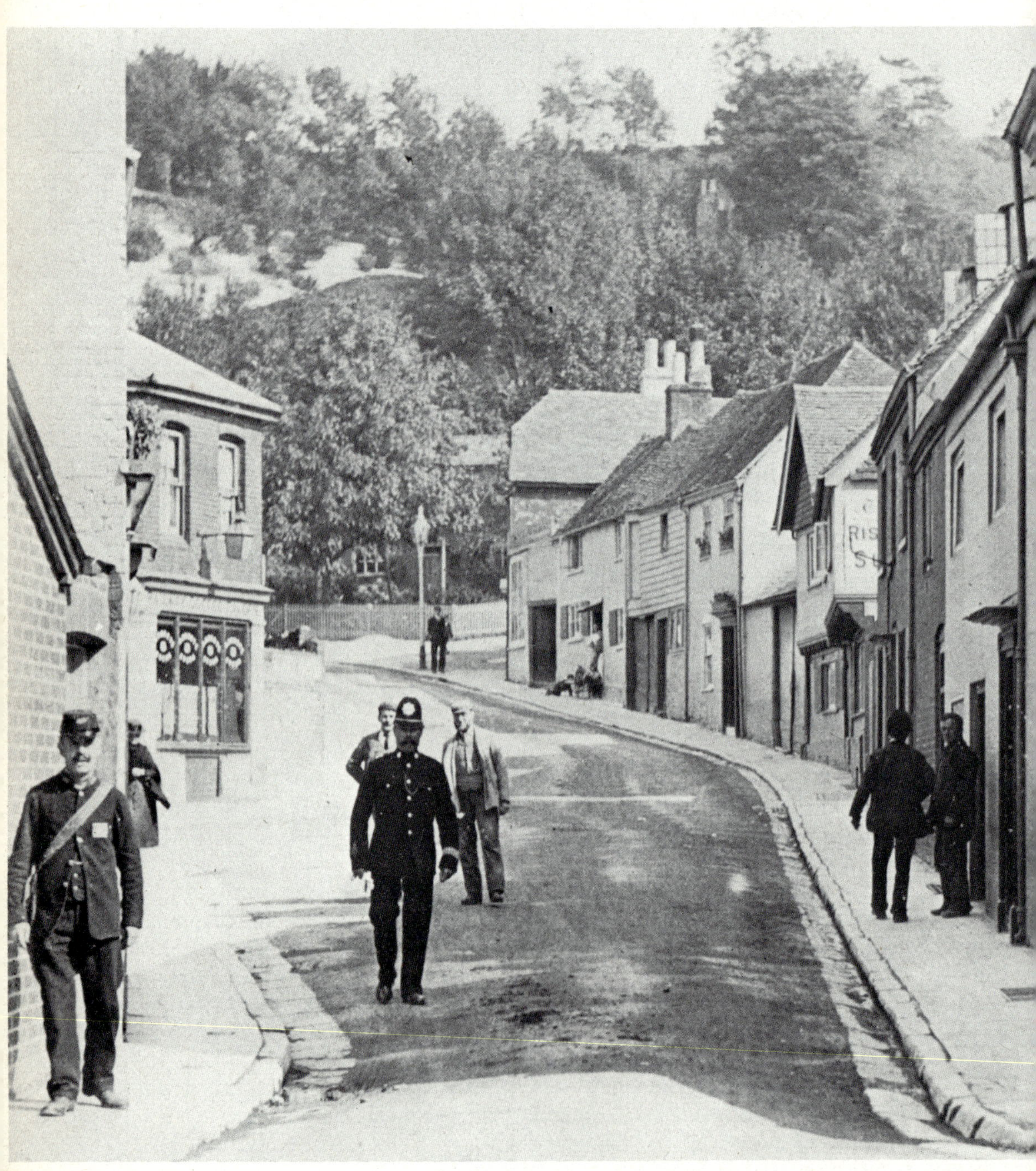

14 (Left) Bridge St. looking towards St. Giles's Hill, c. 1900. As well as illustrating the costume of a Victorian postman and policeman, this picture shows how narrow was the entrance from Bridge St. into Chesil St.

15 (Below) Chesil St. looking north, c. 1895. On the right is the Old Chesil Rectory and adjoining it are the houses that were demolished when Bridge St. was widened.

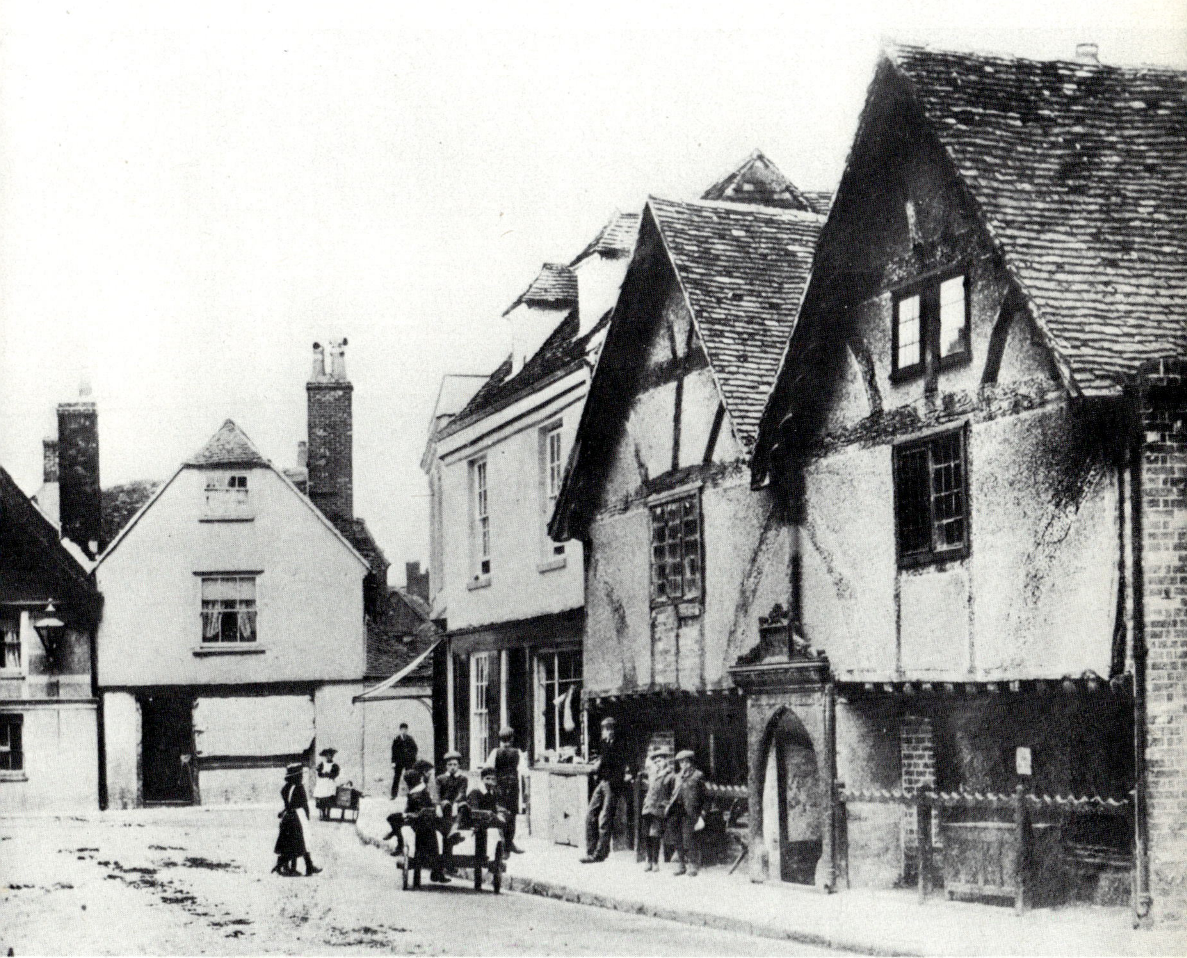

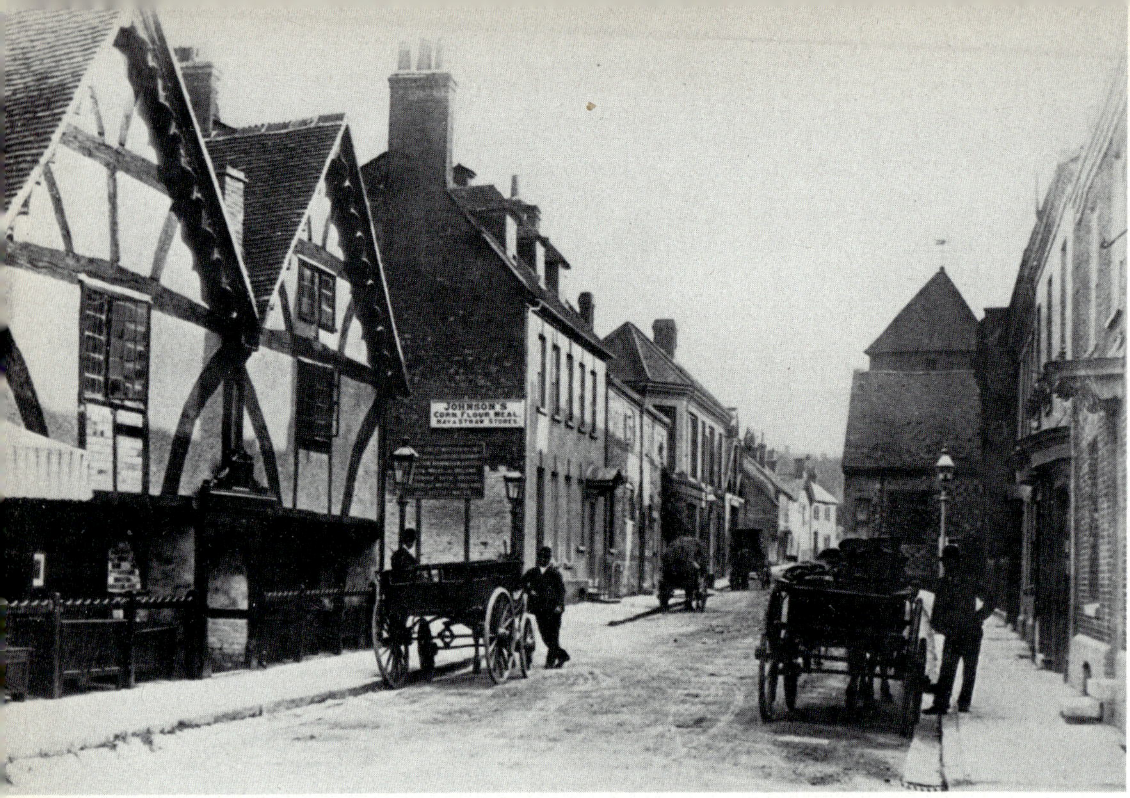

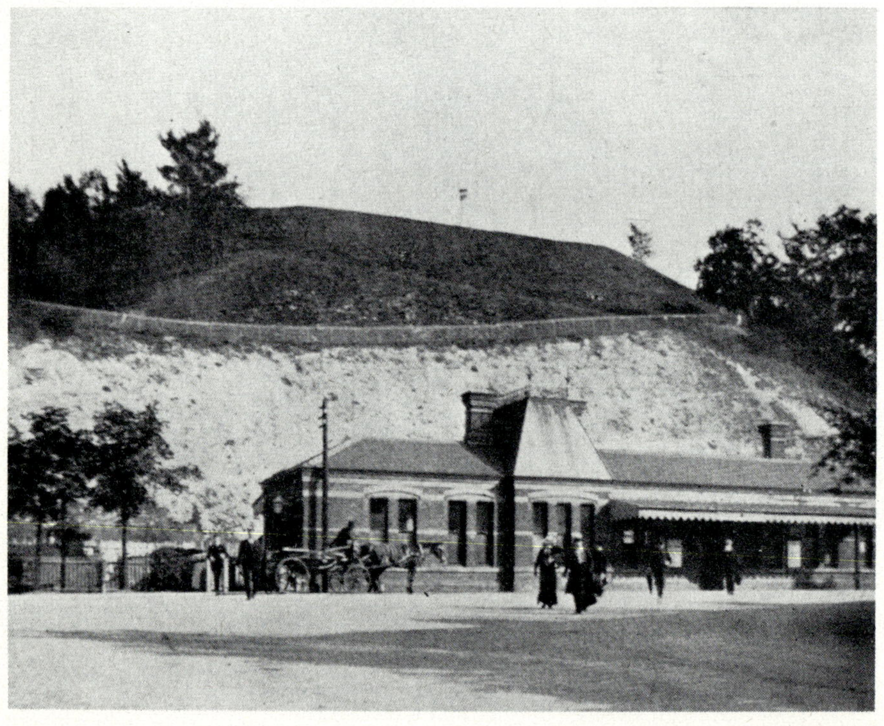

16 (Above left) About 1900, Chesil St. looking South towards St. Peter's Church. On the left, just beyond the Old Chesil Rectory is the entrance to the G.W.R. station (now closed).

17 (Below left) Chesil St. station c. 1900. The G.W.R. line from Newbury to Chesil St. Winchester was opened in 1885.

18 (Below) c. 1880. Looking across Chesil St. and down Wharf Hill. The tower of Winchester College can be seen in the distance. The man on the far left is Mr. Ballard, the blacksmith, standing outside his shop. A little further down is his assistant holding blacksmith's tongs.

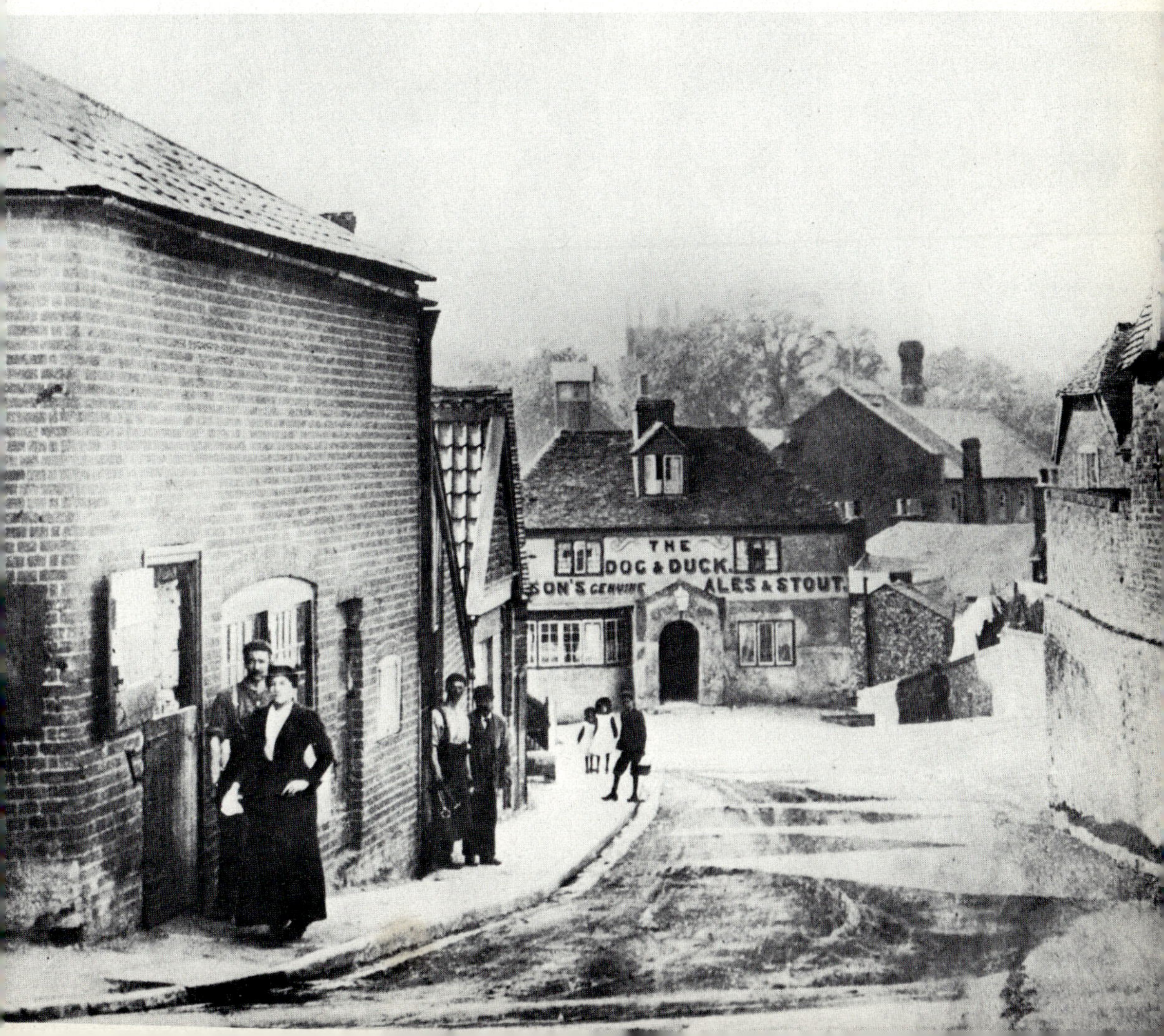

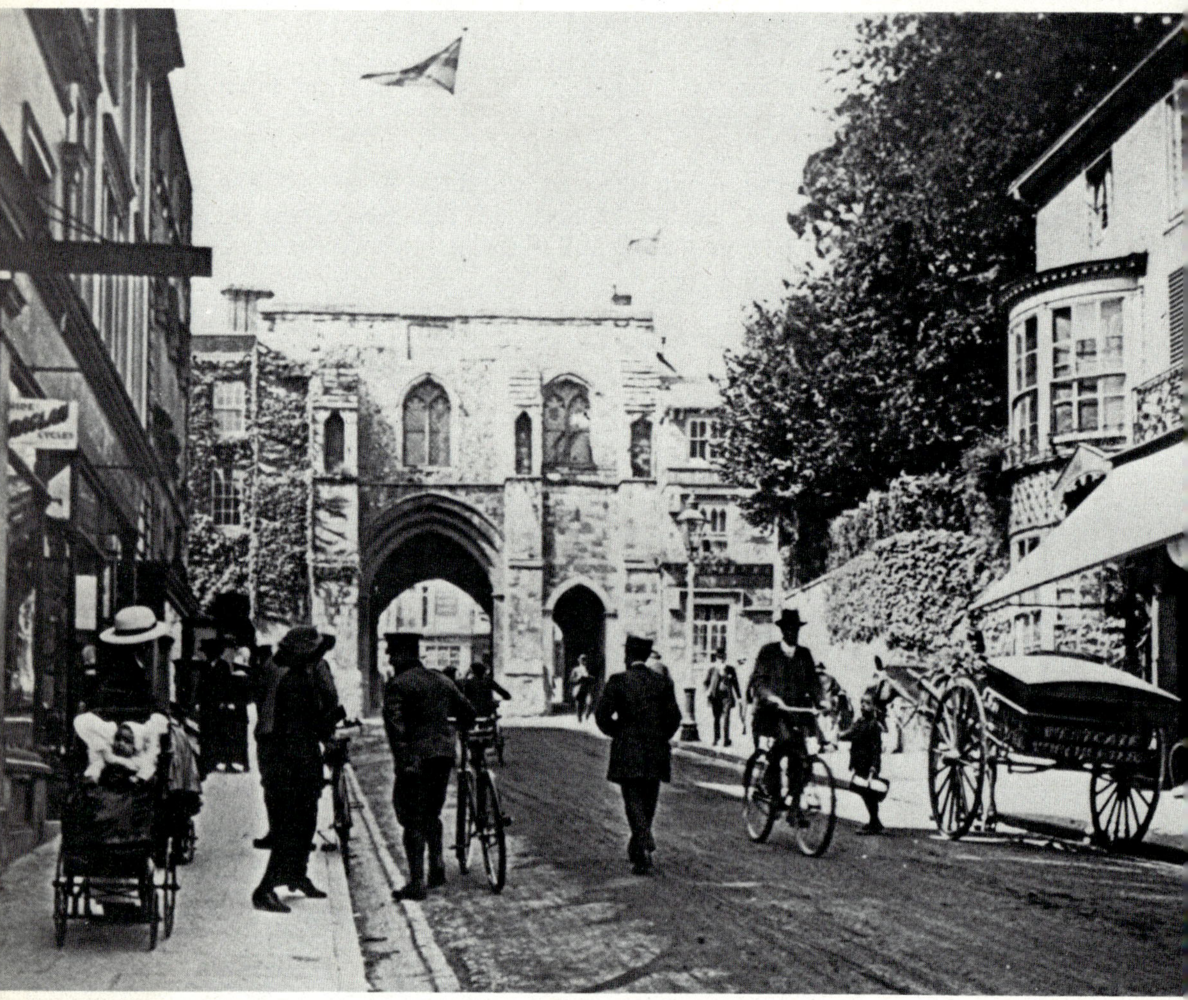

19 (Above) The Westgate seen from the High St., c. 1911. The building adjoining the Westgate on the right is The Plume of Feathers Inn. This has now been demolished to allow the road to go around the Westgate. The shop on the extreme right belonged to Salter & Son the butchers. One of their carts stands outside the shop which has since been demolished.

20 (Right) c. 1900. Looking up the High St. to the Westgate. The two men with the delivery cart on the right are standing outside the shop of T. A. Brown & Sons, the drapers of 102 High St.

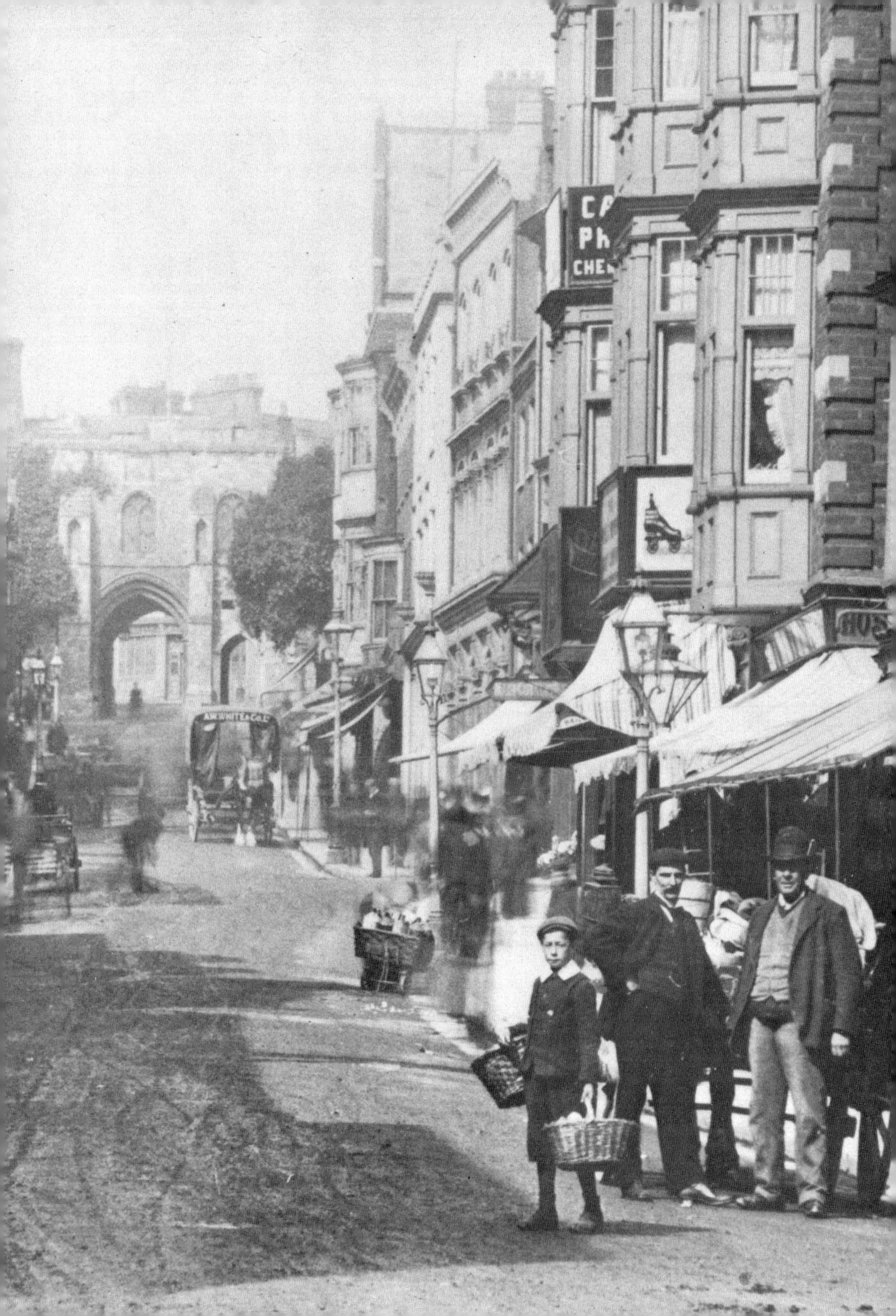
CA
PH
CHE

21 (Below) The Westgate viewed from the Romsey Rd, c. 1880. The house on the right had been demolished by 1895 to make way for the County Offices. On the right of the picture is a baker's cart.

22 (Above right) Another view above the Westgate in c. 1874, looking towards the Great Hall of Winchester Castle on the extreme right of the picture.

23 (Below right) The High Sheriff's coach outside the Great Hall of Winchester Castle in c. 1908.

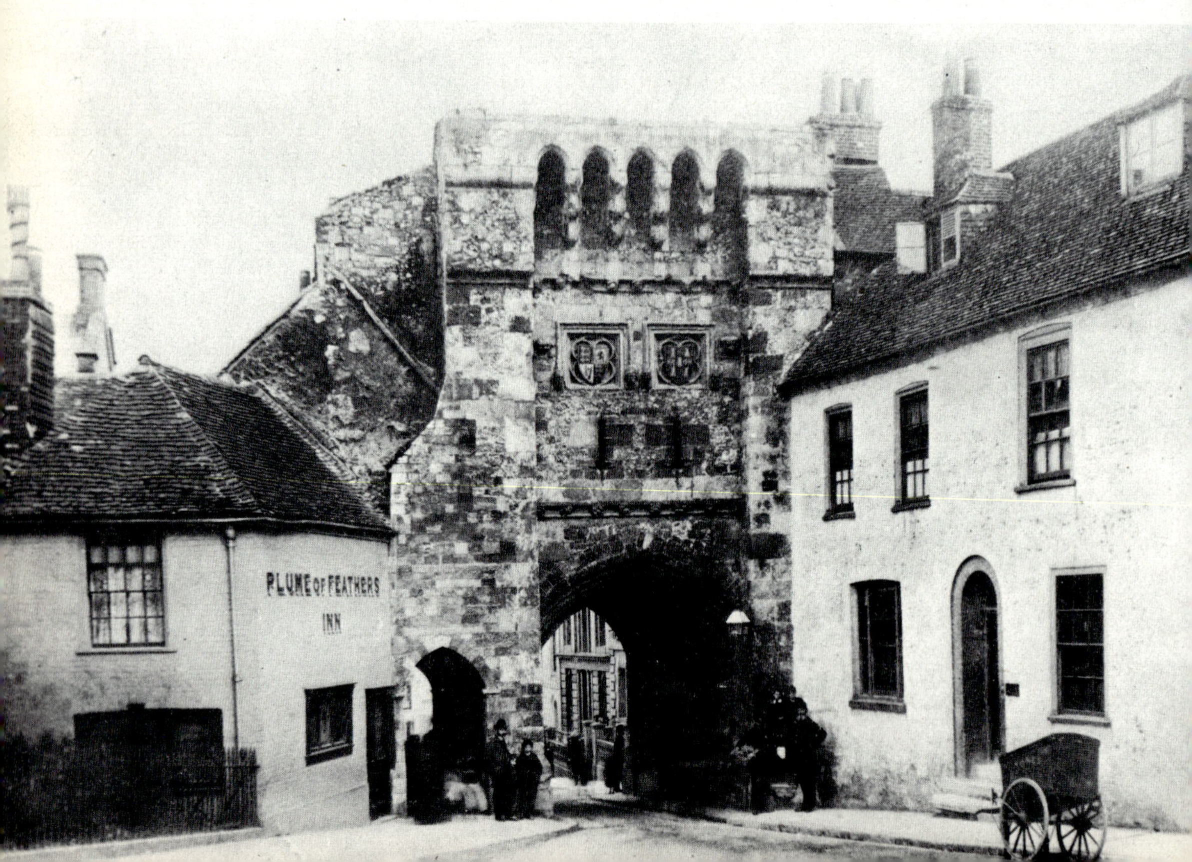

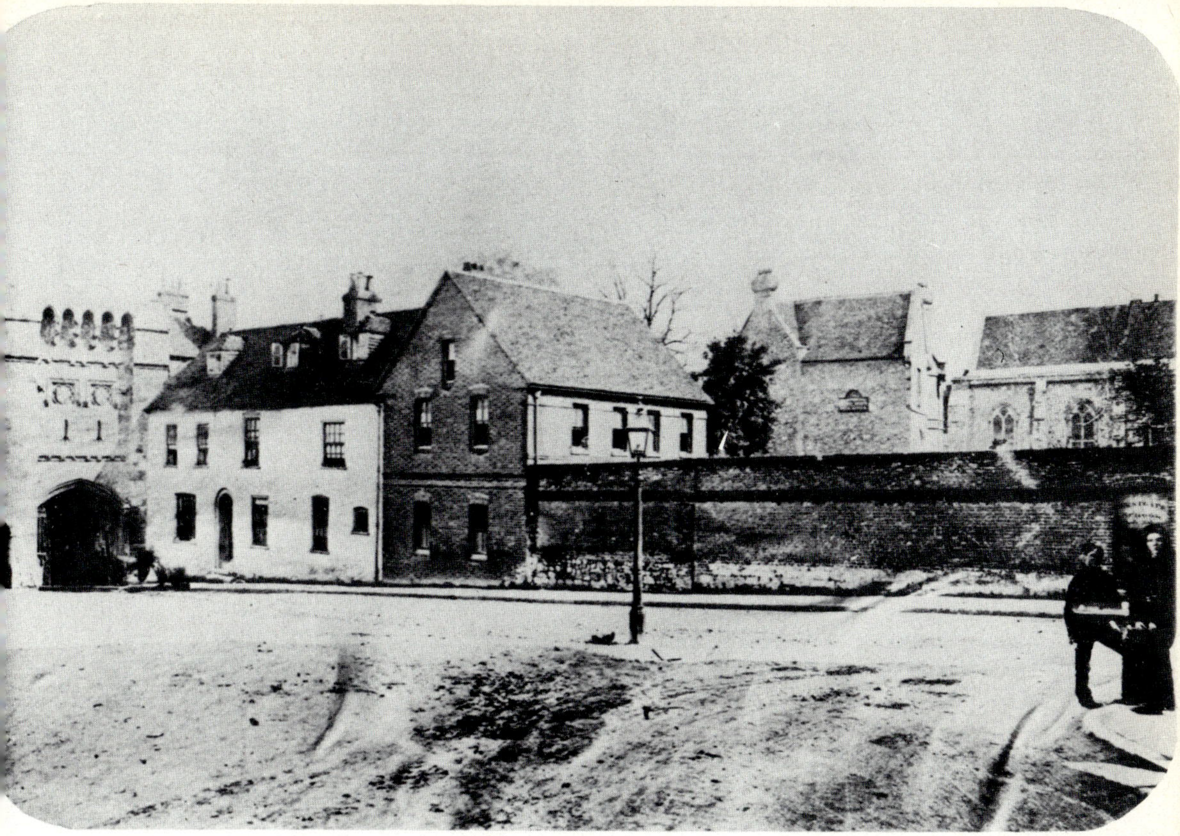

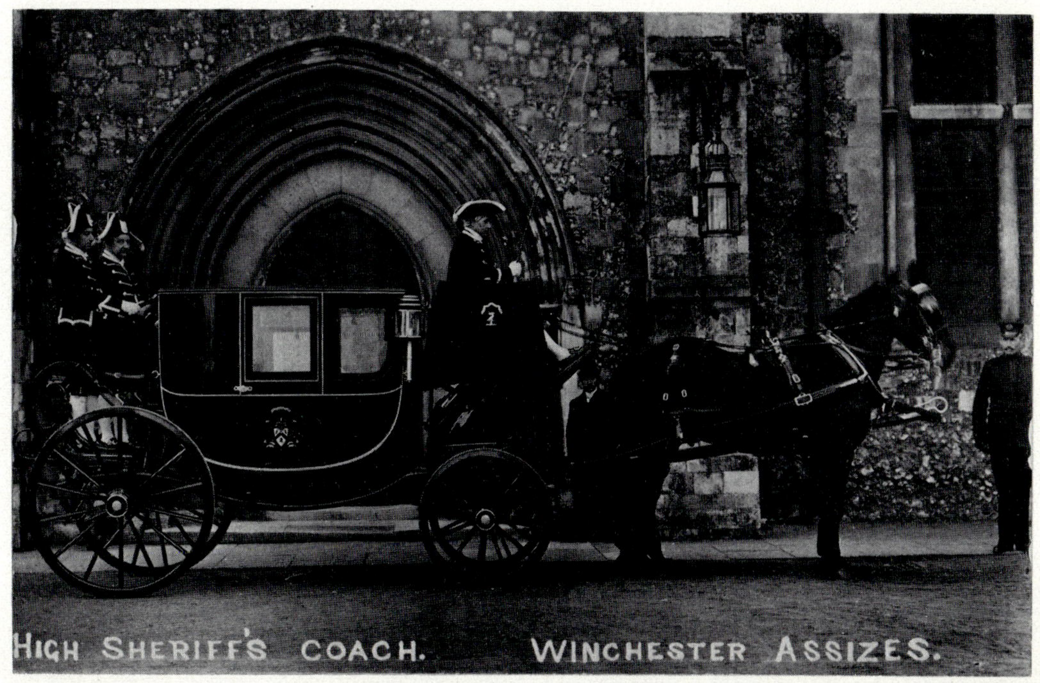
HIGH SHERIFF'S COACH.
WINCHESTER ASSIZES.

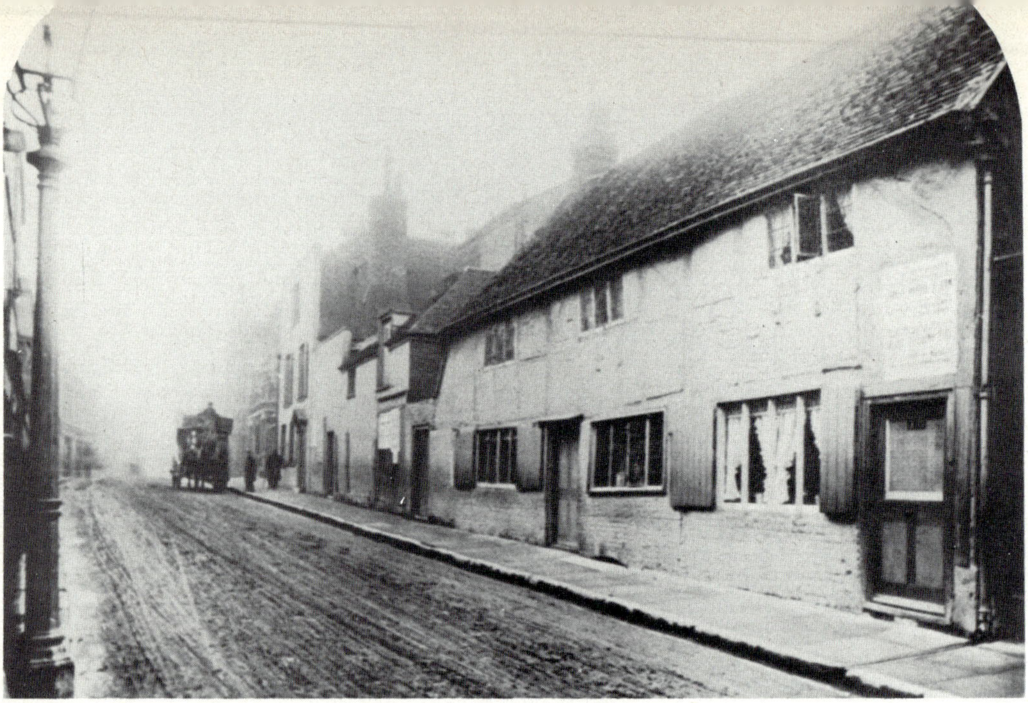

24 (Above) Jewry St. looking south in 1902, before the road had a tarmac surface. The rather drab building on the right is now the Elizabethan Restaurant.

25 (Below) Jewry St. looking north c. 1900. On the far left is the entrance to Andrews the coach builders. Next door is the shop of Mr. A. G. Rider. Many of the photographs in this book were originally taken by him. Just beyond is the facade of the Congregational Church (see Plate 26).

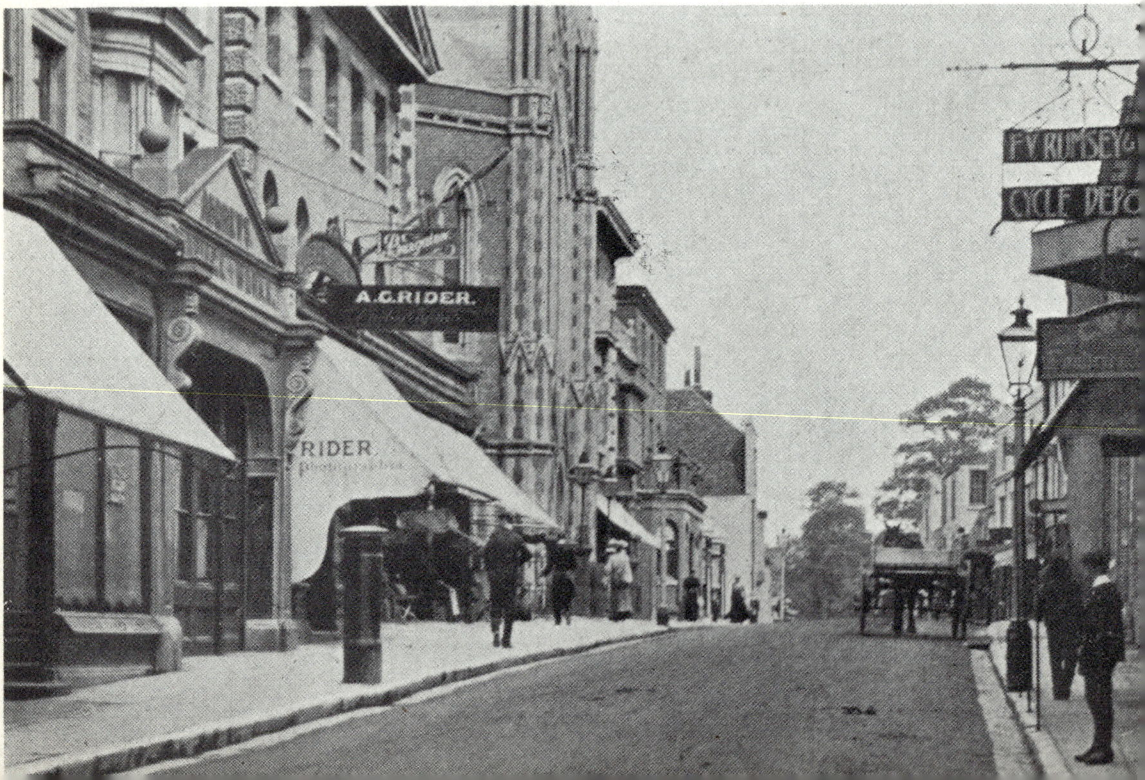

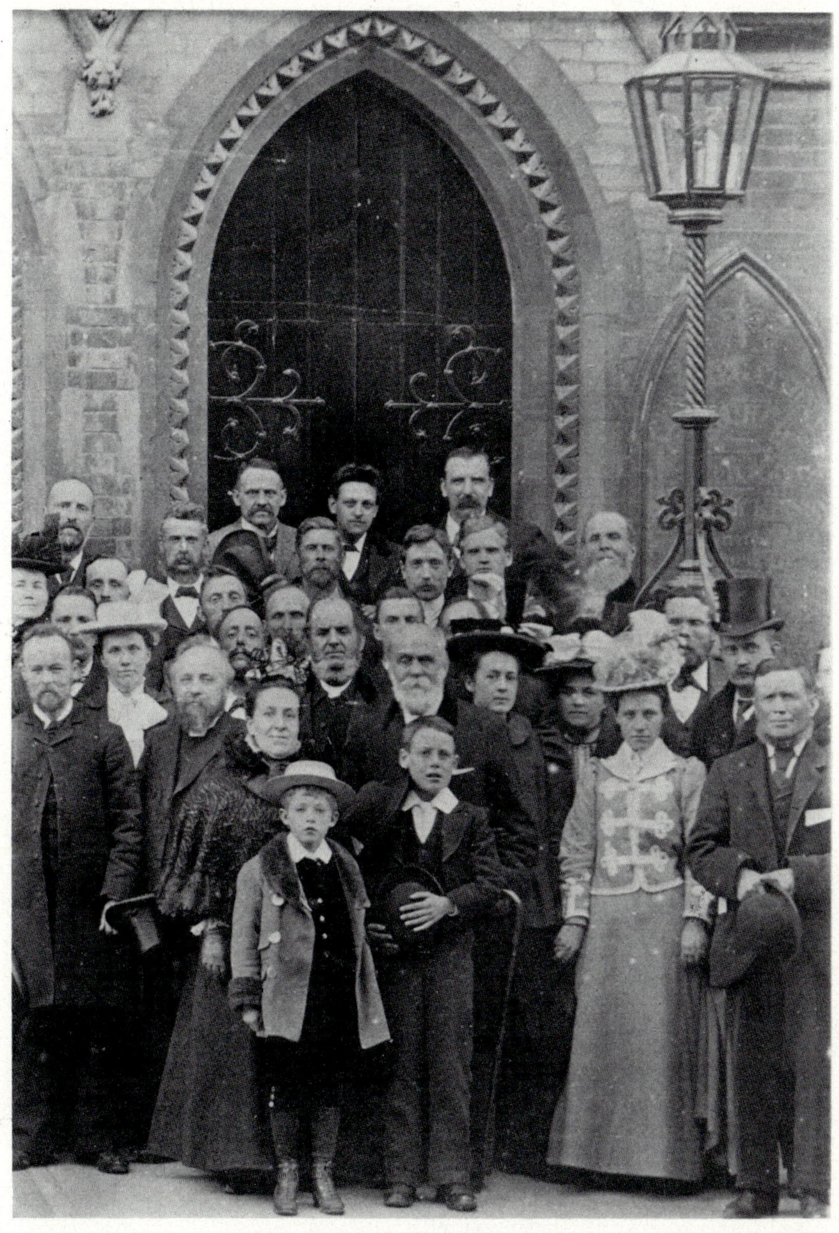

26 (Above) c. 1900, Primitive Methodists in their Sunday best outside the Congregational Church in Jewry St., which they had borrowed for the occasion of their quarterly meeting. On the extreme left front is the Rev. John Shepherd, the minister, and on the extreme right is Mr. Goodall the coal merchant of Ropley. The boy in the straw hat is Master Charles Prangnell. Next to him, holding a bowler hat, stands his elder brother Cecil and behind him stands his mother who kept a baker's shop in Eastgate St. (see plate 85).

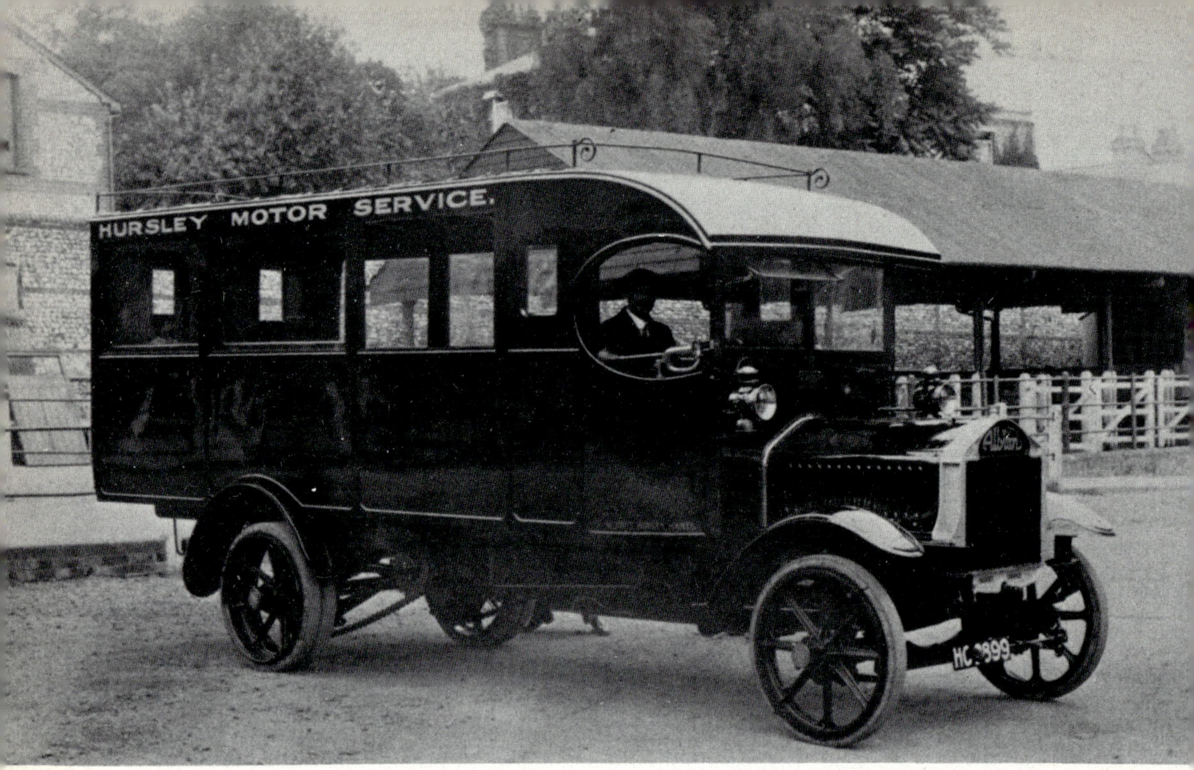

HURSLEY MOTOR SERVICE.

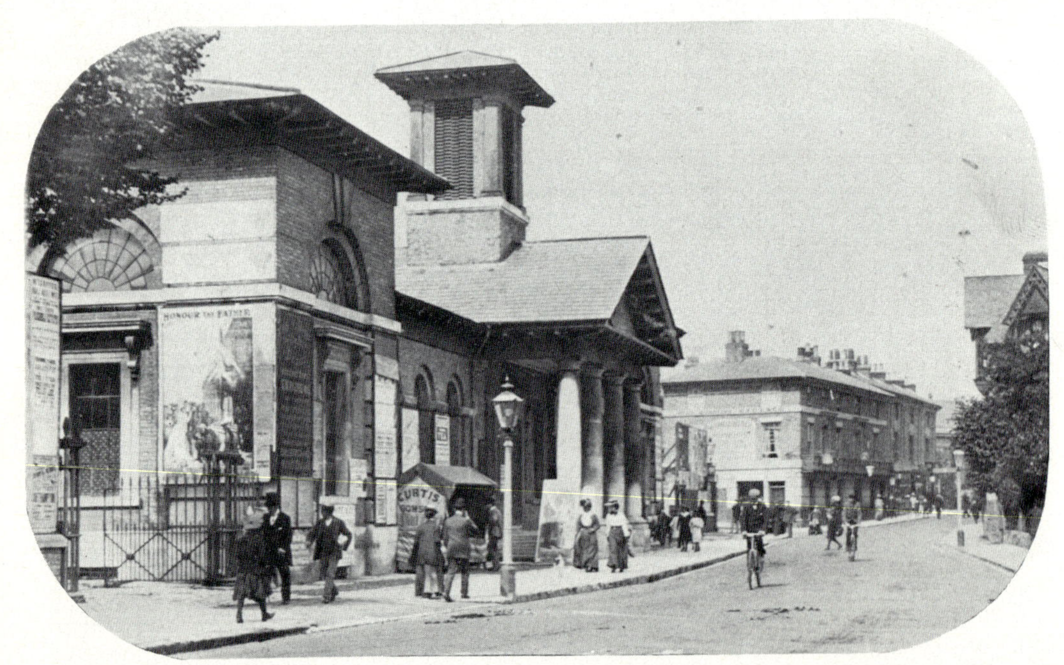
HONOUR THY FATHER
CURTIS

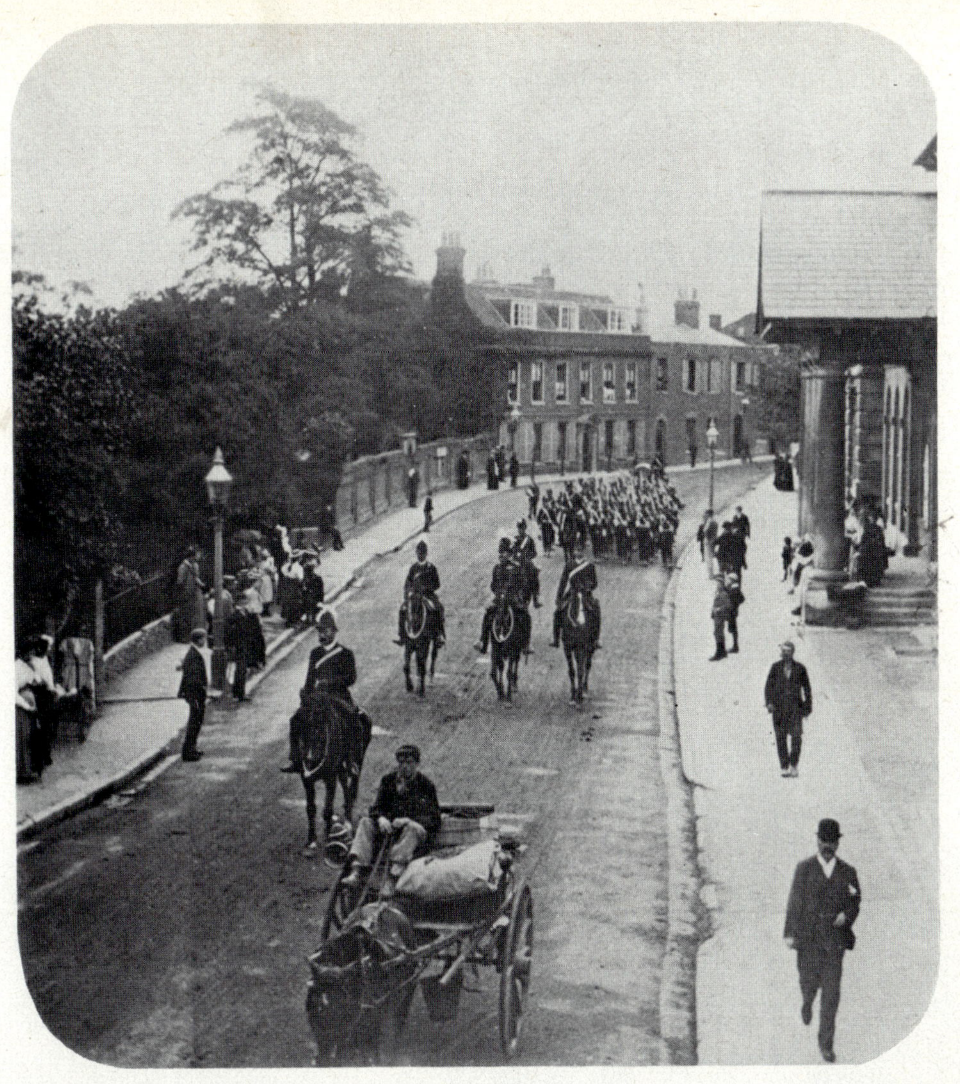

27 (Above left) Mr. William Jones of Hursley seated on one of the buses with which he provided a regular service between Hursley and Winchester for many years. This picture was taken in 1921 in the cattle market behind Winchester Corn Exchange. The pens have been taken down and the space is now used as a car park. Note the solid tyres and chain drive on the bus.

28 (Below left) Jewry St. c. 1900, with the Corn Exchange (now the City Library).
The Market Hotel can be seen just beyond on the left. It was later converted to a cinema.

29 (Above) Jewry St. in 1895. The Rifle Brigade on the march. The horse and cart in the foreground were not an official part of the parade! On the right is the Corn Exchange. The gardens on the left are now occupied by shops.

30 (Below) Looking eastwards down North Walls c. 1900.

31 (Above right) c. 1900. The Crown and Cushion Inn on the corner of North Walls and Jewry Street. E. Batchellor, to whom the hand cart belonged, was a confectioner in the High St.

32 (Below right) Wales St. Winnall c. 1900.

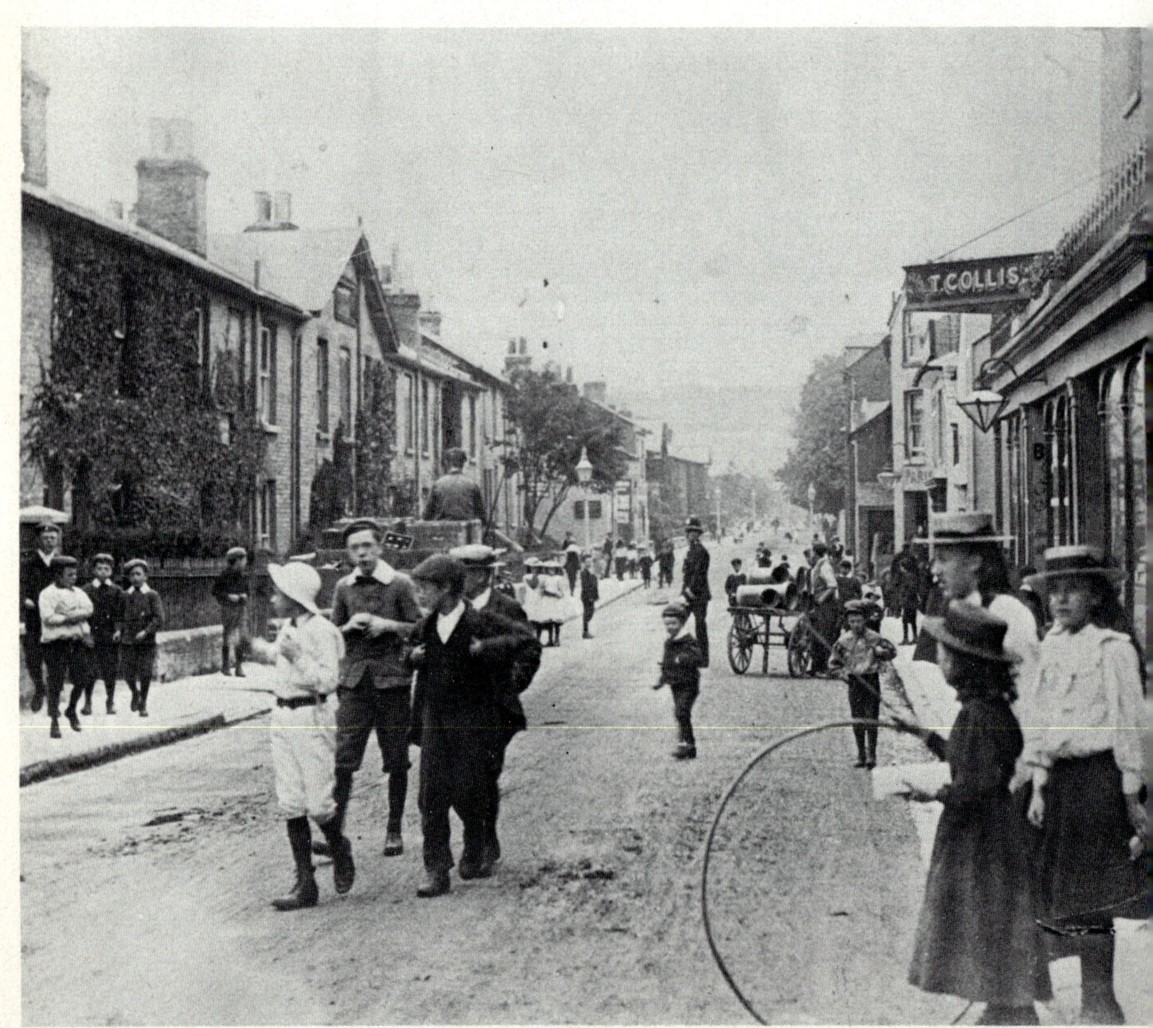

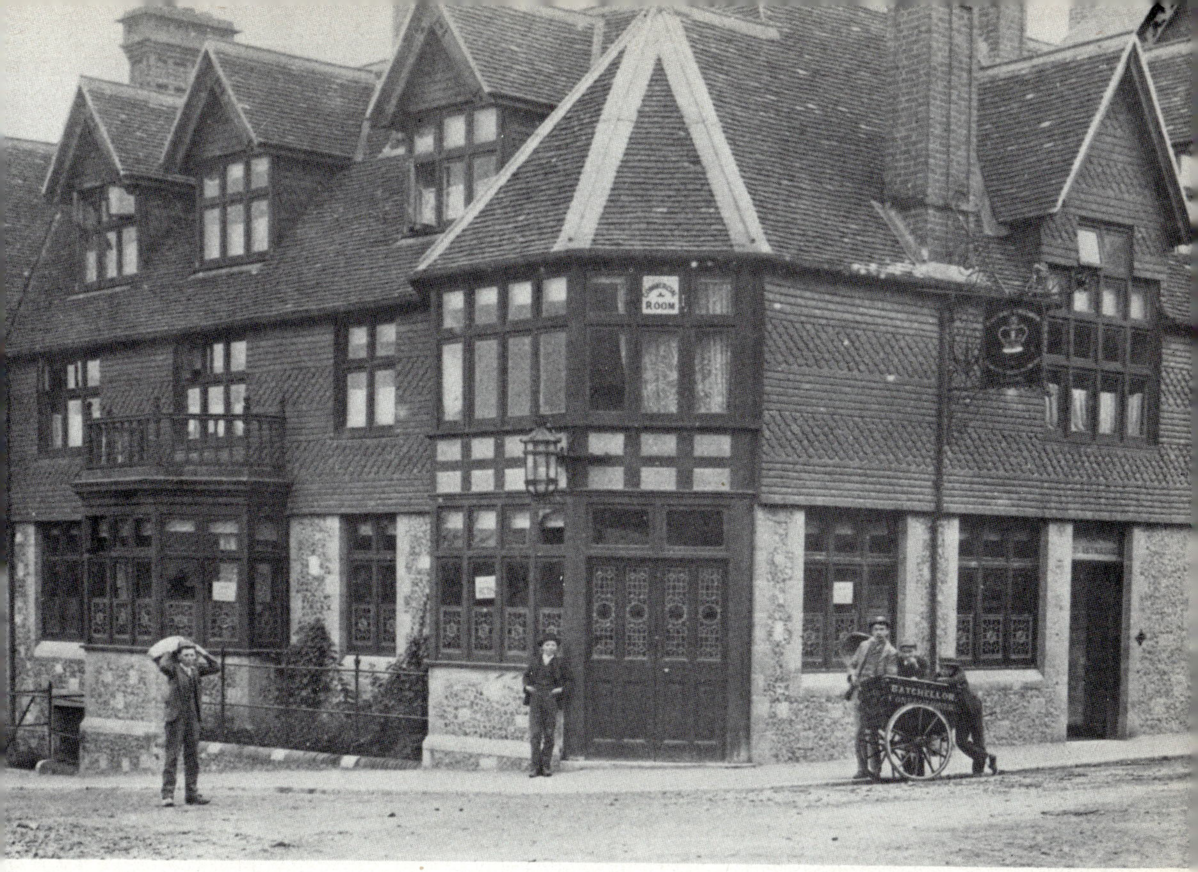

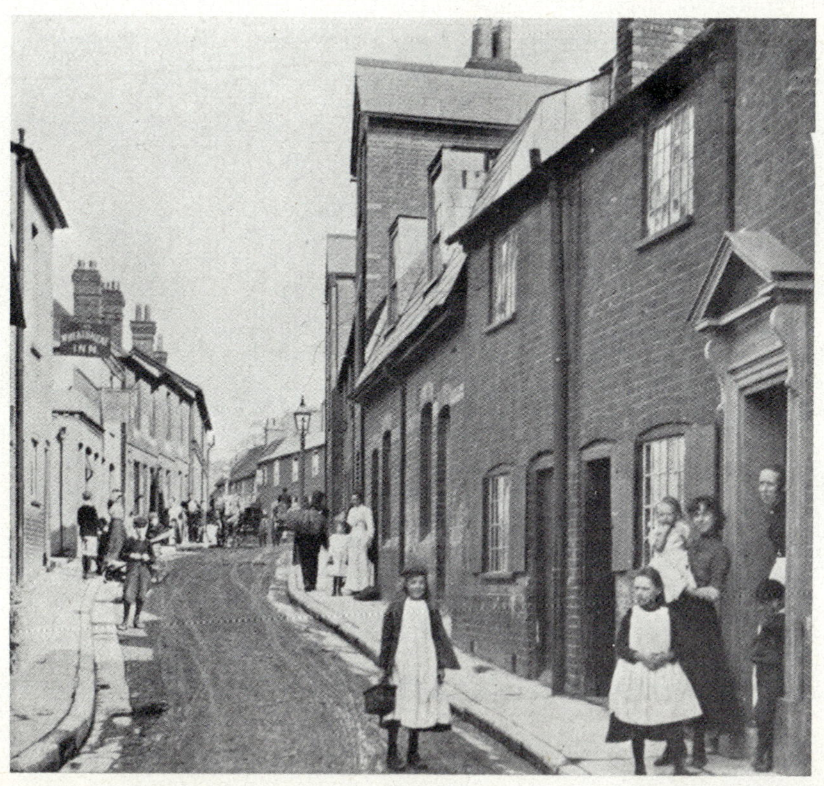
INN

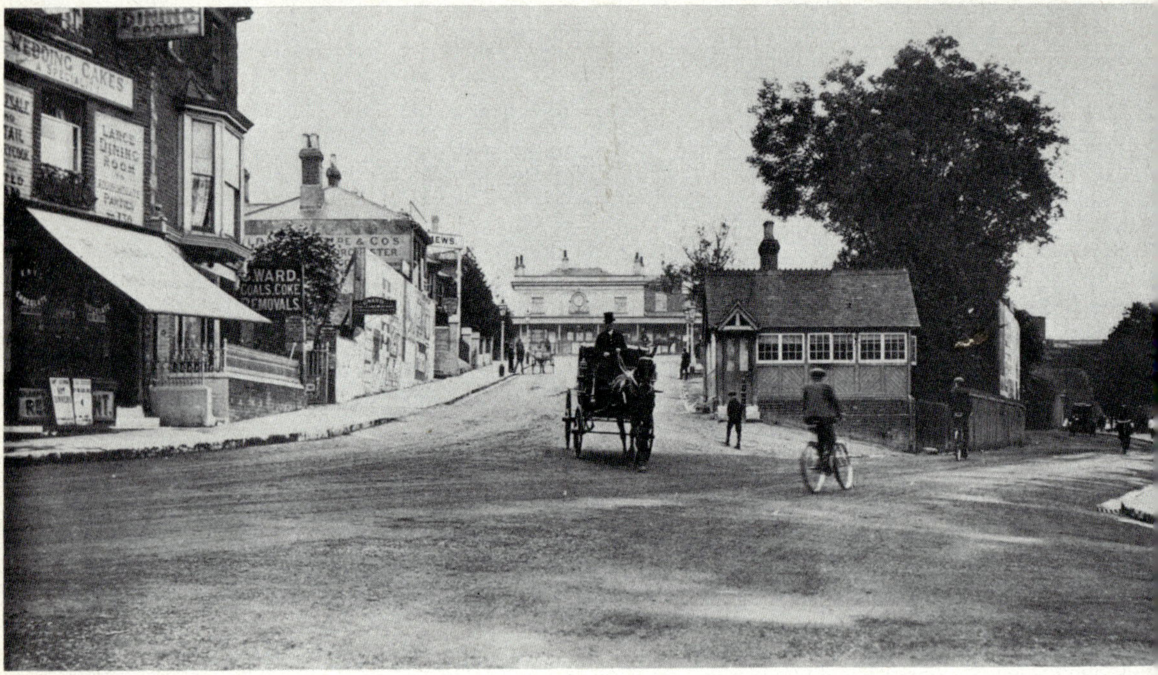

WEDDING CAKES
LARGE DINING ROOM
G. WARD.
COALS, COKE
REMOVALS.
NEWS

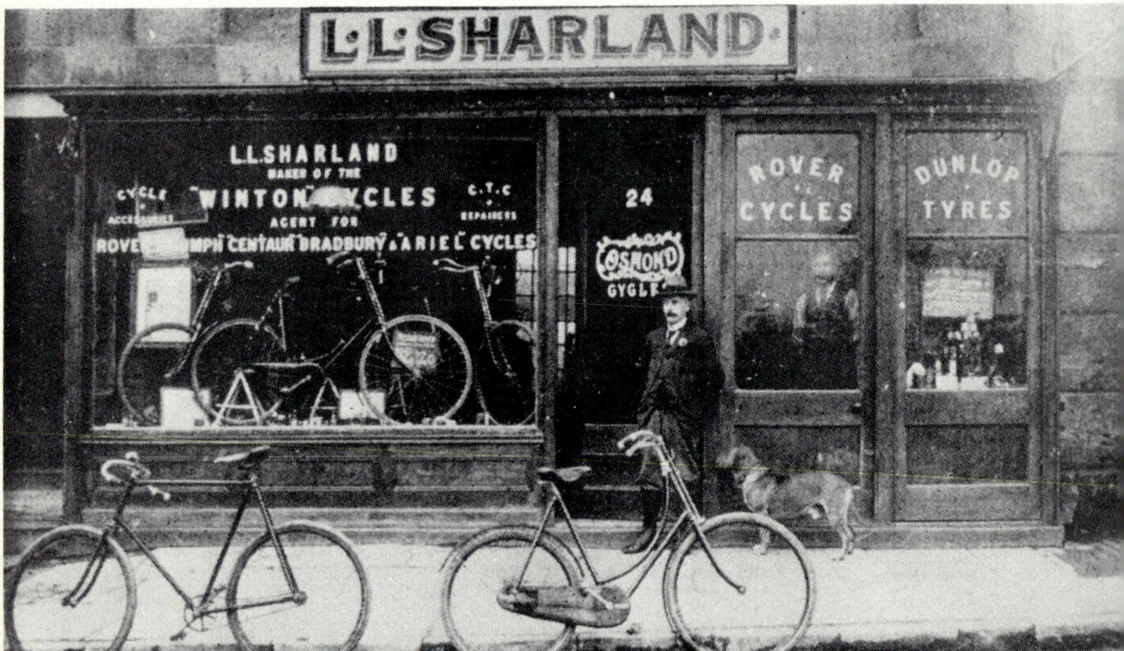

L·L·SHARLAND·
L.L.SHARLAND
MAKER OF THE
WINTON CYCLES
AGENT FOR
CYCLE ACCESSORIES
C.T.C. REPAIRERS
CENTAUR BRADBURY & ARIEL CYCLES
24
OSMOND CYCLES
ROVER CYCLES
DUNLOP TYRES

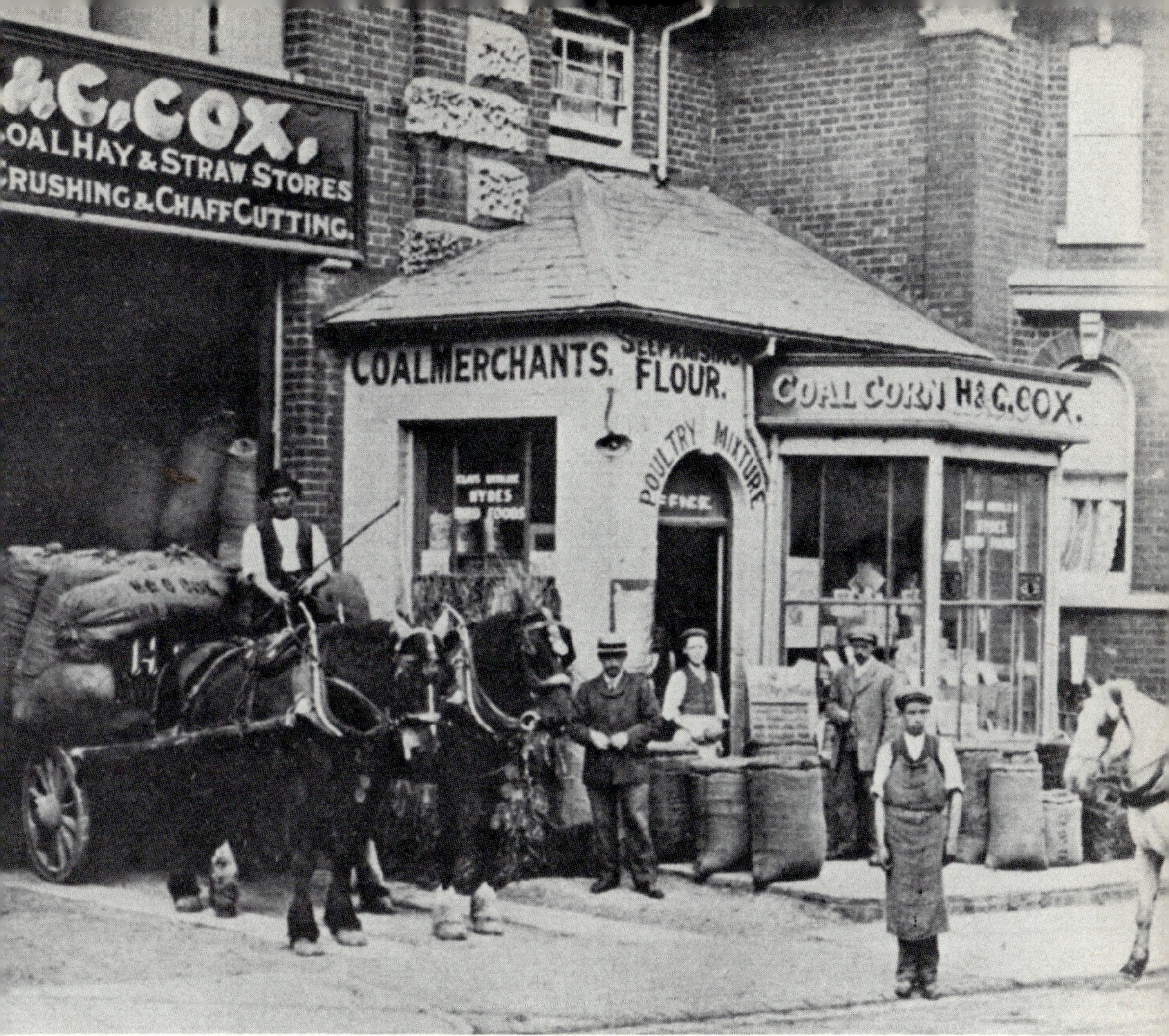

33 (Above left) The approach to Winchester City Station c. 1900. The shop awning on the left belonged to R. Sharp's restaurant. On the right is the cab-driver's hut.

34 (Below left) C. 1903. Mr. L. L. Sharland, maker of the celebrated "Winton" cycle, outside his shop at 24, Jewry St. (now the Star of Bengal Indian Restaurant). Among his many advertised services were "cycles for hire and riding taught".

35 (Above) H. & C. Cox of 9 City Rd. c. 1907. The Employment Exchange now stands on the site of this building.

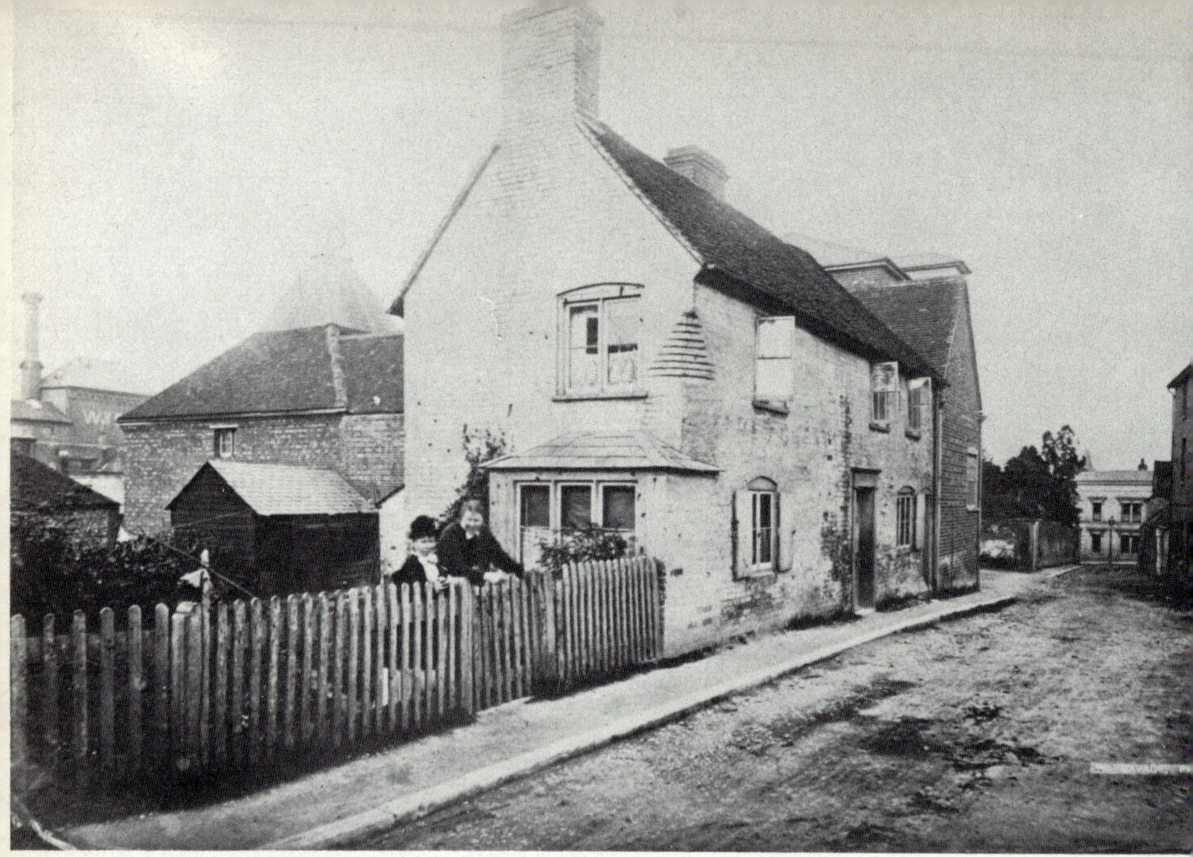

36 (Above) Swan Lane looking east towards Hyde St., c. 1880. The White Swan in Hyde St. can just be seen at the end of the street and the chimney of Wyeth's brewery is on the far left. The gardens in the foreground have been replaced by the Eagle Hotel car park.

37 (Above right) c. 1907. H. Collis's dairy at 68 Hyde St. The dairy was supplied from Mr. Collis's dairy farm at Headbourne Worthy.

38 (Below right) Inside the yard of Chaplin & Co., the general carriers of Hyde St. c. 1900. The wagon which usually carried goods is here preparing for a charity parade, possibly a mile of pennies appeal for Winchester Hospital. These fine old buildings still remain.

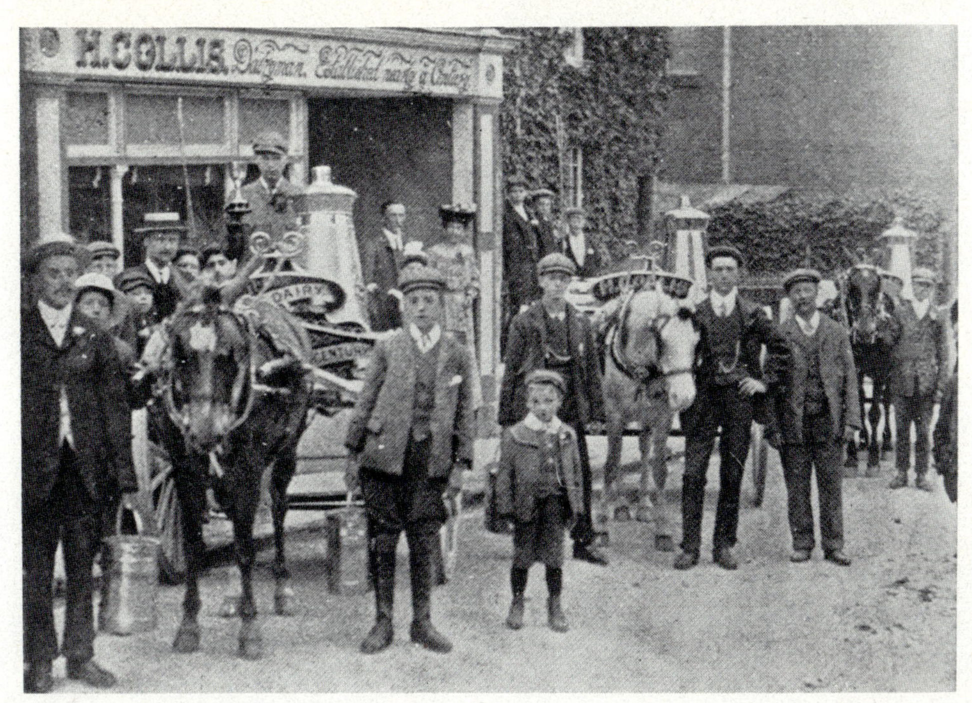
H.COLLIS,

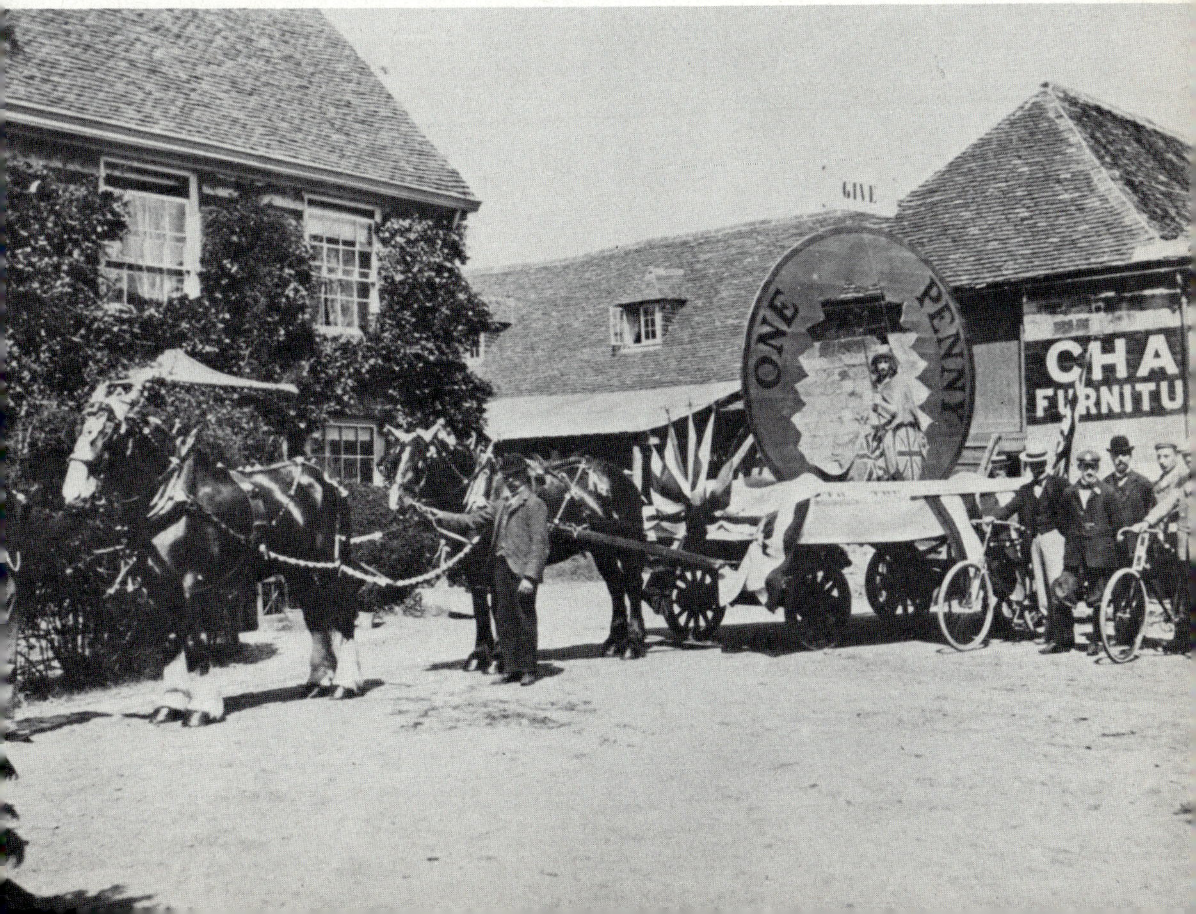

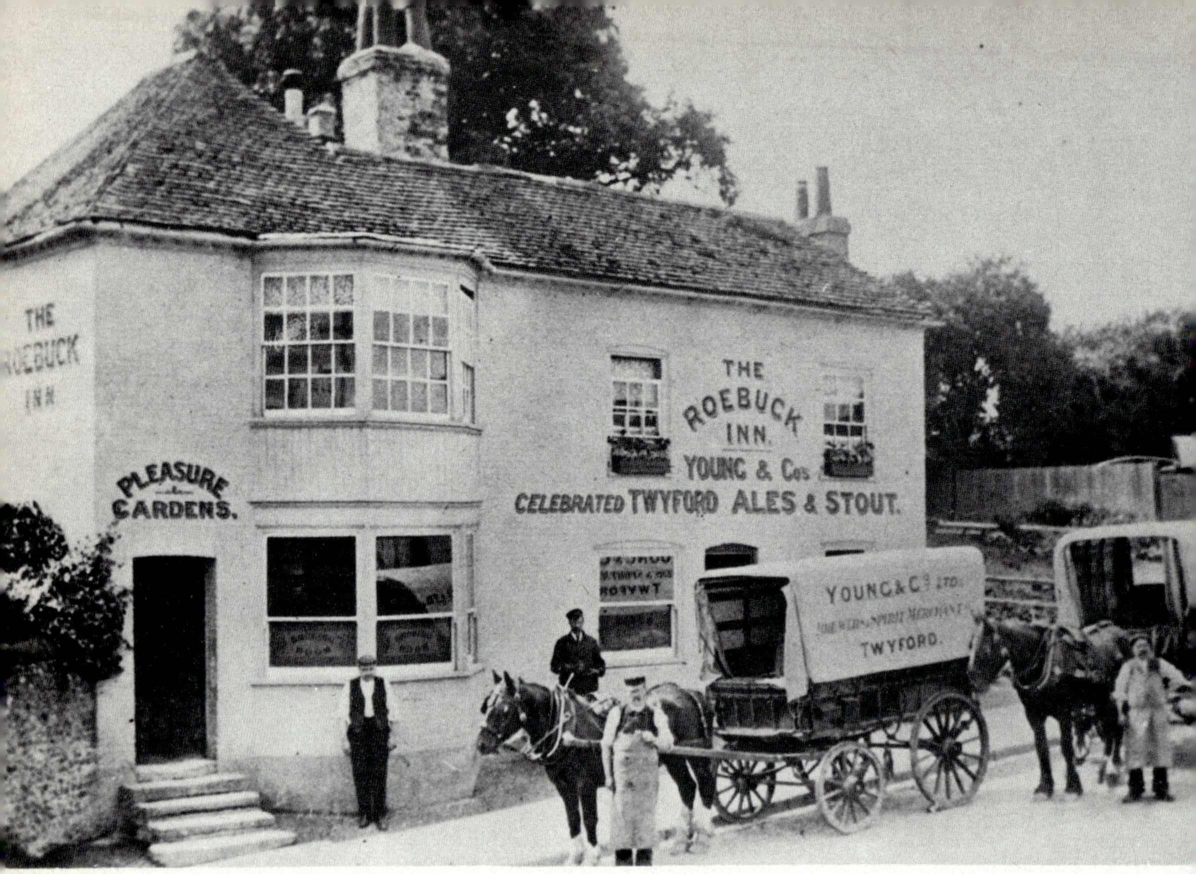

THE
ROEBUCK
INN
PLEASURE
GARDENS.
THE
ROEBUCK
INN.
YOUNG & Co's
CELEBRATED TWYFORD ALES & STOUT.
YOUNG & Co LTD.
TWYFORD.

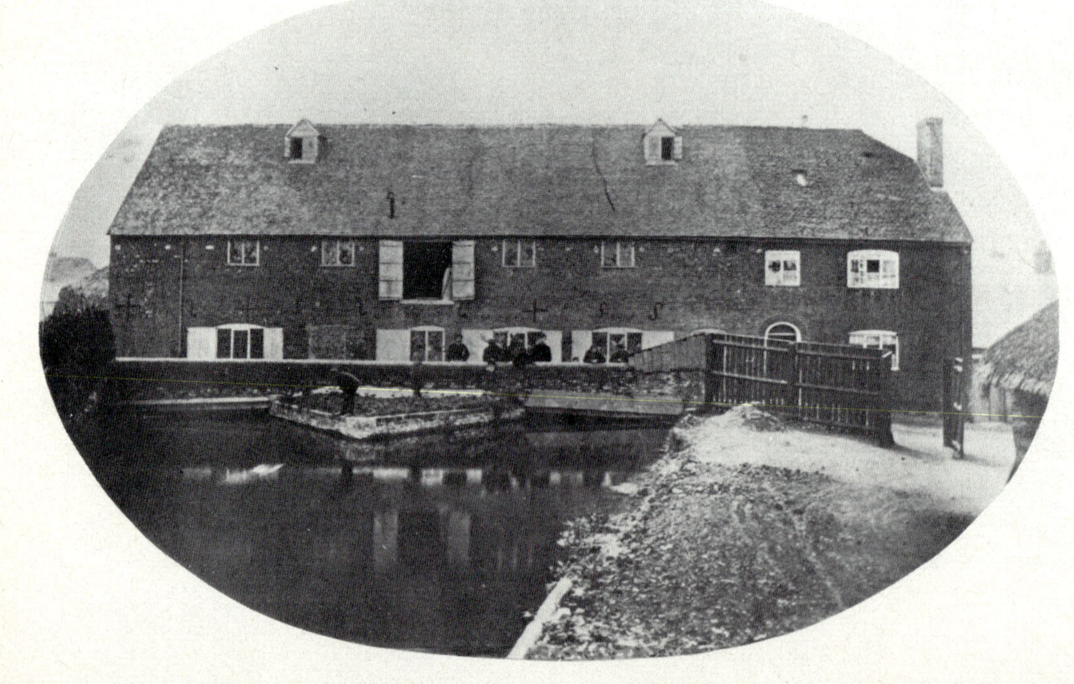

39 (Above left) c. 1910. Twyford brewery owned by Mr. Thomas Young, was at that time a thriving industry. Here, two waggons deliver beer to the Roebuck Inn,, Stockbridge Rd., Winchester.

40 (Below left) Durngate Mill from the north c. 1870. This late 18th century building was demolished in 1967. A mill had stood on the site since the 13th century.

41 (Below) Old houses in Middle Brook St. c. 1880.

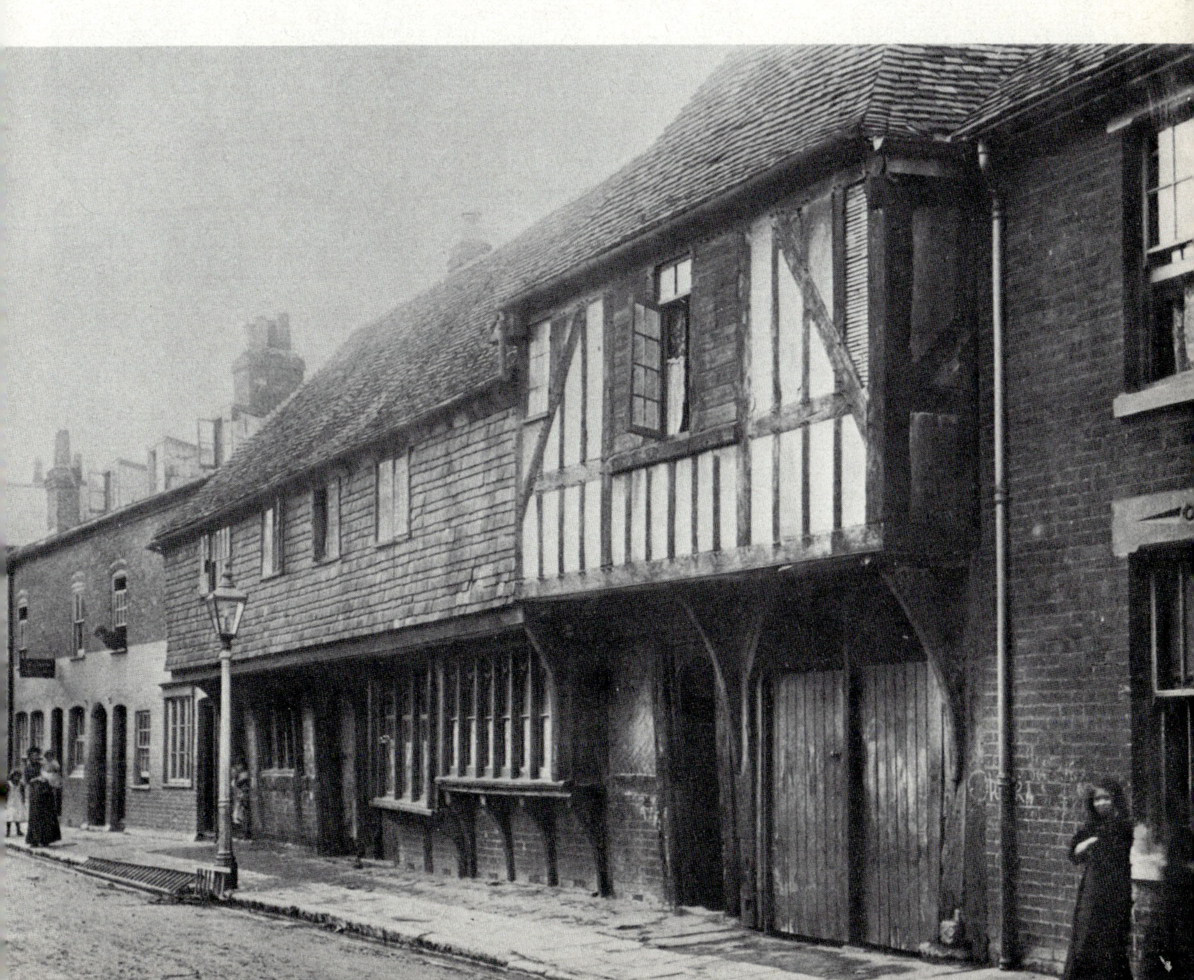

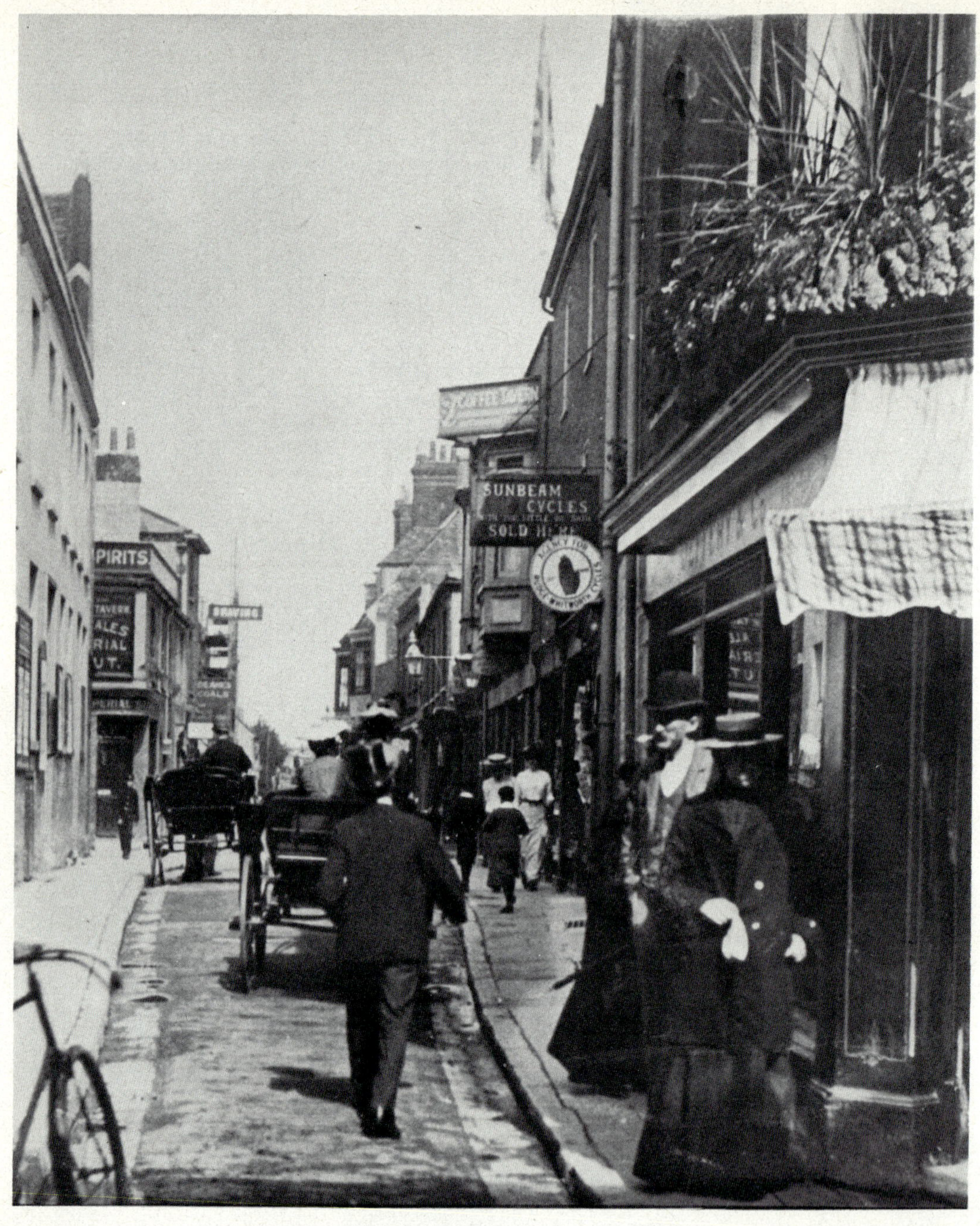

42 (Above) The entrance to Parchment St. from High St. c. 1900. The shop on the far right belonged to Jeffery & Co. the florists and nurserymen (now occupied by Hepworth's).

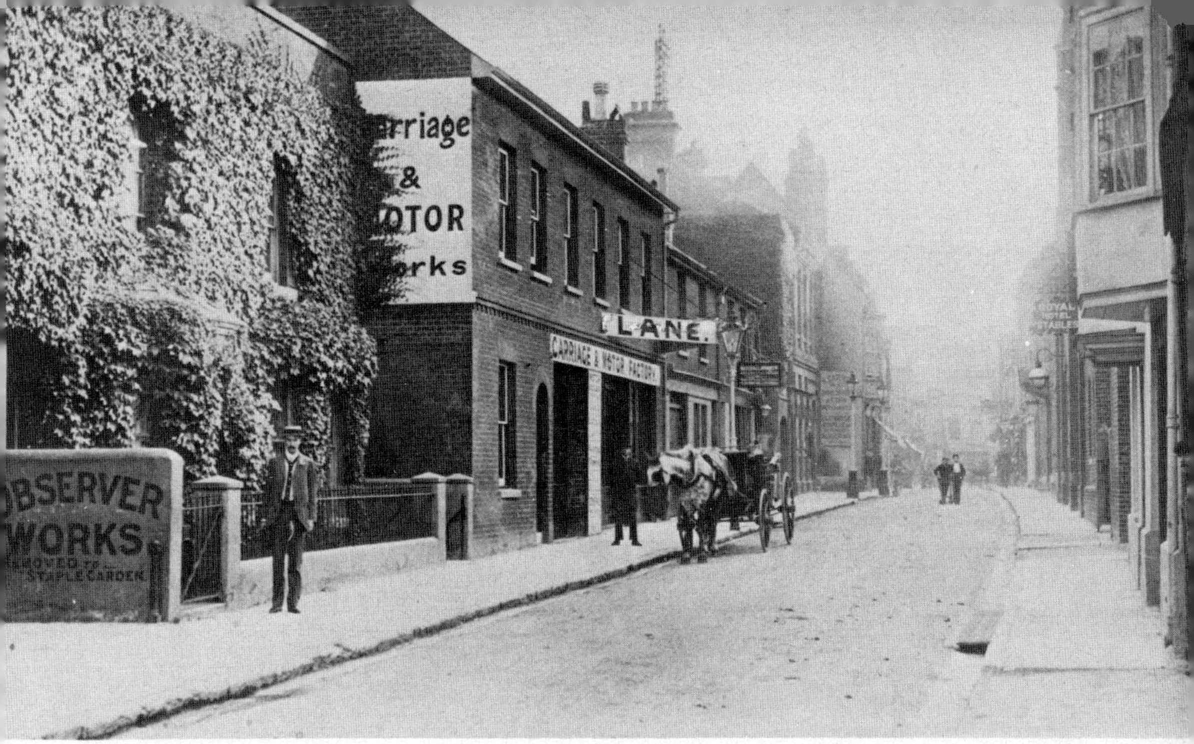

43 (Above) Parchment St. looking towards High St. c. 1905. The sign on the left refers to the Hampshire Observer which was then printed by Warren & Son at Staple Garden (see plate 59).

44 (Right) c. 1909. Will Short's carriage and motor factory in Parchment St. This site is now occupied by Blackwell & Moody the masons, Will Short's garage having moved to Southgate St. (see plate 61).

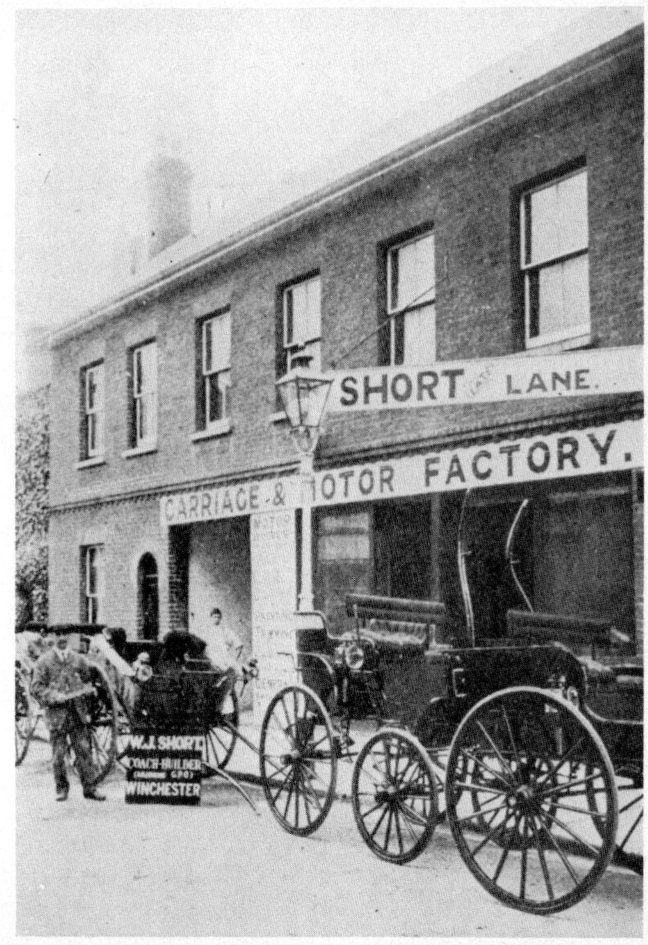

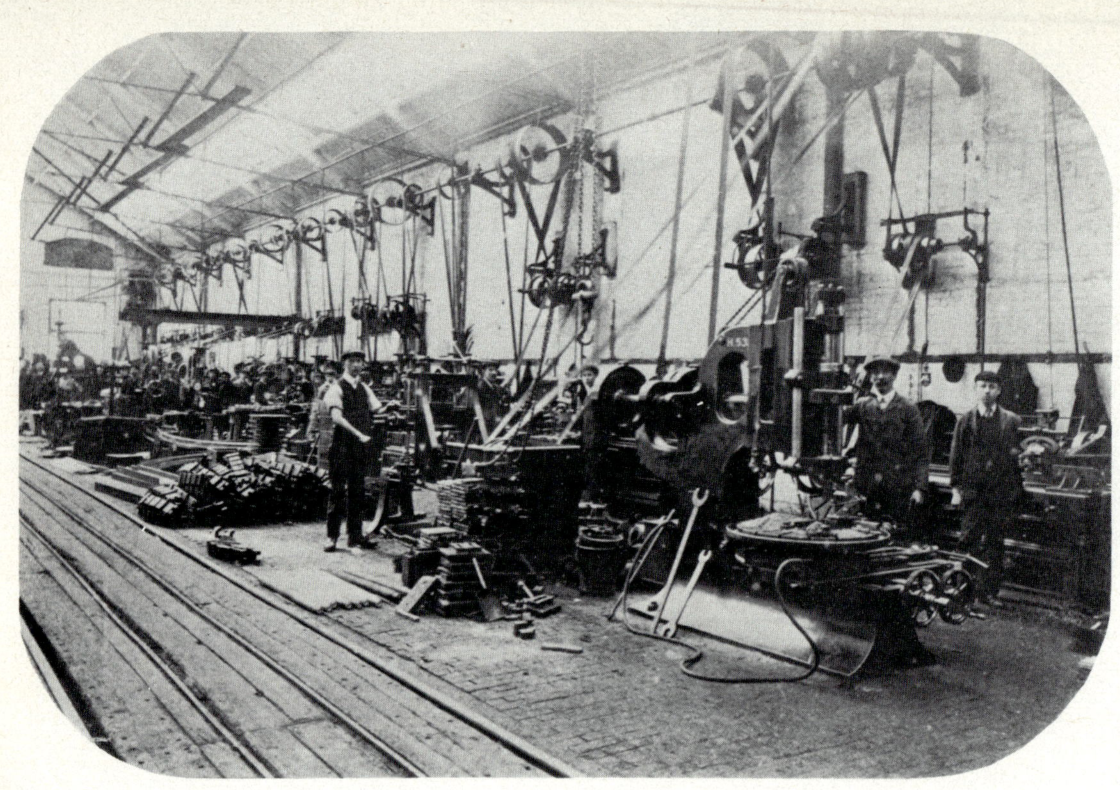

45 (Above) c. 1900. Inside the City Engineering Works between Middle and Lower Brook St. (now a car park). It was owned by the Jewell family for several generations and, among other things, made components for the G.W.R. Winchester – Newbury line. The man with his sleeves rolled up in the centre foreground is probably Mr. H. P. M. Jewell, grandson of the founder of the business.

46 (Above right) c. 1920. Mr. G. W. Piper (1863–1944) stands on the left of this picture outside his office at 6 Parchment St. He was a shipping agent and took an active part in an emigration scheme for the unemployed after the Great War.

47 (Below right) Mr. Piper was also a coal merchant and a manufacturer of mineral waters (in Upper Brook St.) Here in about 1920 is one of his delivery wagons loaded with crates and bags of coal.

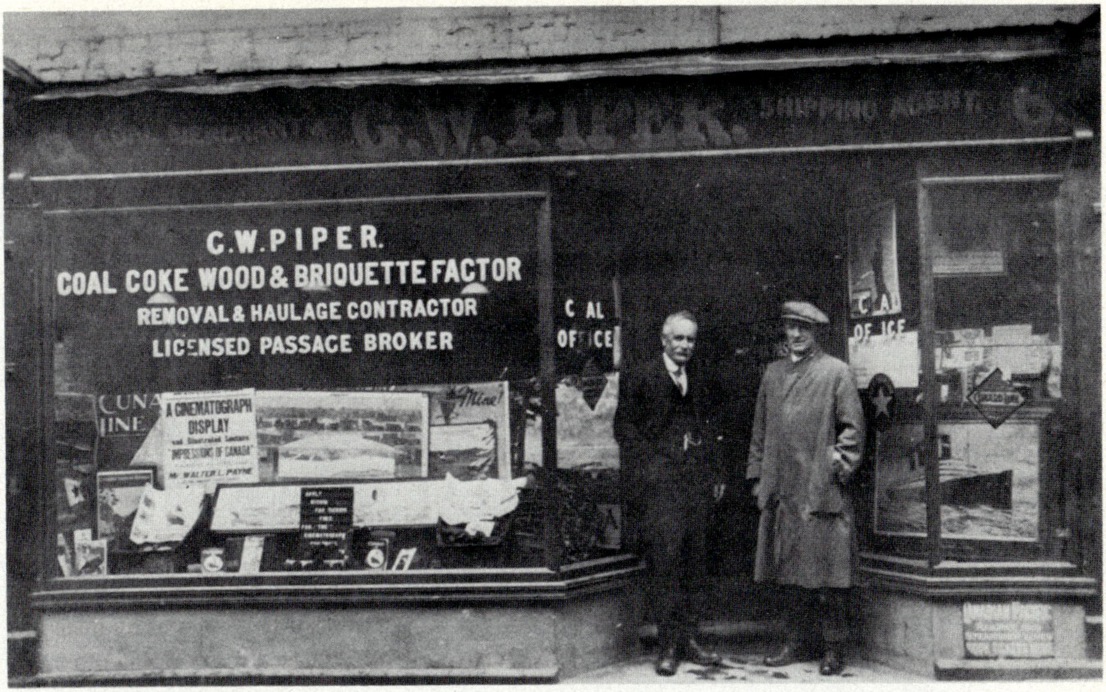

G.W. PIPER.
COAL COKE WOOD & BRIQUETTE FACTOR
REMOVAL & HAULAGE CONTRACTOR
LICENSED PASSAGE BROKER
A CINEMATOGRAPH DISPLAY
IMPRESSIONS OF CANADA
COAL OFFICE

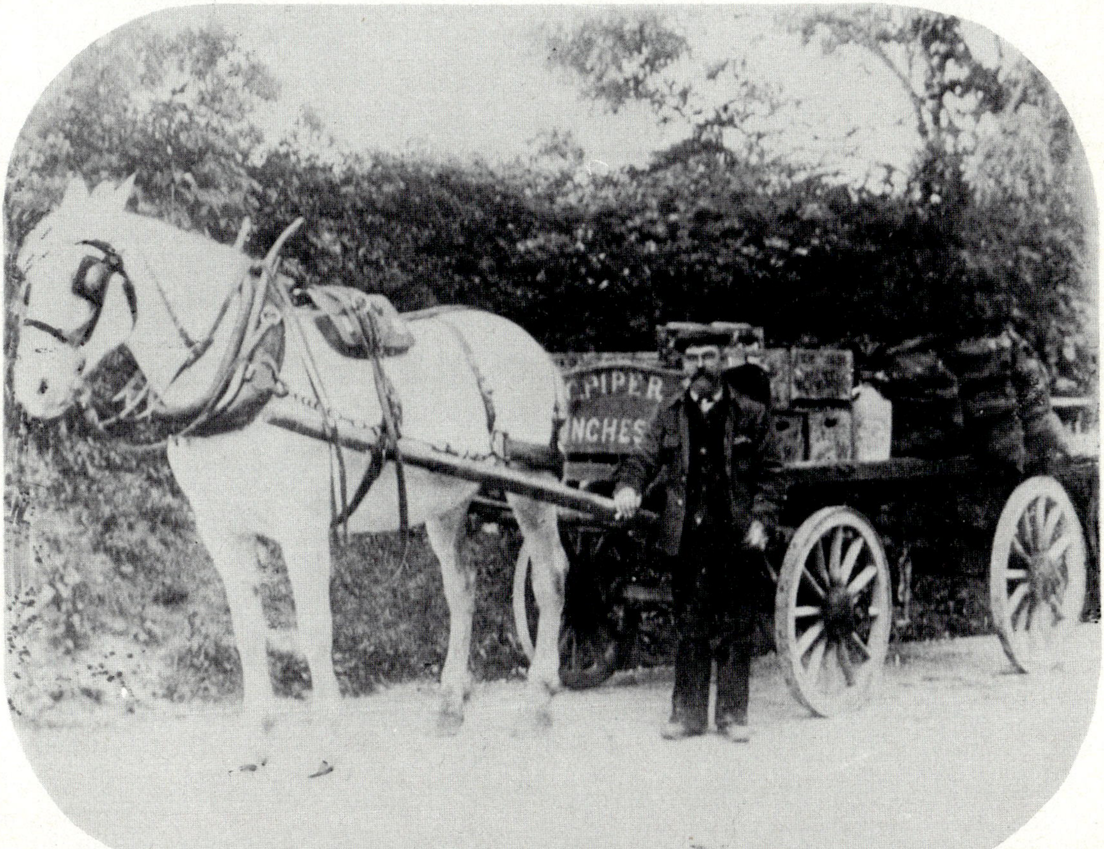

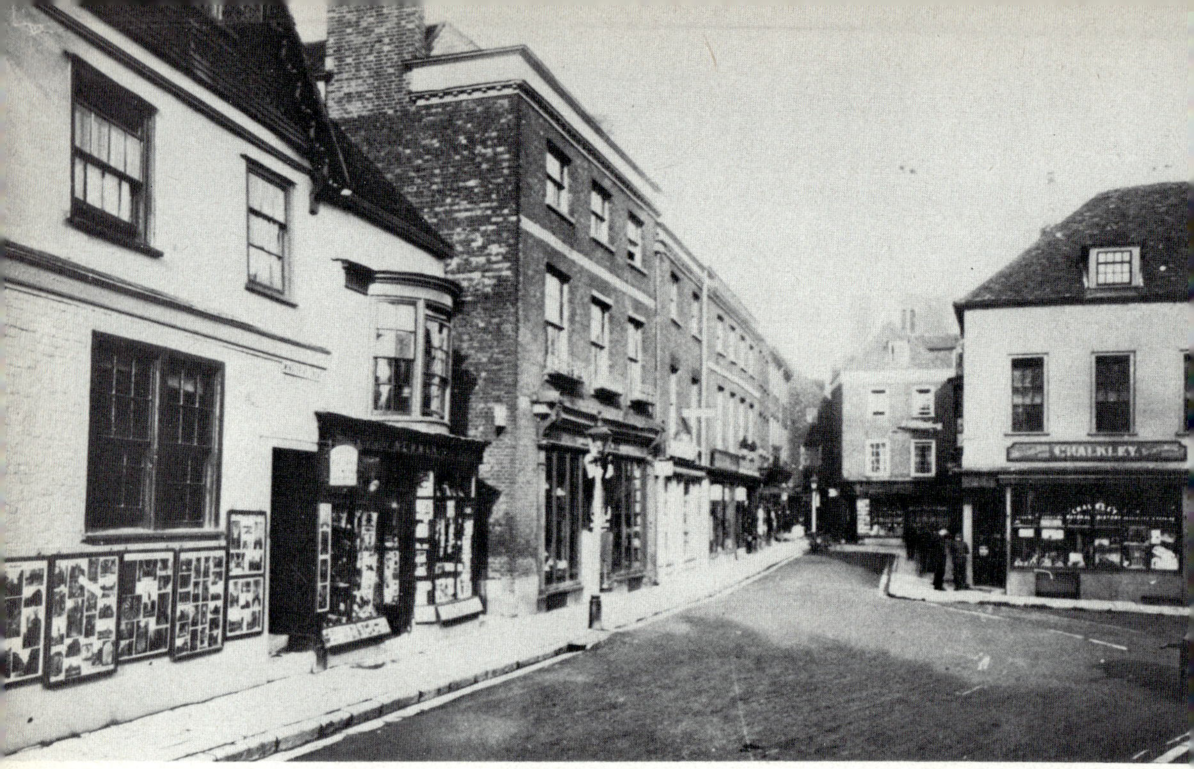

CHALKLEY

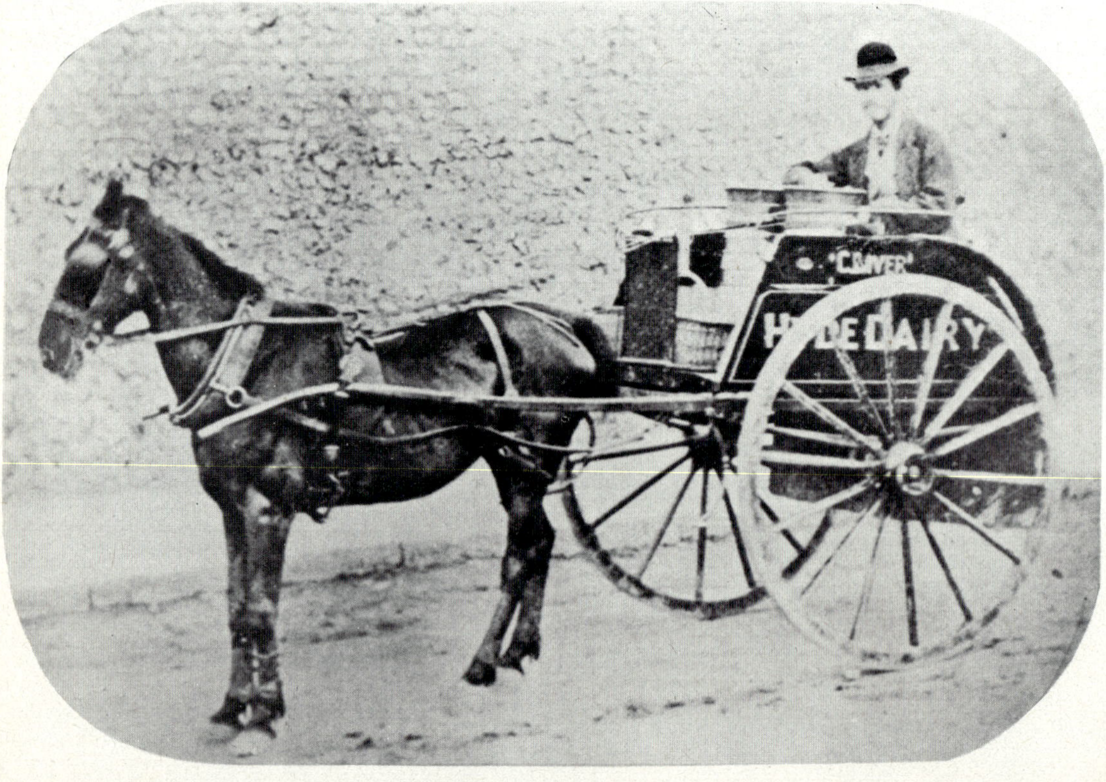

48 (Above left) The Square c. 1900. On the far left is Mrs. Newman's toy and fancy goods shop. On the right is the shop of Mr. W. Chalkley, taxidermist, gun and fishing tackle maker.

49 (Below left) Mr. C. Driver the dairyman in St. Swithun's St. c. 1885. Mr Driver's dairy farm was at Fulflood. His daughter, who was also the milkmaid, sat beside him in the cart and took the milk and eggs from door to door (The egg basket can be seen beside the two churns). This is thought to be the first milk float in Winchester. Previously Mr. Driver's family had delivered the milk from buckets suspended from a yoke.

50 (Below) David Frost's shop in The Square c. 1895. This is now The Camera Exchange although D. Frost is still inscribed on the door step. On the left is Freddie Frost who was a world champion cyclist. He did his training in the cellar which was lit through the grill that can be seen in this picture.

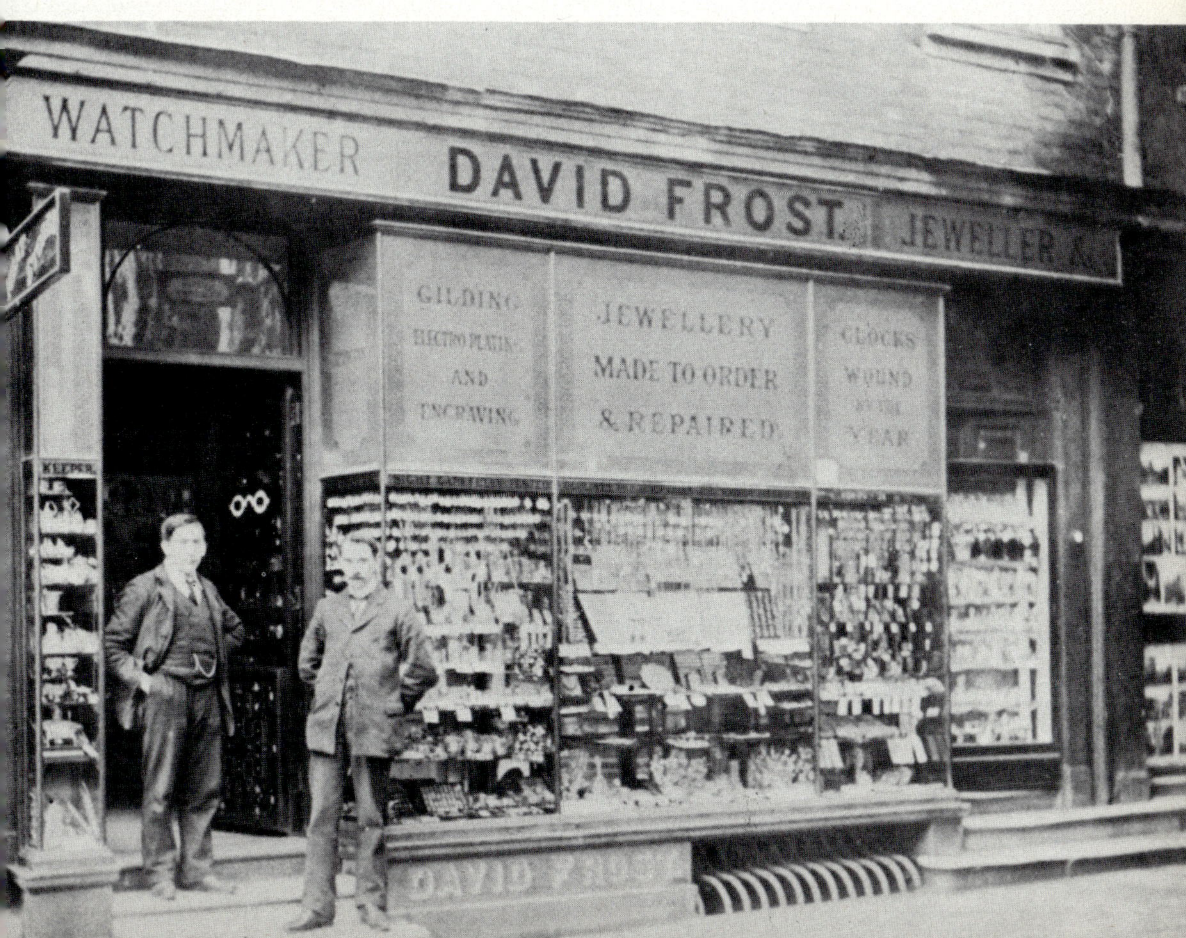

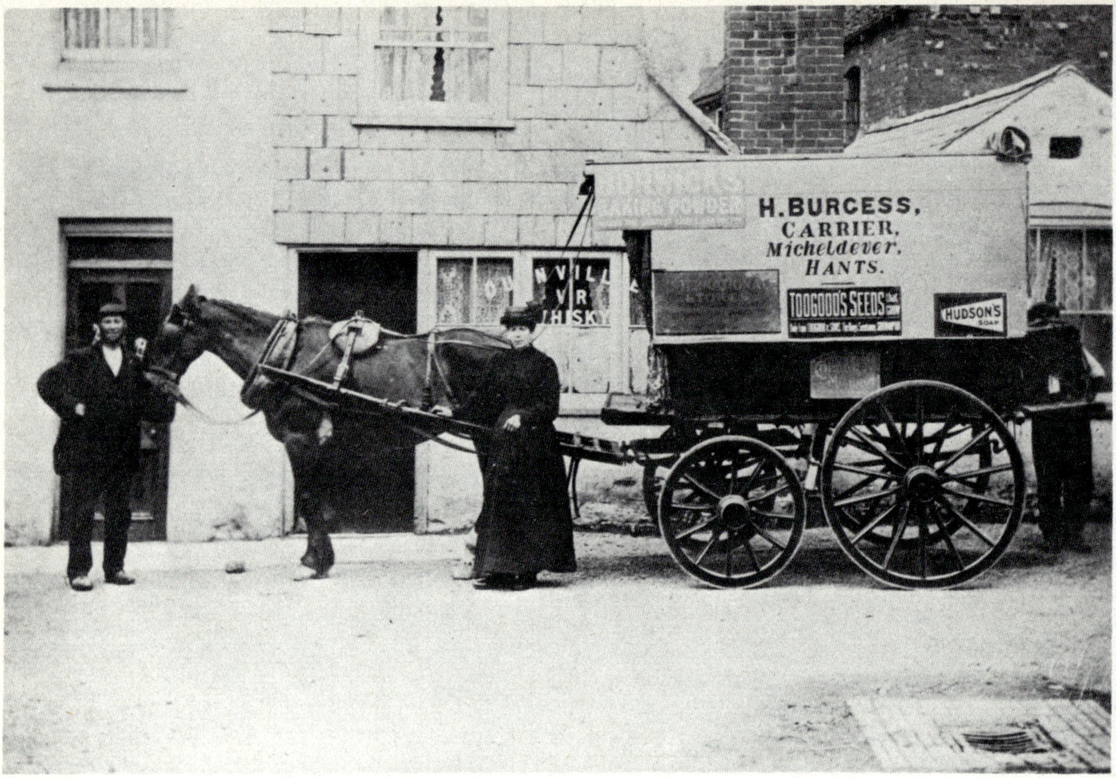

H. BURGESS,
CARRIER,
Micheldever,
HANTS.
TOOGOOD'S SEEDS
HUDSON'S

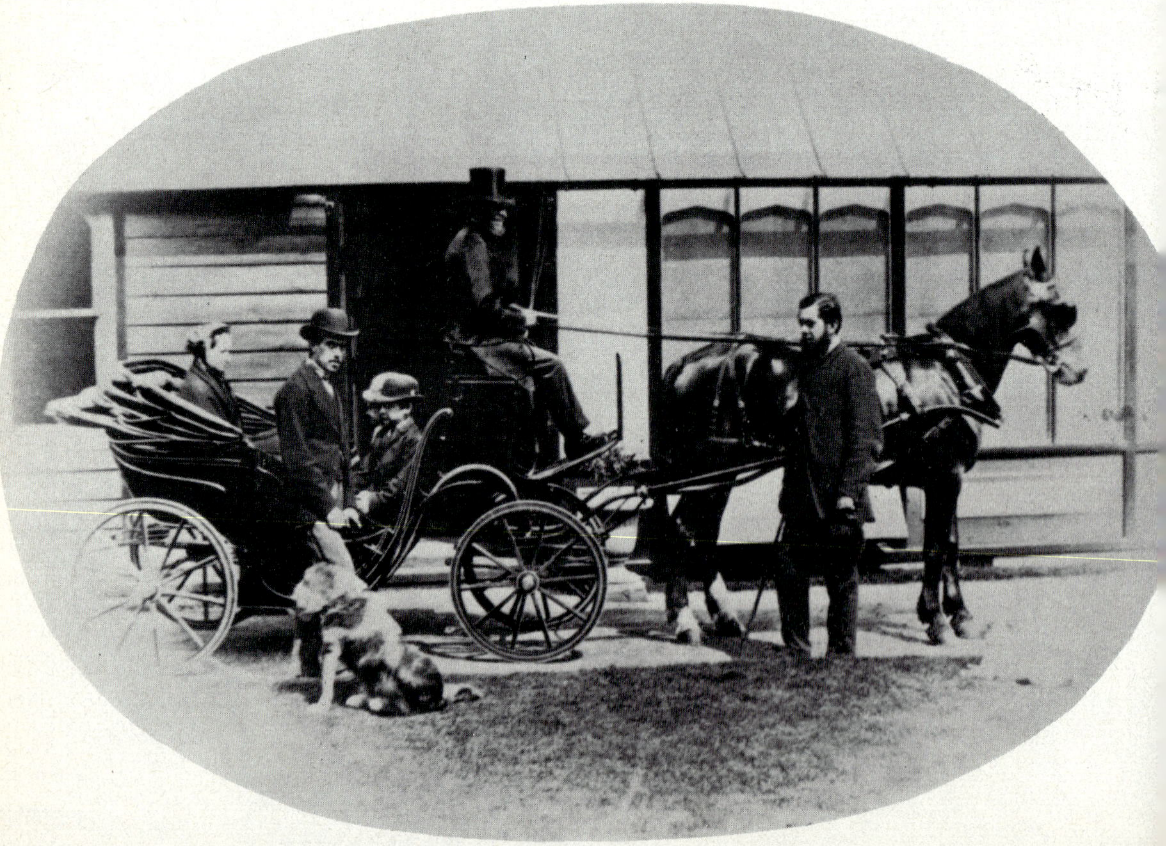

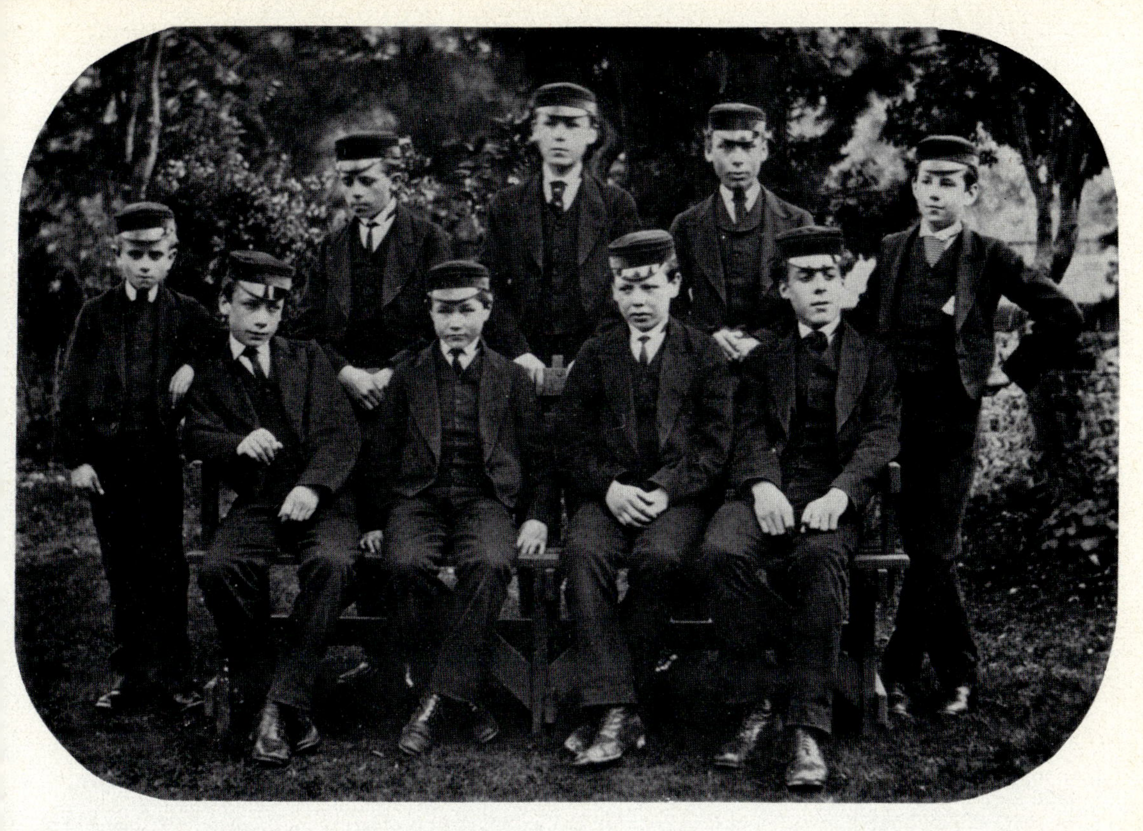

51 (Above left) c. 1910. Mr. and Mrs. Burgess, the carriers from Micheldever, took their cart to Winchester every Monday, Wednesday and Saturday and left the City Arms, near the Guildhall, at 3.30 p.m. for the long and slow return journey.

52 (Below left) c. 1870 "Moon's Carriage". John Moon had a livery stable in Edgar Rd. where horses and this carriage could be hired.

53 (Above) Winchester Cathedral choristers. October 1872.

54 (Below) A typical ward in the Royal Hampshire County Hospital, c. 1895. The Hospital was built in 1868 to the design of the architect William Butterfield, but the lay-out of the wards as shown here, was based on the recommendations of Florence Nightingale, who was a friend of the chairman of the Hospital's board of governors.

55 (Above right) Collecting for the hospital c. 1910.

56 (Below right) Du Boulay's, Edgar Rd. c. 1870. During the 19th century, Winchester College commoners were dispersed from the College itself and lodged in boarding houses situated on higher and healthier ground. Du Boulay's is one such boarding house, named after the first house master, the Rev. James Du Boulay who may be the man with the newspaper in this picture.

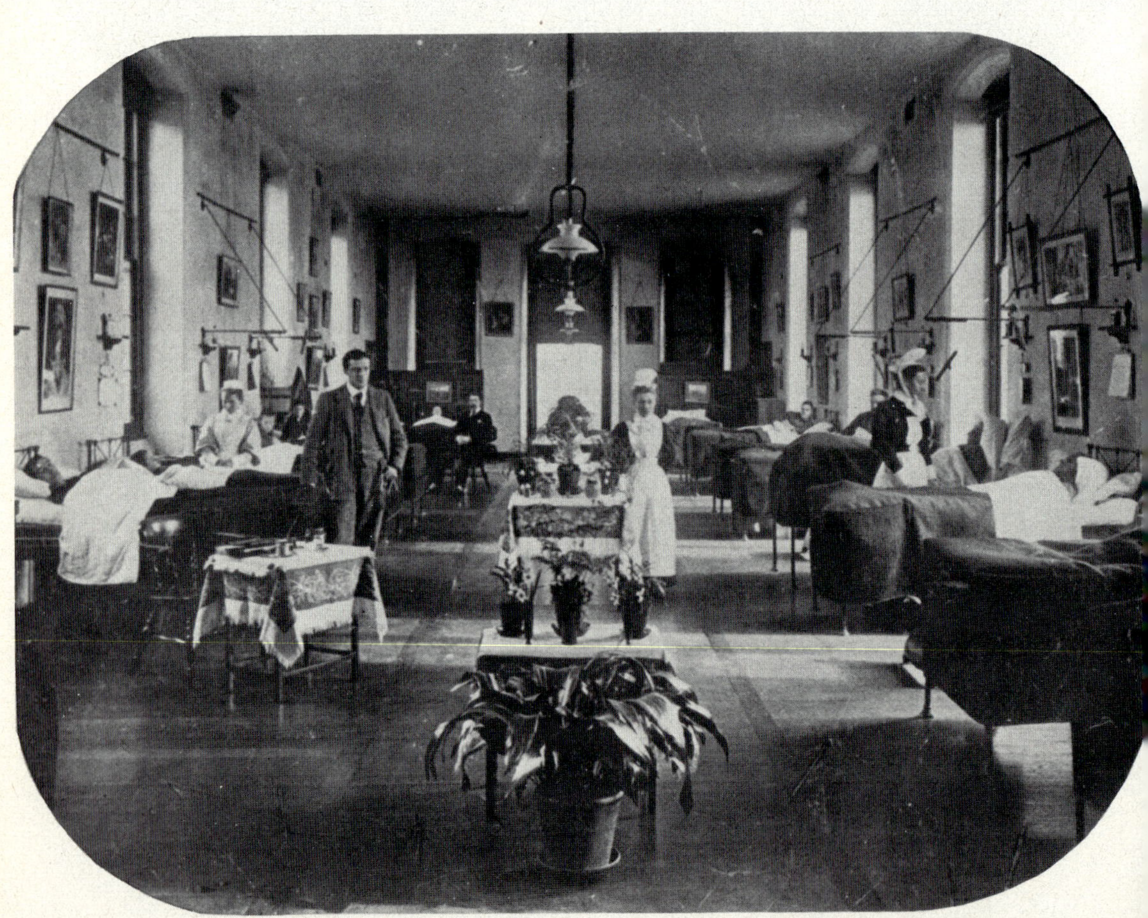

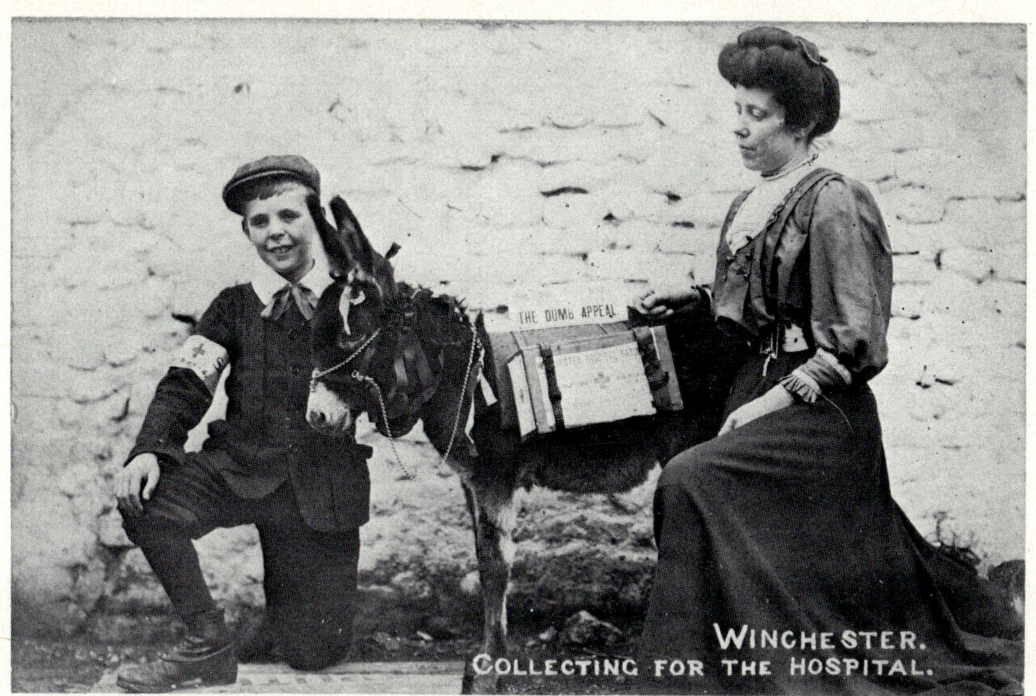

WINCHESTER.
COLLECTING FOR THE HOSPITAL.

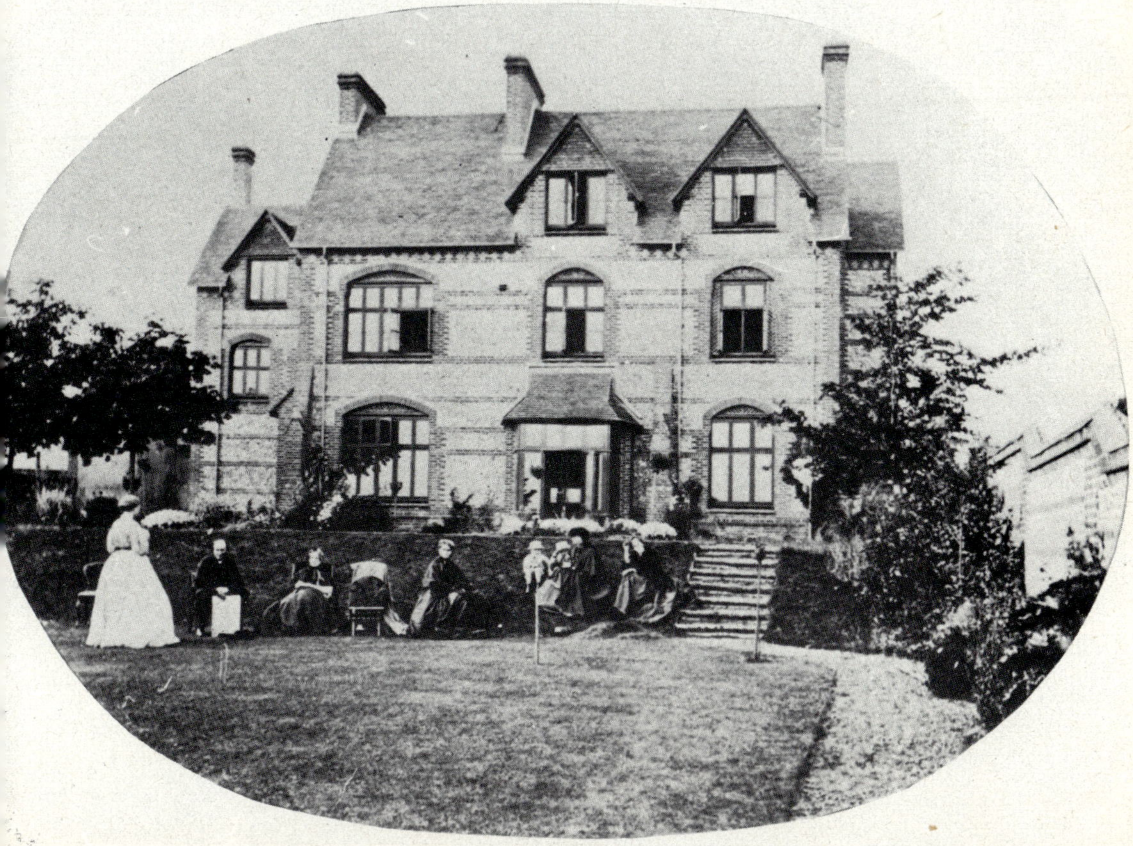

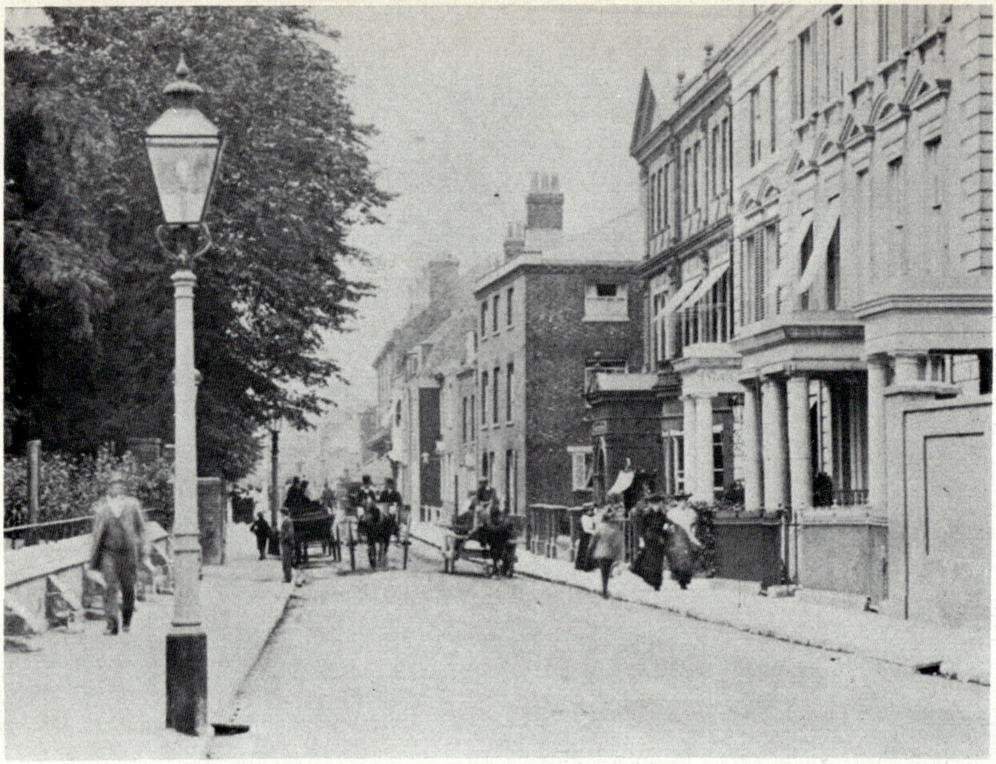

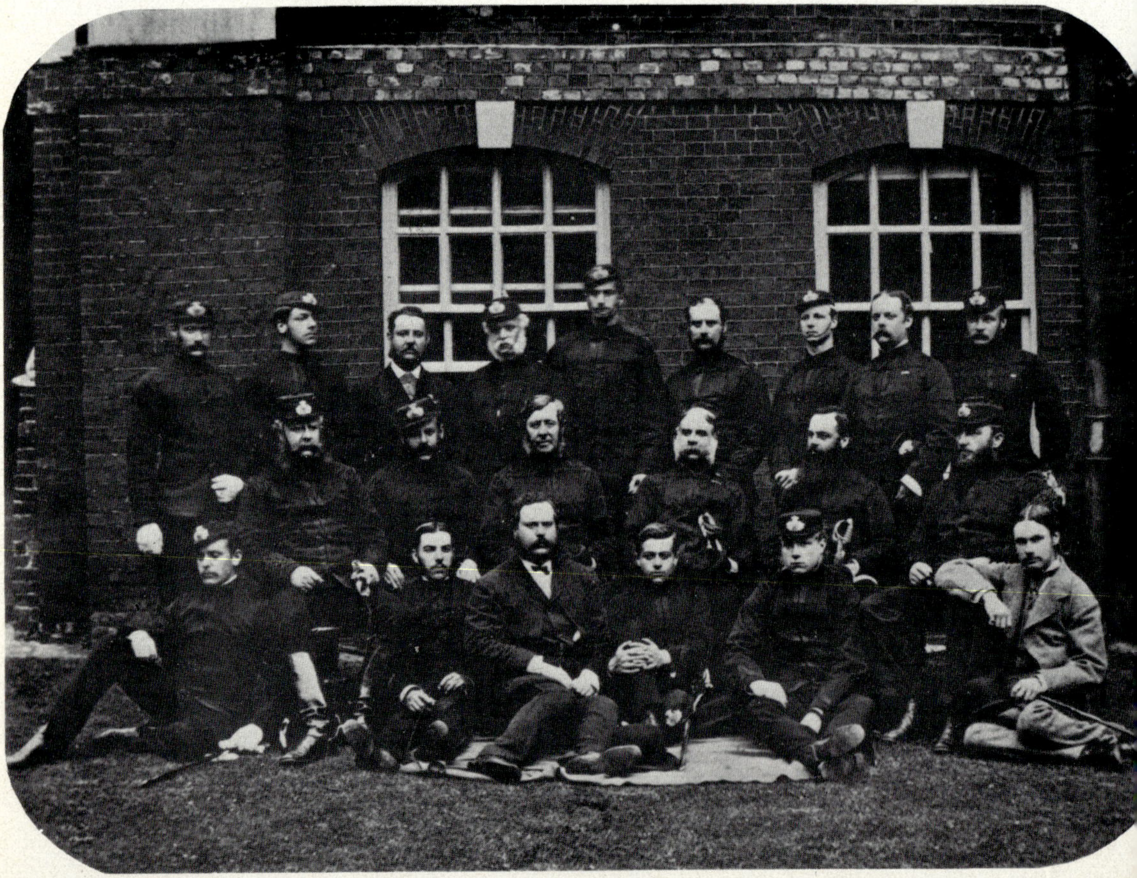

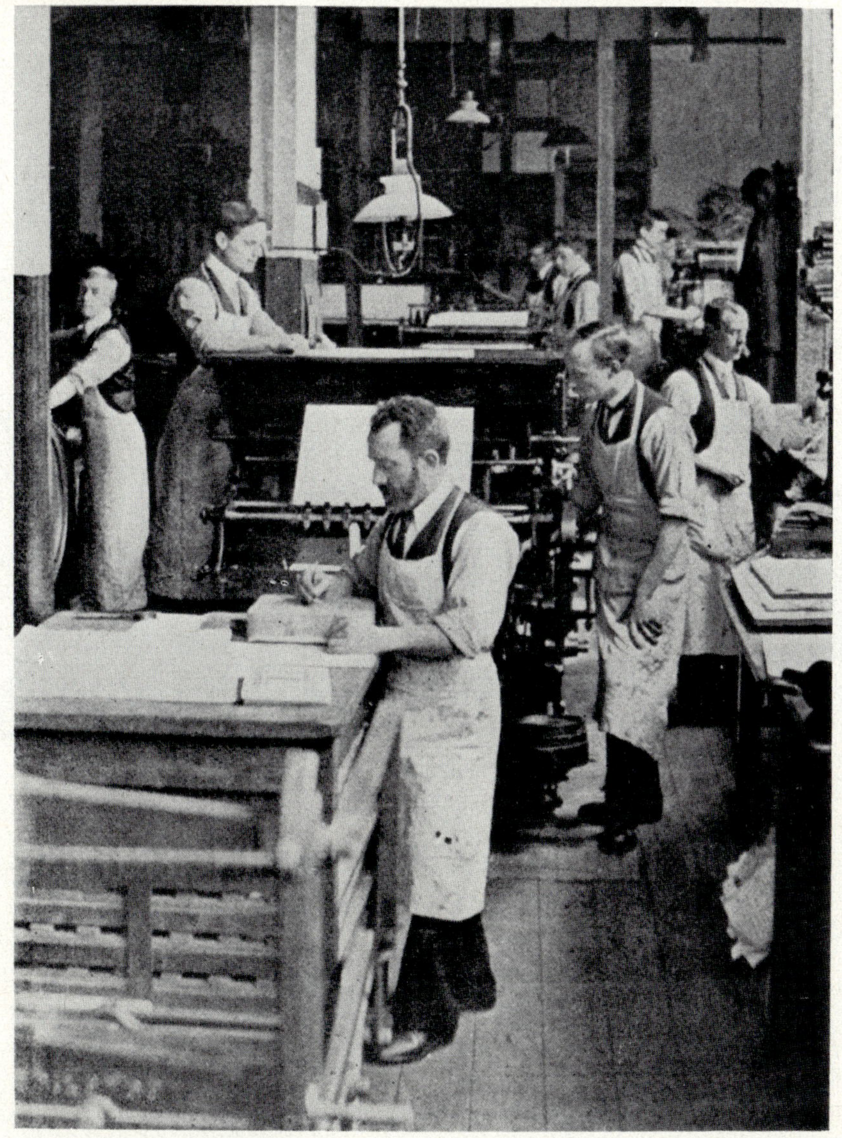

57 (Above left) Southgate St. looking towards High St., c. 1900. The wall on the left belongs to St. Thomas's Church (now the County Archives) and the trees beyond stand in the garden of Serles House.

58 (Below left) c. 1881. Officers of the Hants. Militia on the lawn in front of Serles House (now the museum of the Royal Hampshire Regiment).

59 (Above) c. 1909. Inside the lithographic and copper-plate department of Warren and Son in Staple Garden. The Hampshire Observer newspaper, guides, directories and books were all printed here.

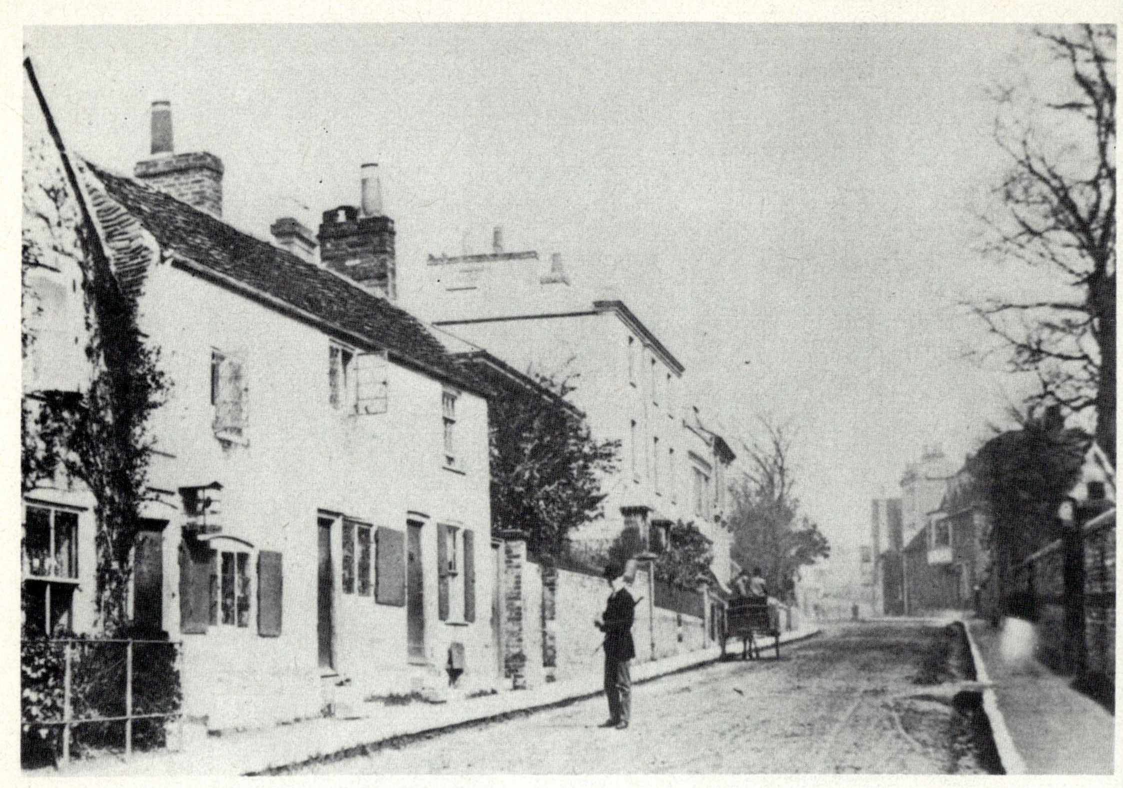

60 (Above) Southgate Rd. looking north c. 1871. The Oriel window of the Oriel Hotel can just be seen on the right. The house on the left with shutters has been demolished and replaced by the Southgate Rd. Post Office.

61 (Right) c. 1890. The stable yard belonging to G. Parker in Southgate St. Mr. Parker was a horse dealer and is said to have made his fortune during the Boer War selling horses to the Army. These buildings are now used by Will Short's garage (see plate 44). The chimney on the left (now demolished) belonged to Dear & Co., the brewers of St. James's Lane.

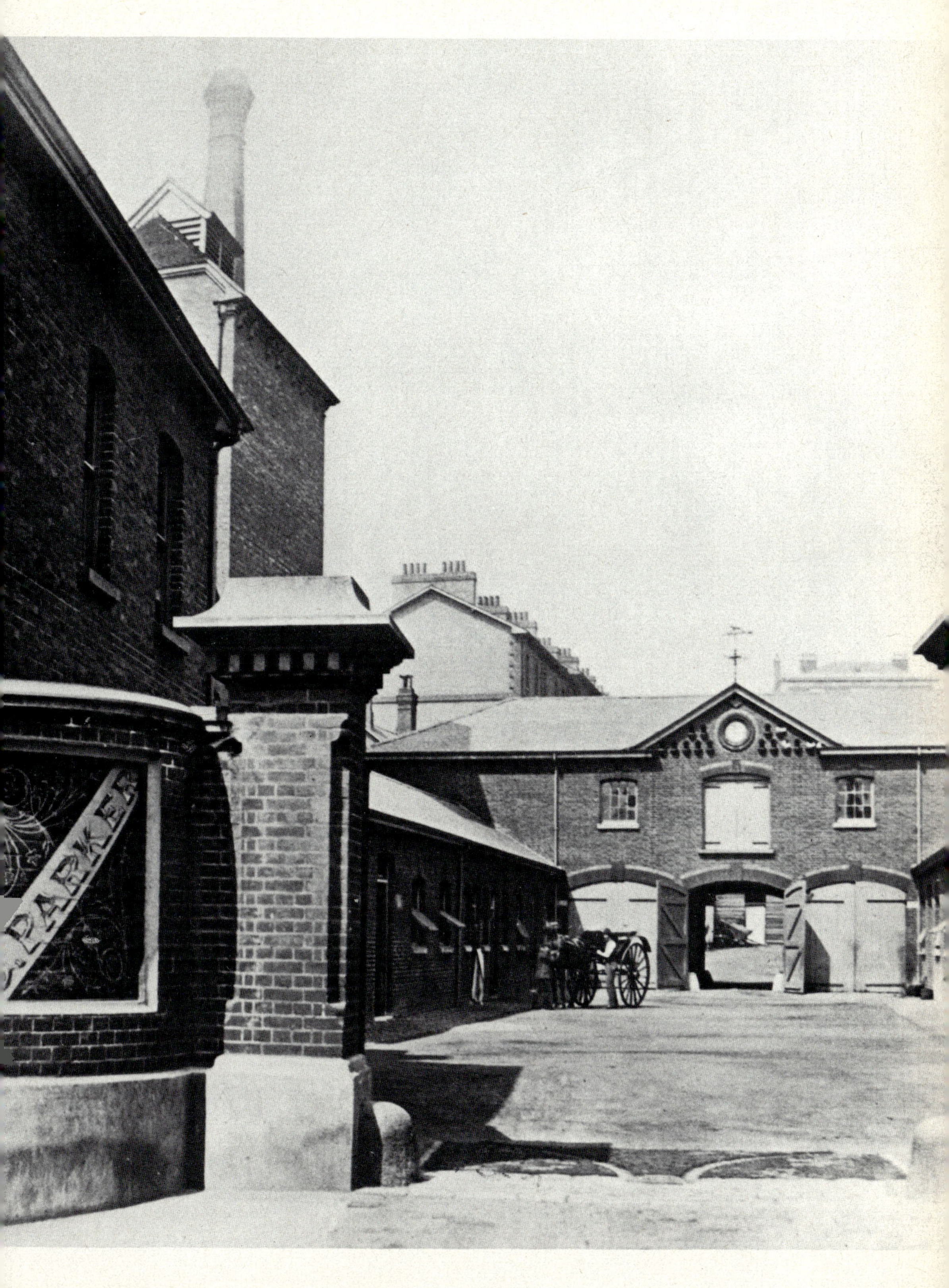
PARKER

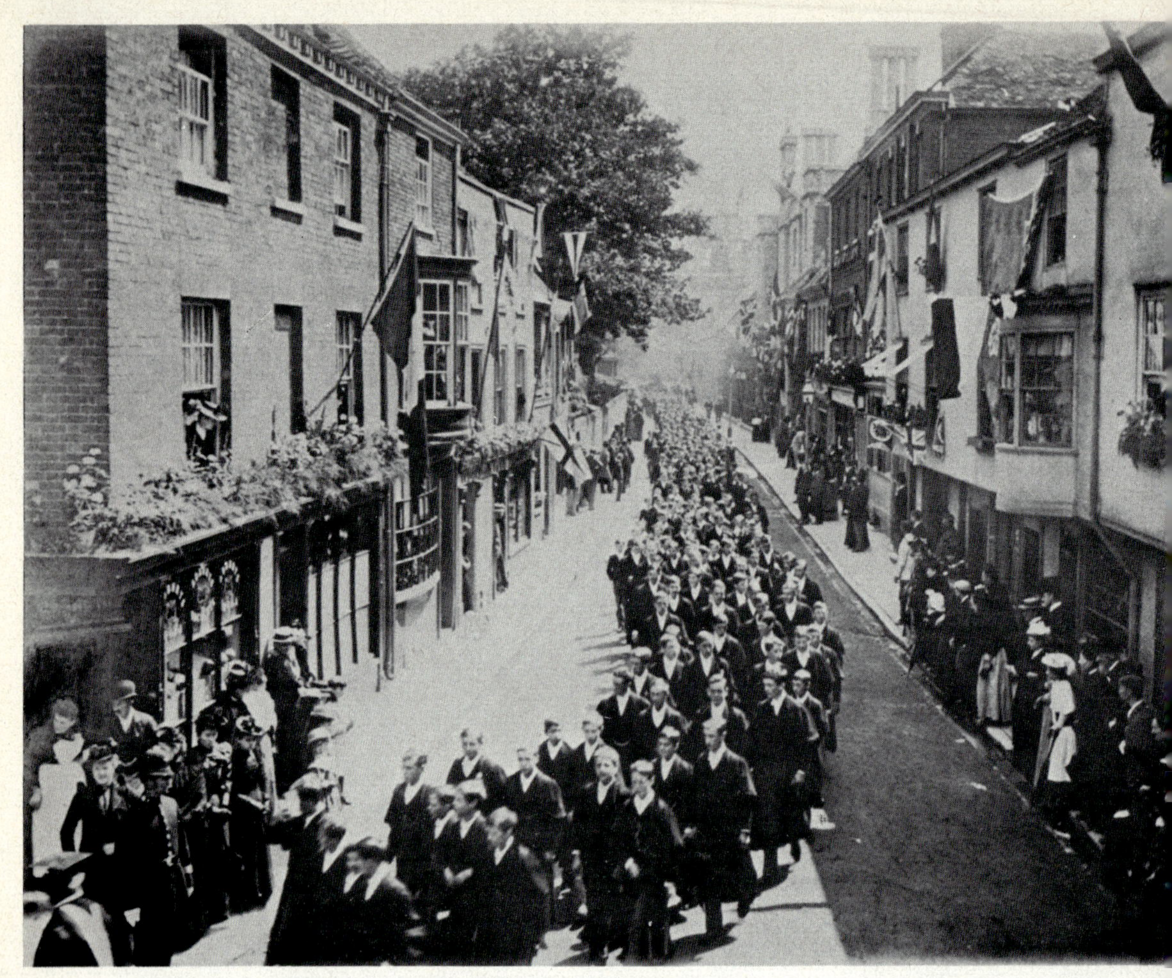

62 (Above) 1893. Members of Winchester College taking part in the celebrations of the 500th anniversary of the founding of the College. The procession began at the College and moved to the Cathedral for a service of thanksgiving. The houses on the left of the picture have been demolished to make way for gardens.

63 (Below) The Eton–Winchester cricket match played on the Winchester College playing fields in 1894.

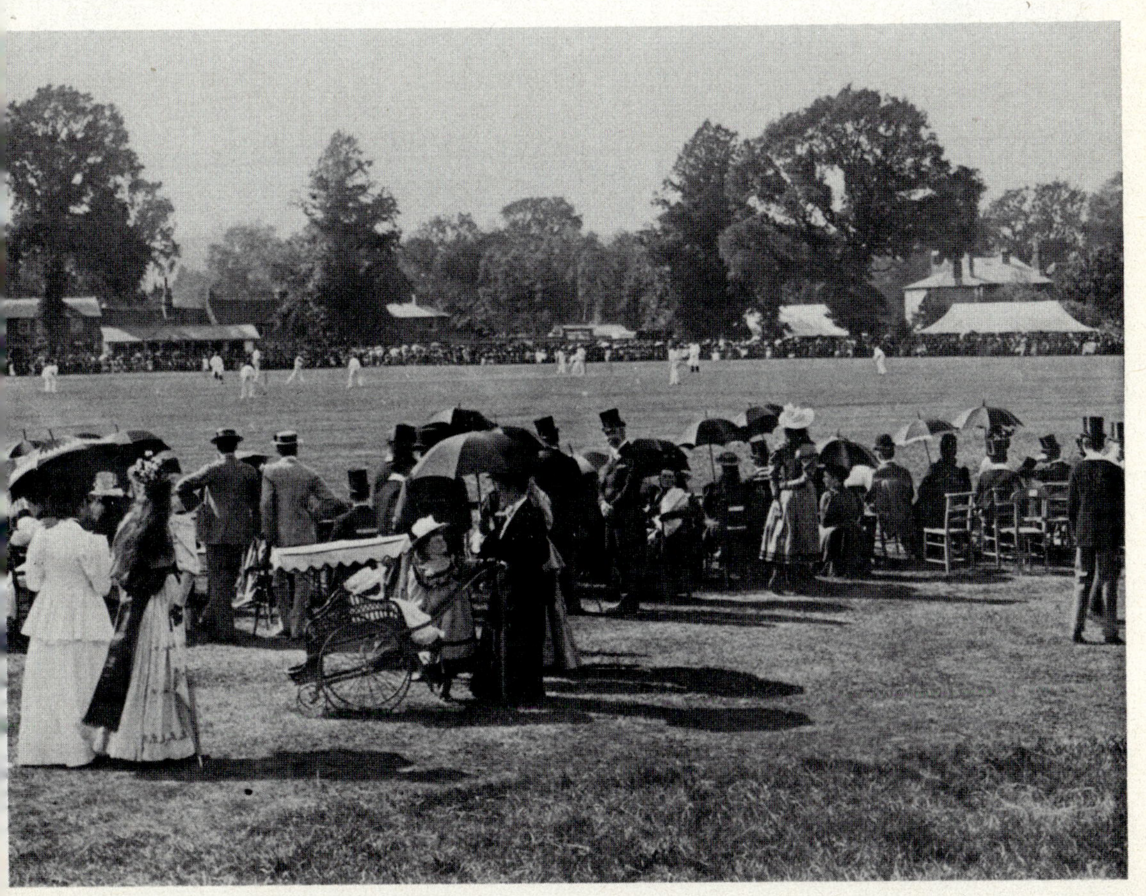

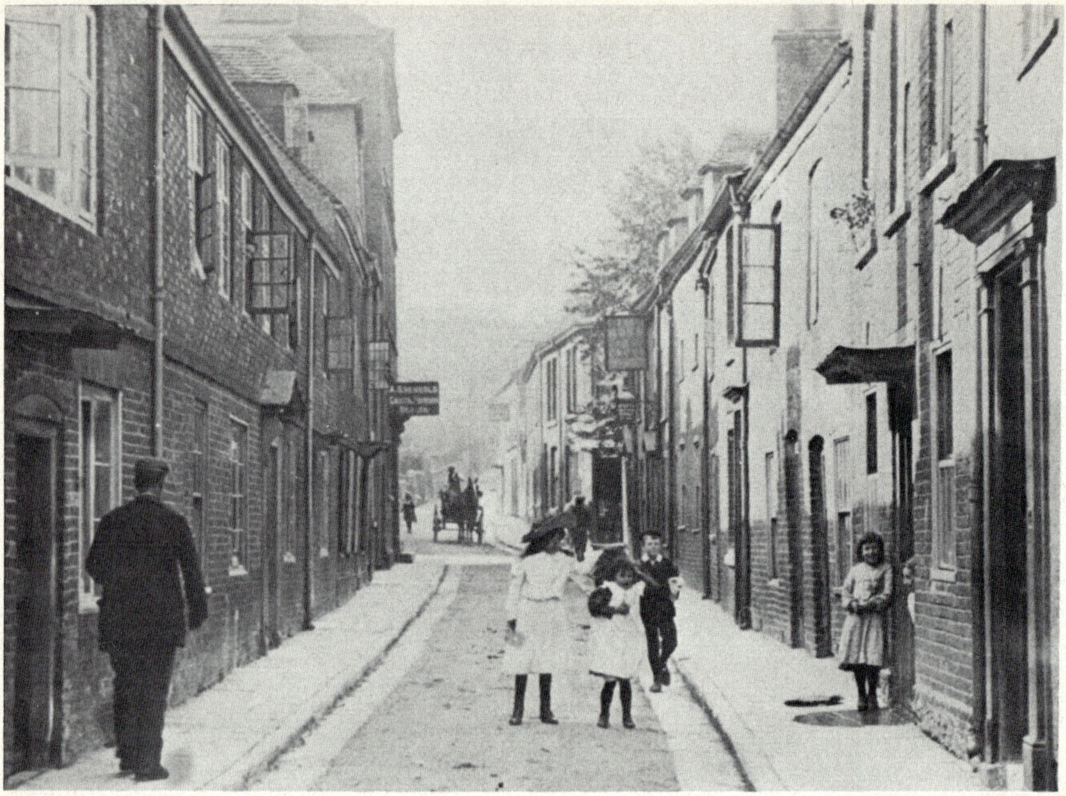

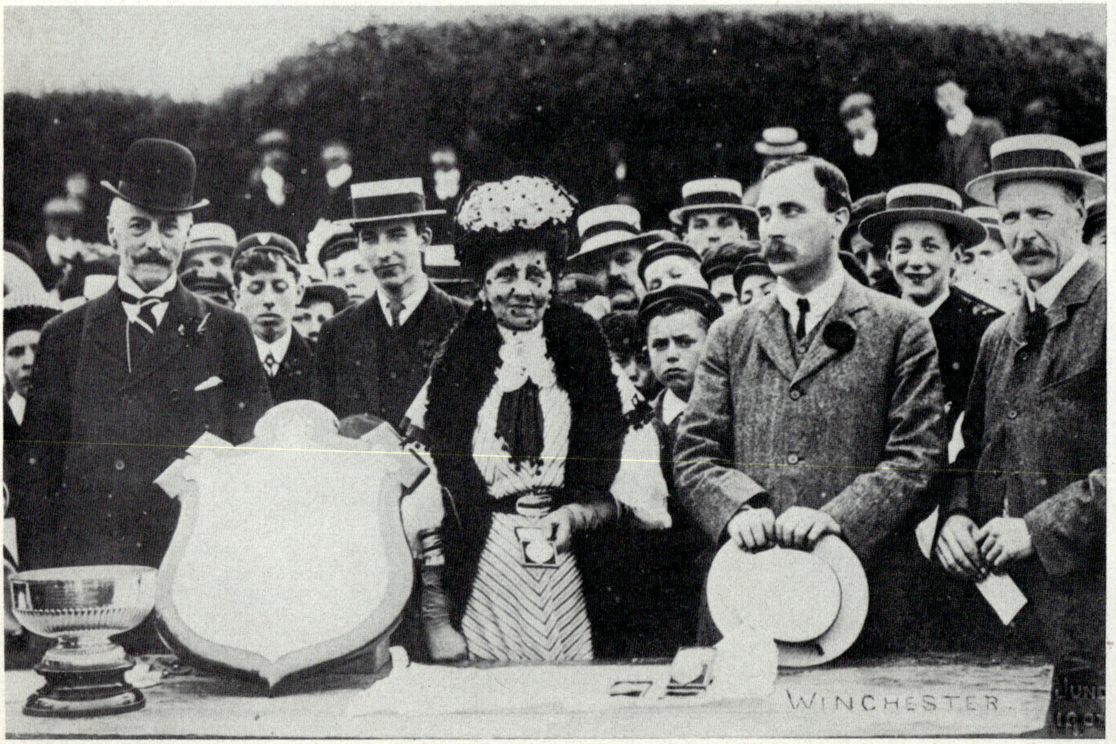

WINCHESTER.

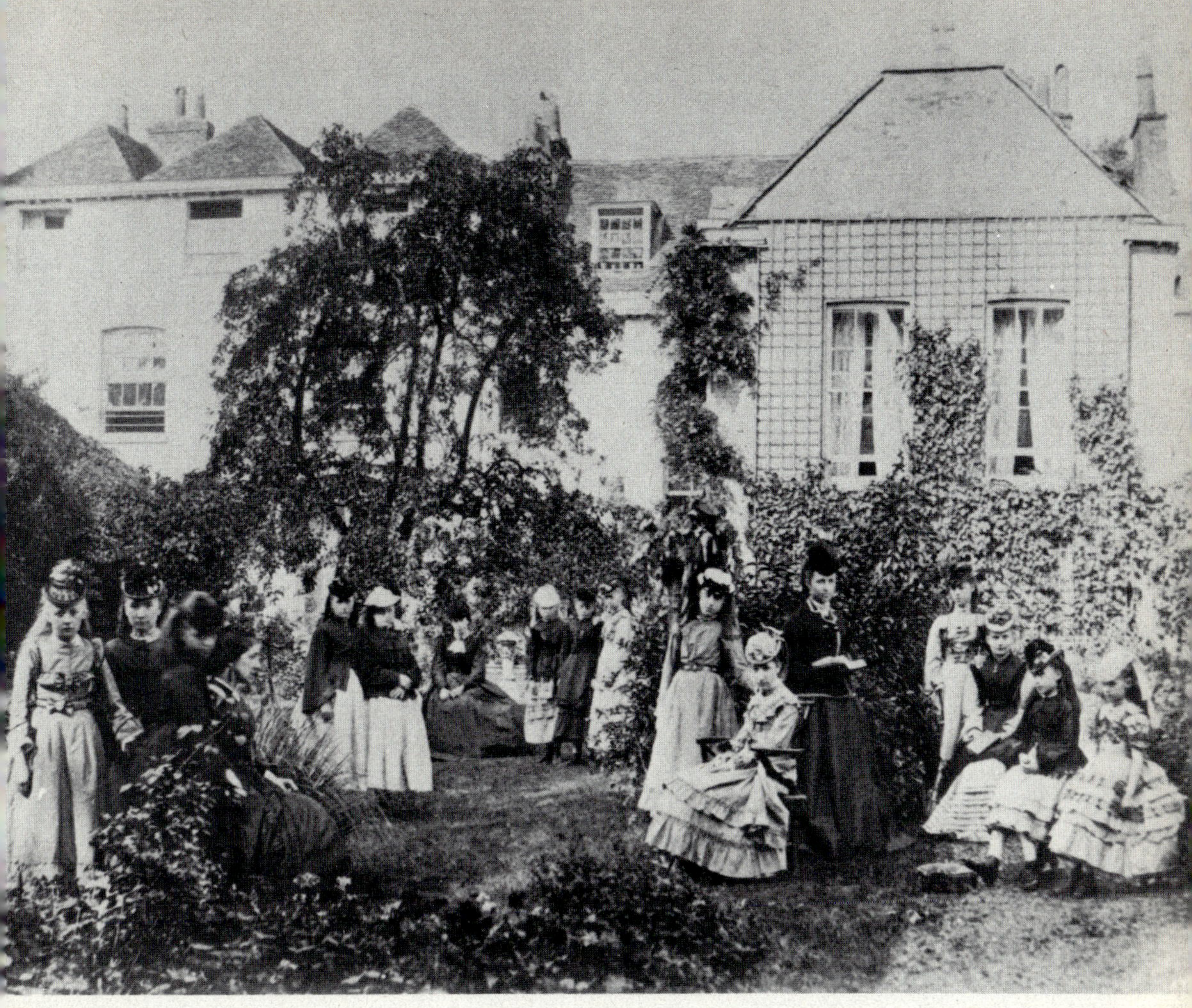

64 (Above left) Canon St. looking north c. 1900. The shop sign on the left bears the name of Mrs. Ann Shergold, grocer, and the sign on the right belongs to the Rose and Crown Inn.

65 (Below left) Lady Portal distributing the prizes at the Hampshire Public Schools Athletics Sports at Bar End, Winchester in June 1907. The sports were an annual event and seven schools competed: Perin's of Alresford, Eggar's of Alton, Andover Grammar, Queen Mary's Basingstoke, Bournemouth School, Gosport Secondary School and Peter Symond's of Winchester.

66 (Above) c. 1872. In the garden of 9 Kingsgate St. where the Misses Lucy, Eliza and Amelia White ran a school for young ladies.

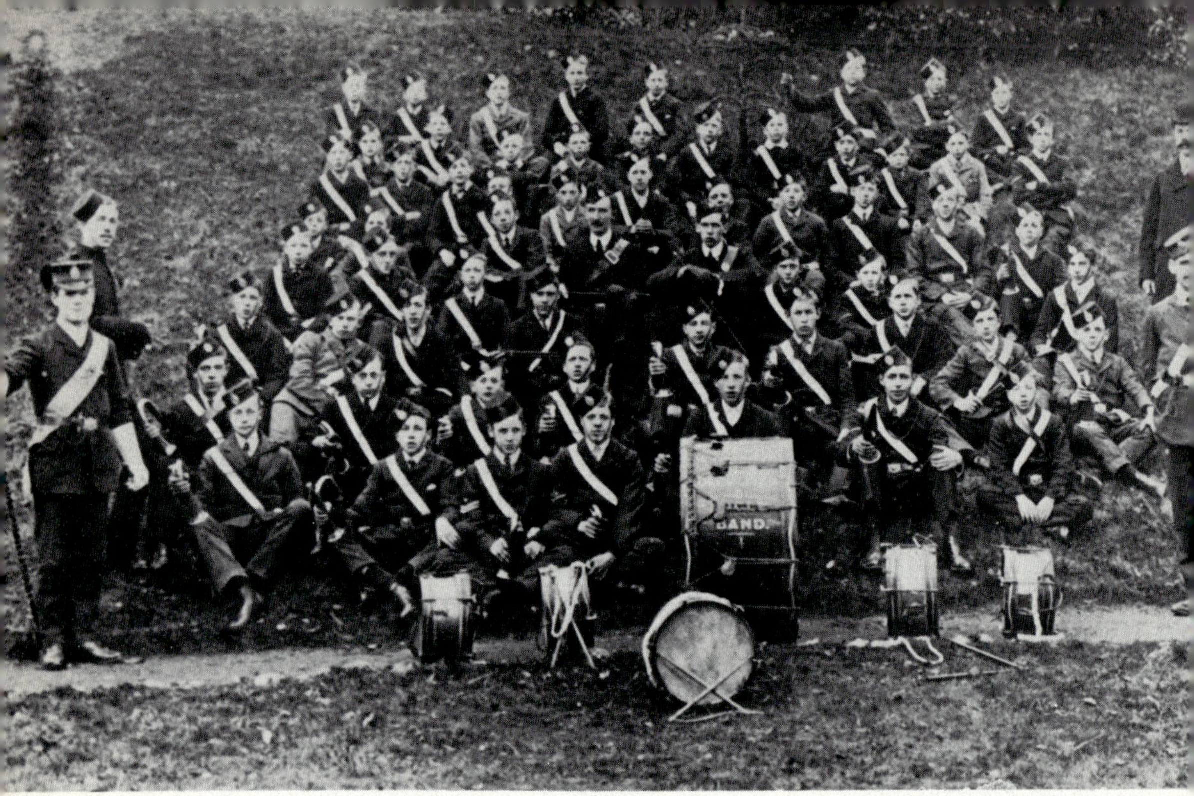

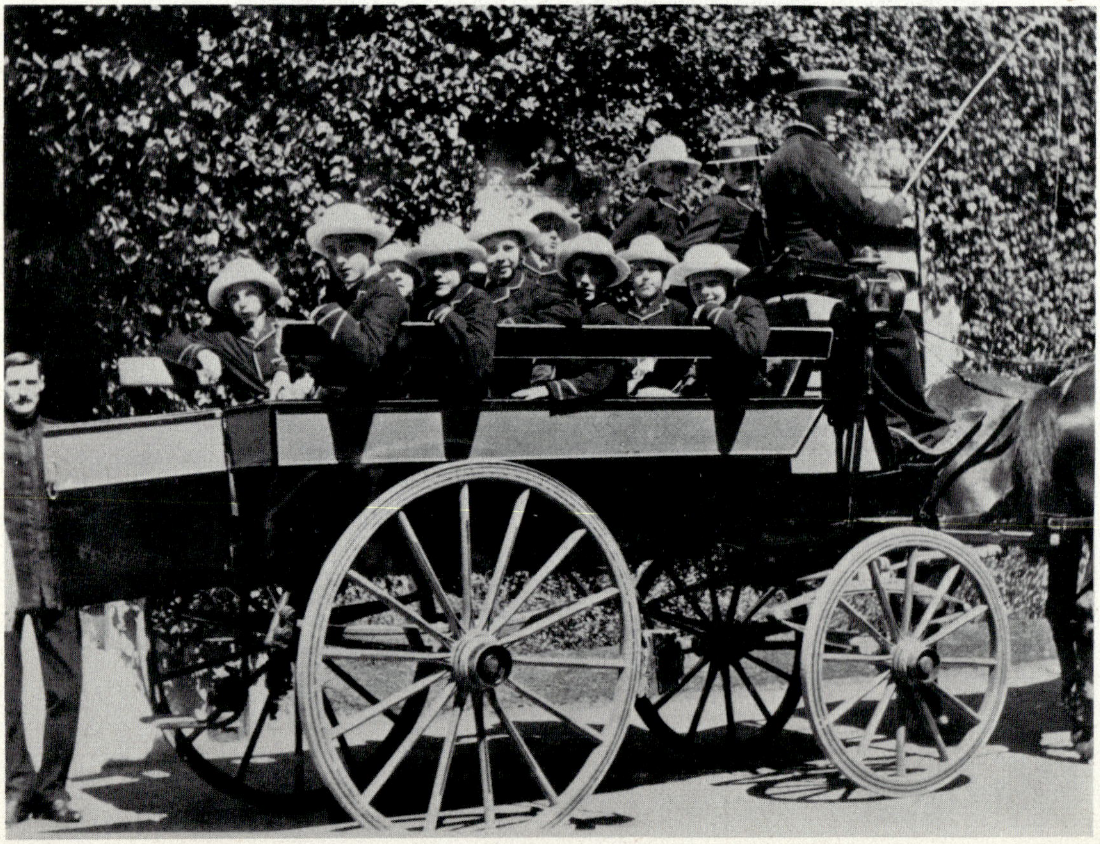

67 (Above left) Winchester Church Lad's Brigade Band c. 1895.

68 (Below left) 1913 Boys leaving Winton House School for an outing in a horse-drawn charabanc.

69 (Below) Winton House c. 1870. Boys playing croquet on the lawn. The figure on the left may be Dr. C. A. Johns the headmaster and well-known author of natural history books.

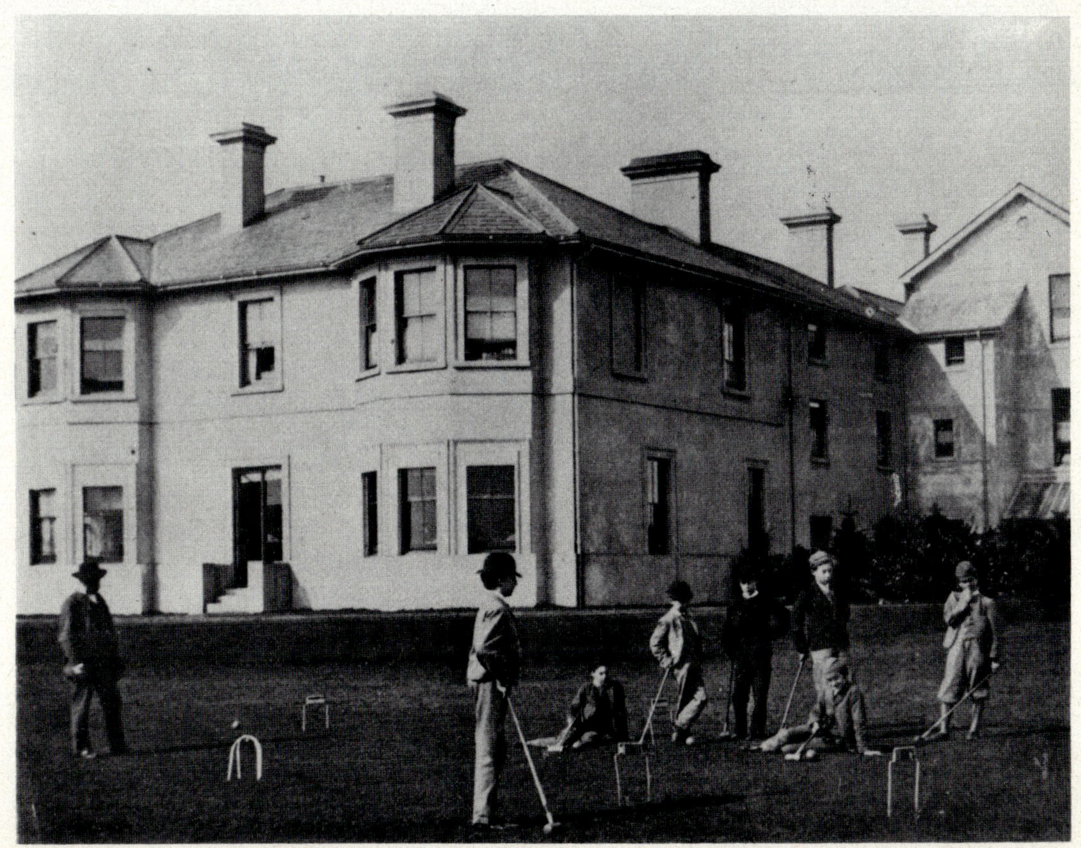

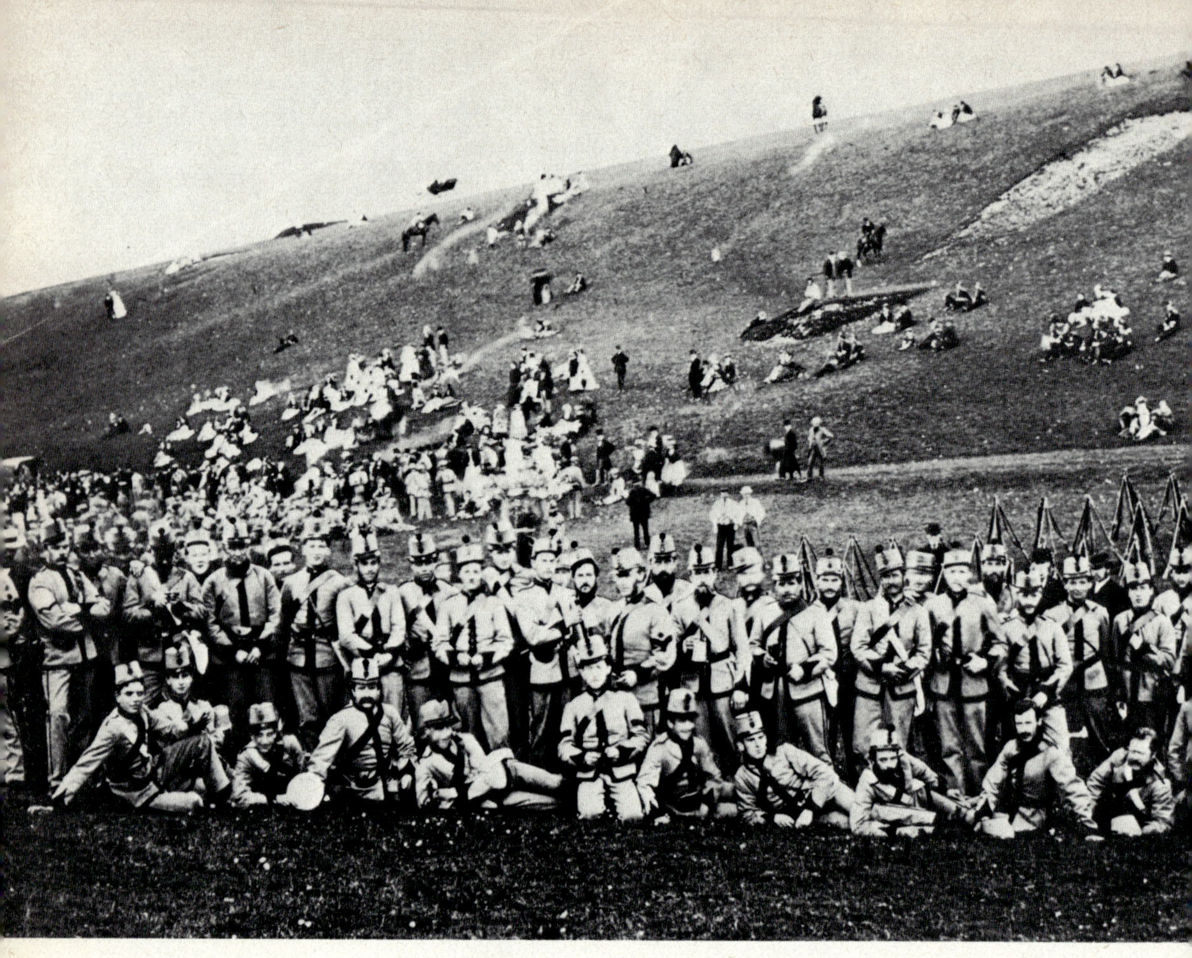

70 (Above) Hampshire Volunteers on Teg Down, 1871.

71 (Above right) The Mayor of Winchester, W. Jacob, sits in the centre of this group at the celebration of the opening of the Abbey grounds in 1890 – Abbey House is the Mayor's official residence.

72 (Below right) A motor mail van which plunged from the Alresford Rd. at St Giles's Hill and came to rest at the top of St. John's St. The accident occurred at 5 a.m. on July 15th 1911 and the guard was killed. The mail van had left London the previous evening and was travelling to Southampton loaded with mail for South Africa.

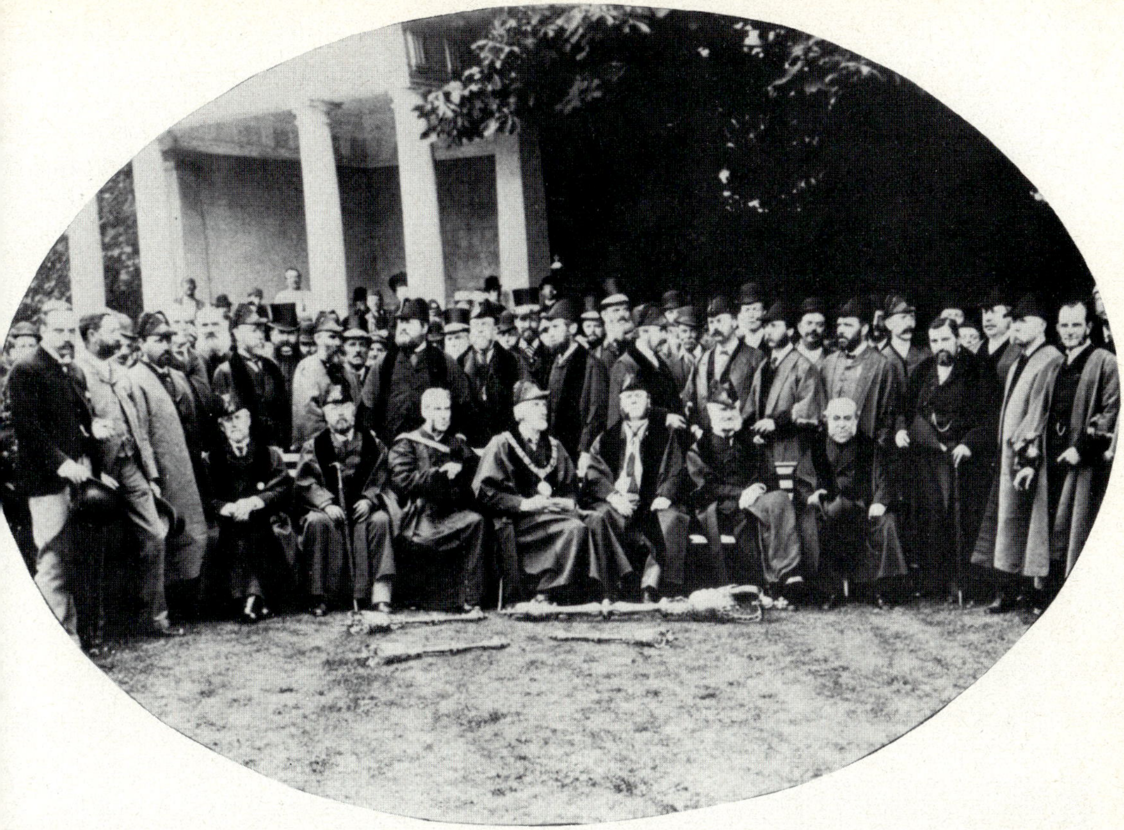

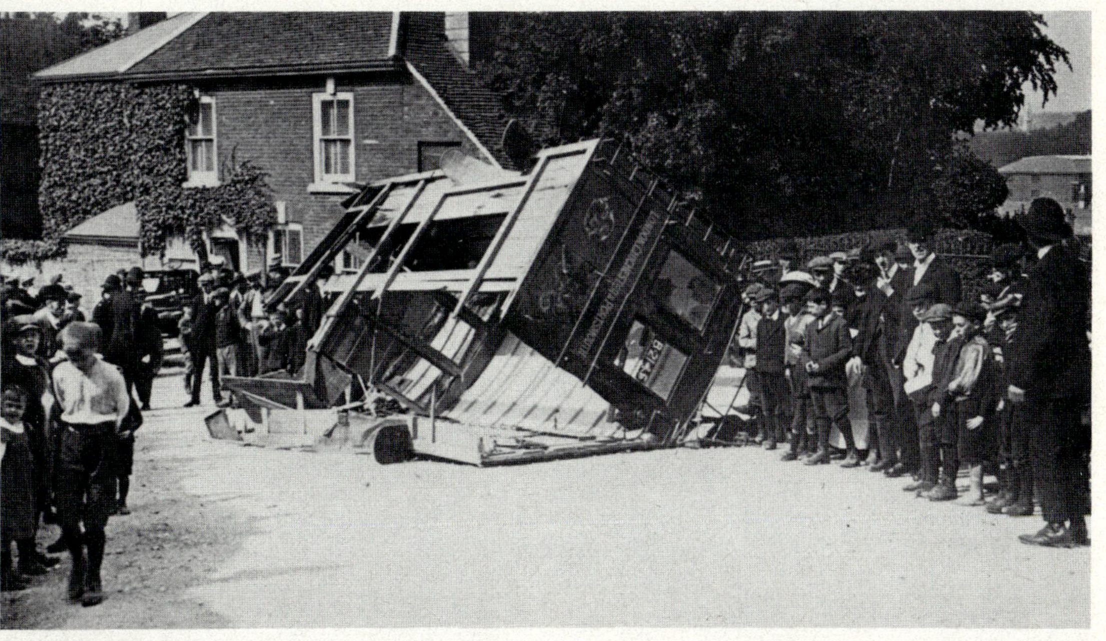

73 (Below) Our forefathers seemed to have had a marked fondness for processions. Apart from celebrating Coronations and Anniversaries in this way (see plate 62) they also had more light-hearted processions. This is believed to be the first procession of motor-cars in Winchester. c1905.

74 (Above right) Also held in the Broadway was the annual Cart Horse Parade. This was discontinued at the outbreak of the First World War.

75 (Below right) A less happy occasion. Soon after the outbreak of the First World War the manager of the Maypole Dairy, just below the pentice in the High Street, was suspected of being a German. He was accused of ridiculing the troops and the public retaliated by smashing the shop windows. Here soldiers have been called in to help the police disperse the crowd.

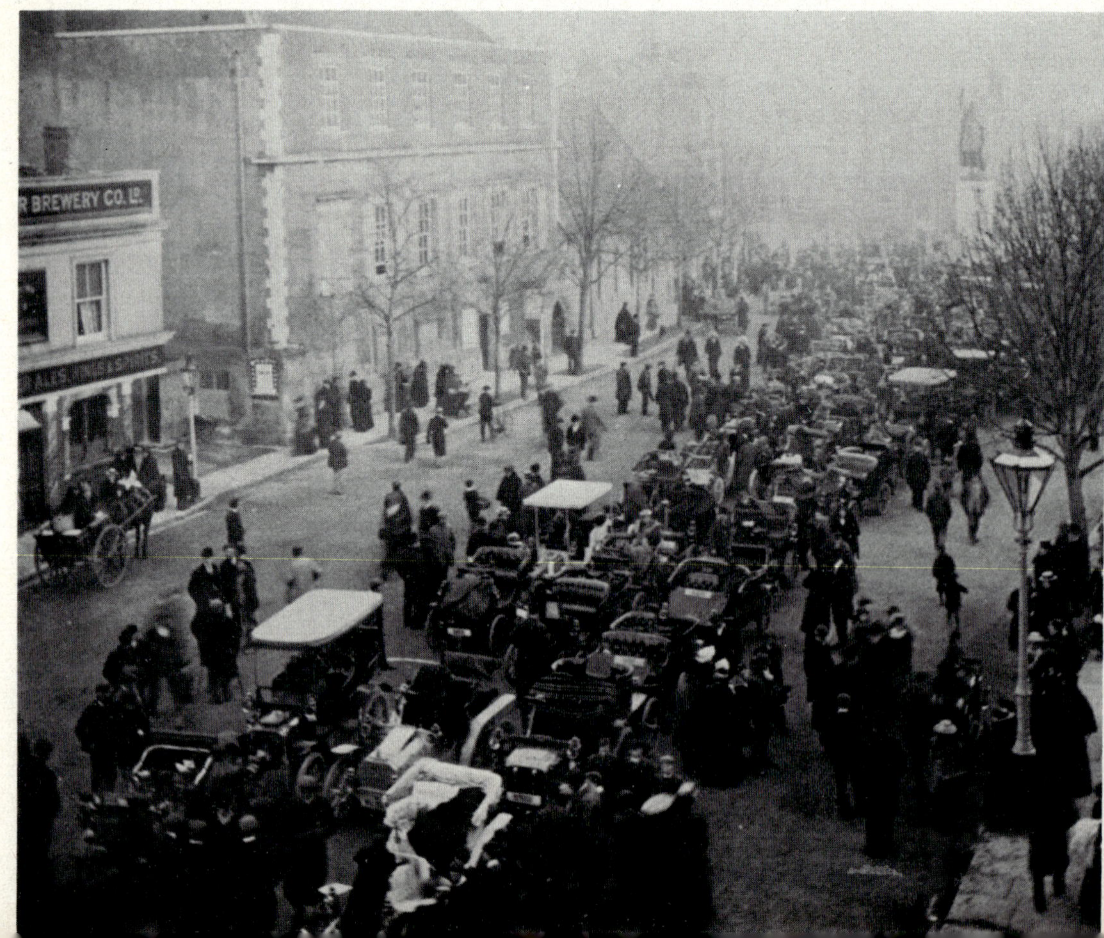

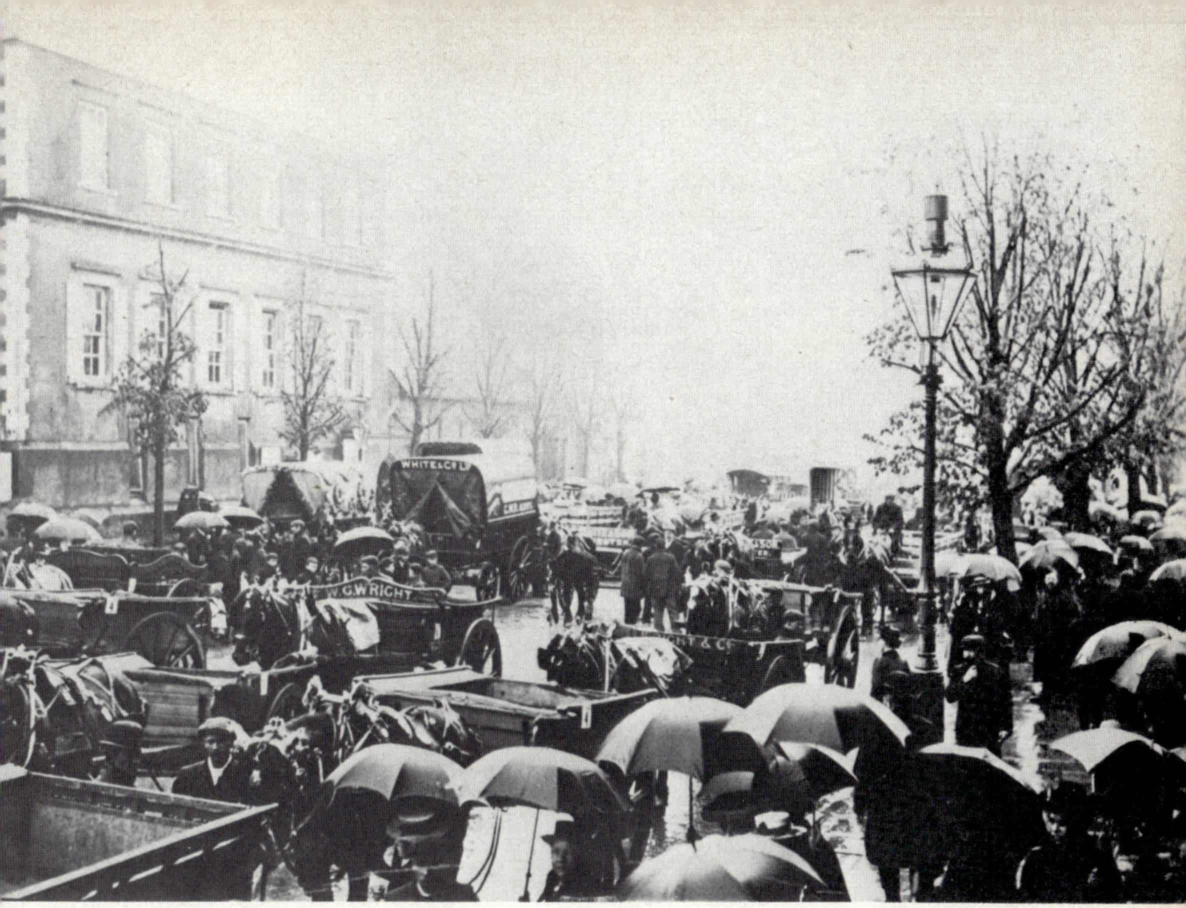

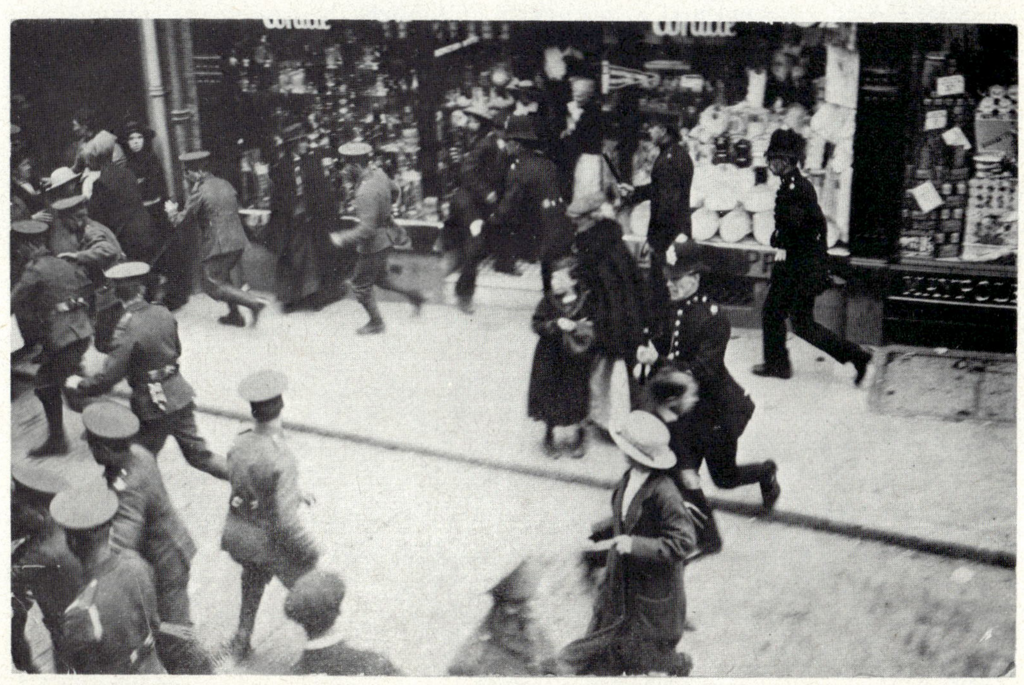

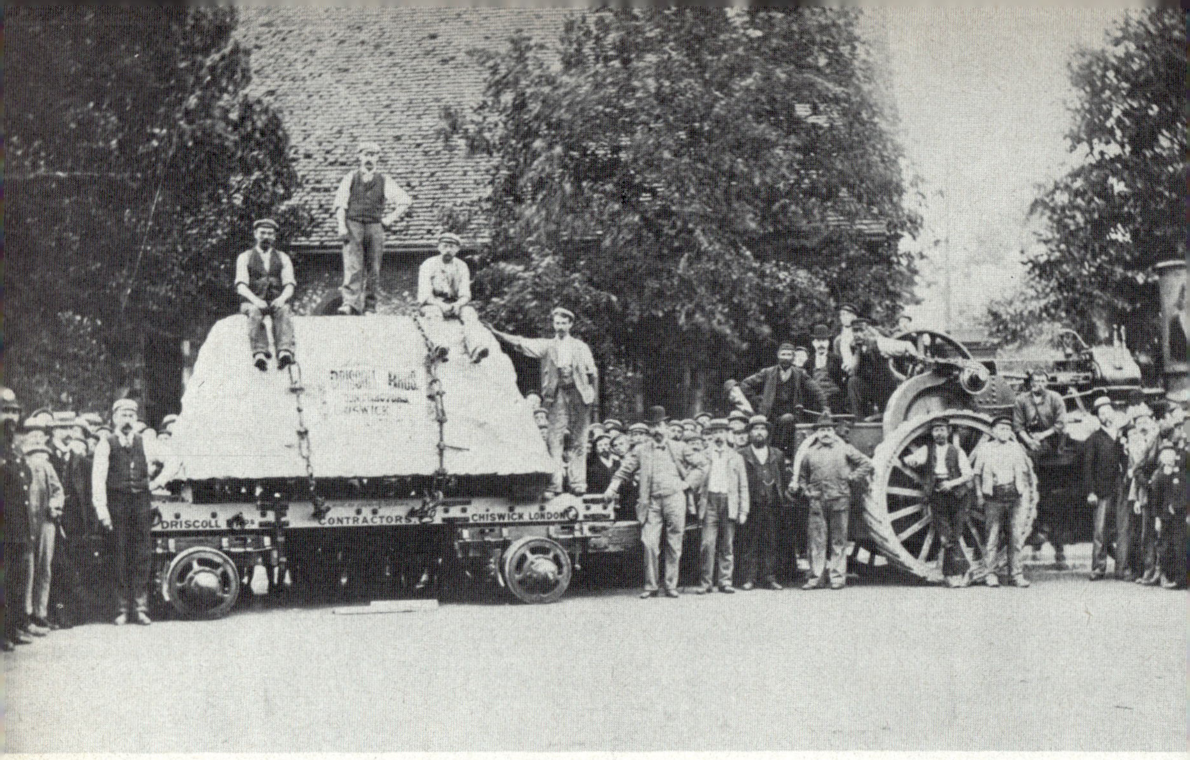

76 and 77 To commemorate the 1000th. anniversary of the death of King Alfred, whose capital city was Winchester, the citizens decided to place a statue of the King in the Broadway. The Statue was designed by Sir Hamo Thornycroft RA and erected in 1901. In Plate 76 (above) the base of the statue, which had been brought from a stone-quarry at Penryn in Cornwall, nears the end of its journey. In plate 77 (right) a group of notable citizens pose in front of the statue shortly after the opening ceremony. The man in the centre of the picture wearing a dark coat and with a heavy black moustache is Councillor Alfred Bowker, the Mayor of Winchester, and the moving force behind the whole enterprise.

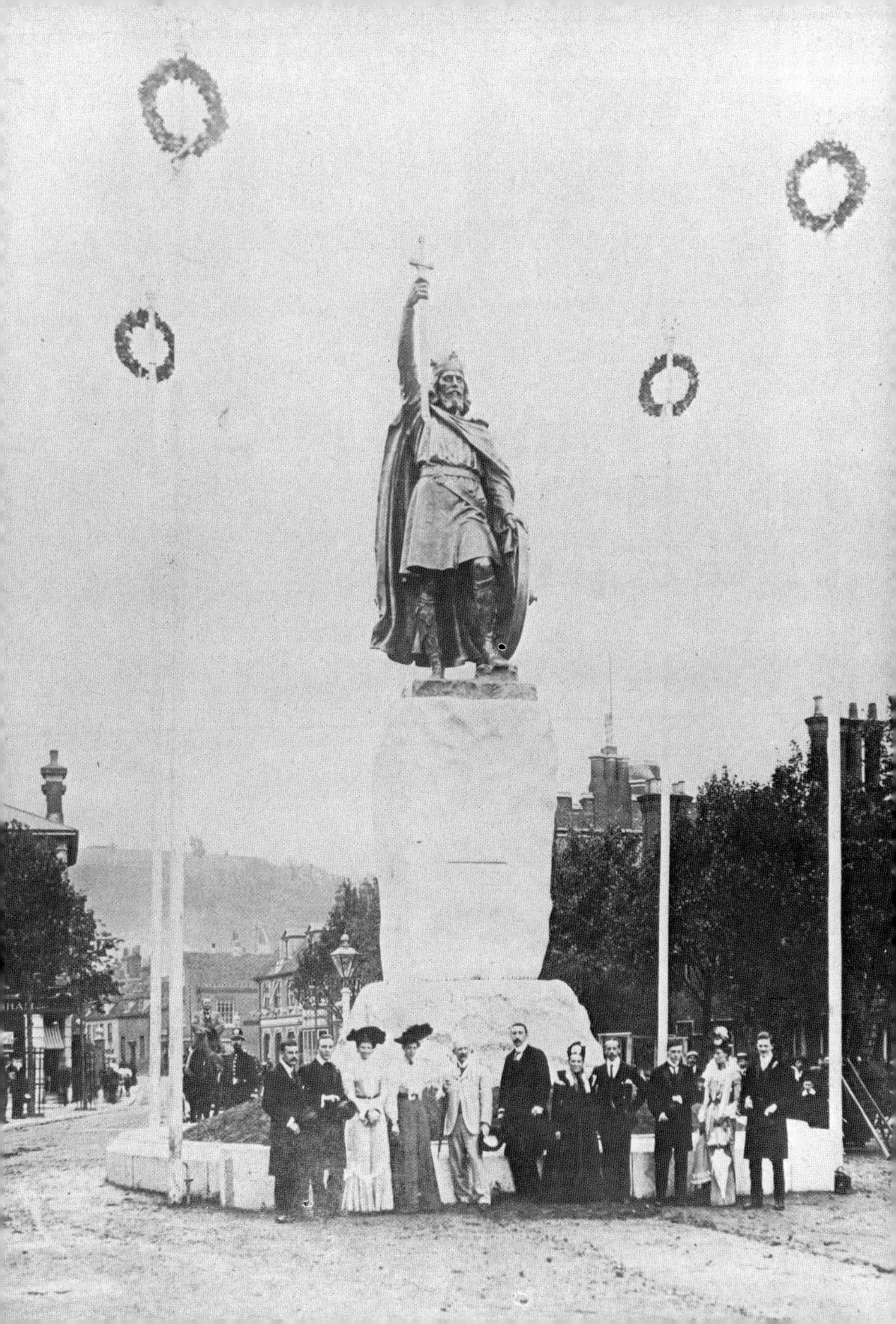

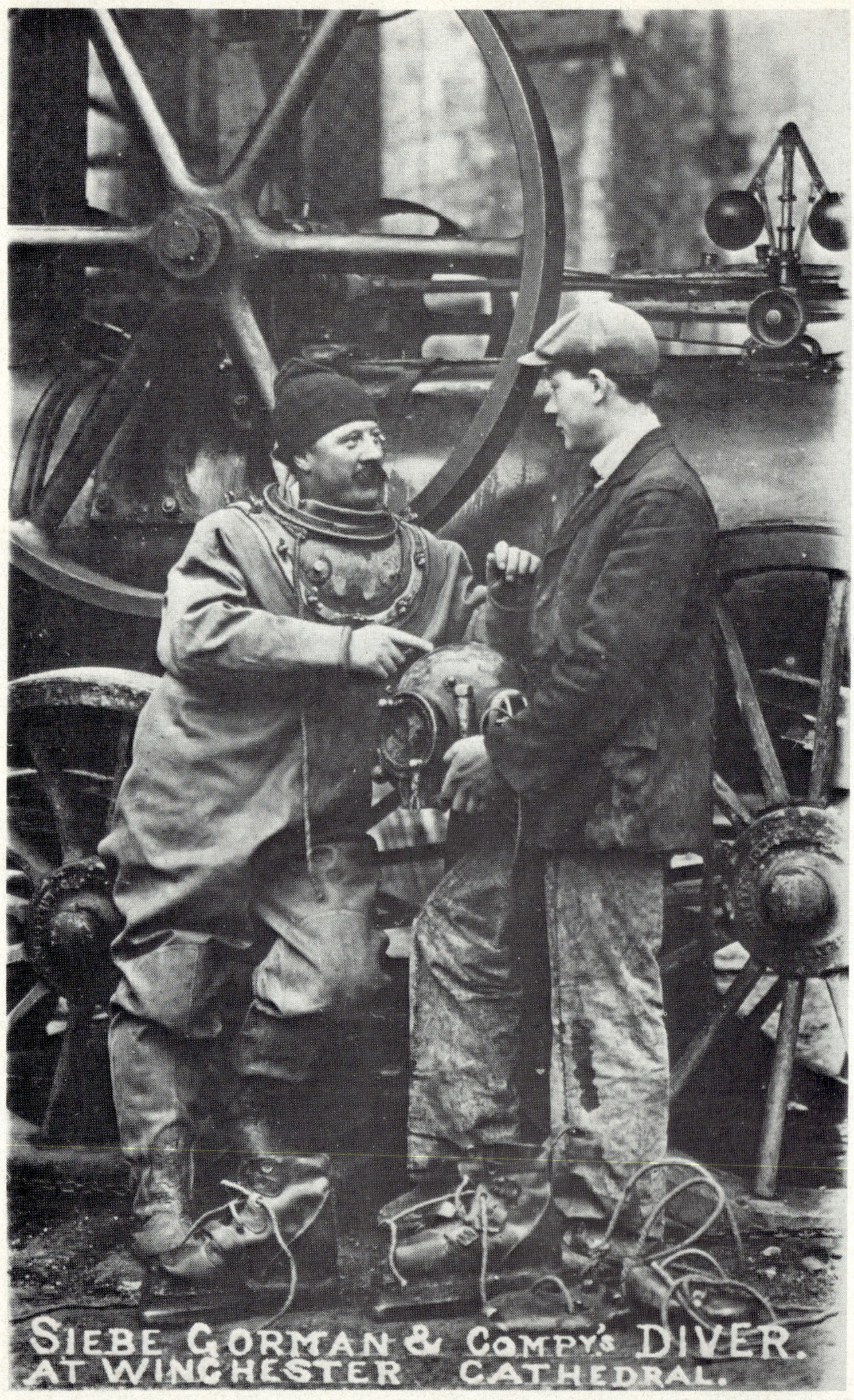

SIEBE GORMAN & COMPY's DIVER.
AT WINCHESTER CATHEDRAL.

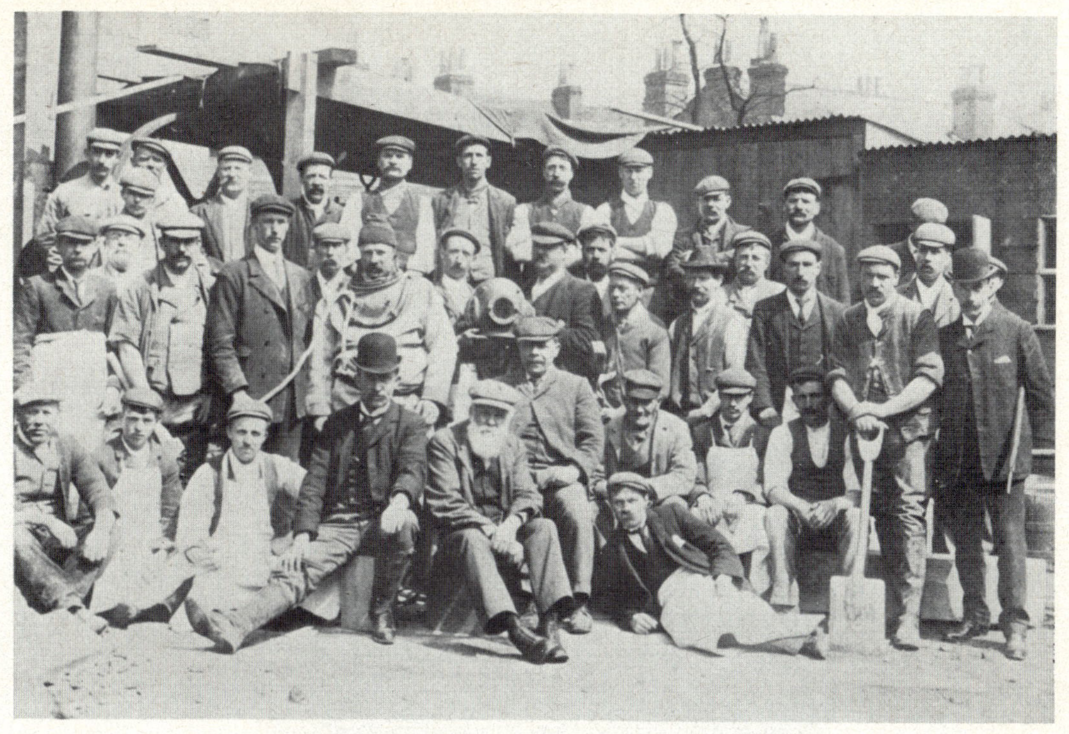

78 (Left) In 1905 it became apparent that Winchester Cathedral was sinking perilously into the marsh on which it was built and that a deep sea diver would have to go beneath the Cathedral to underpin the foundations. The man chosen was William Walker, the chief diver of Siebe Gorman & Co. He had to work in total darkness, wearing a diving suit which weighed 200 lbs. The task took seven years, from 1905 to 1912.

79 (Above) Sometimes as many as 100 men were working on the restoration of the cathedral. Here, some of them pose with the diver. To his left is his personal assistant throughout the entire operation, Will West. Mr. West may also be seen in plates 78 and 80.

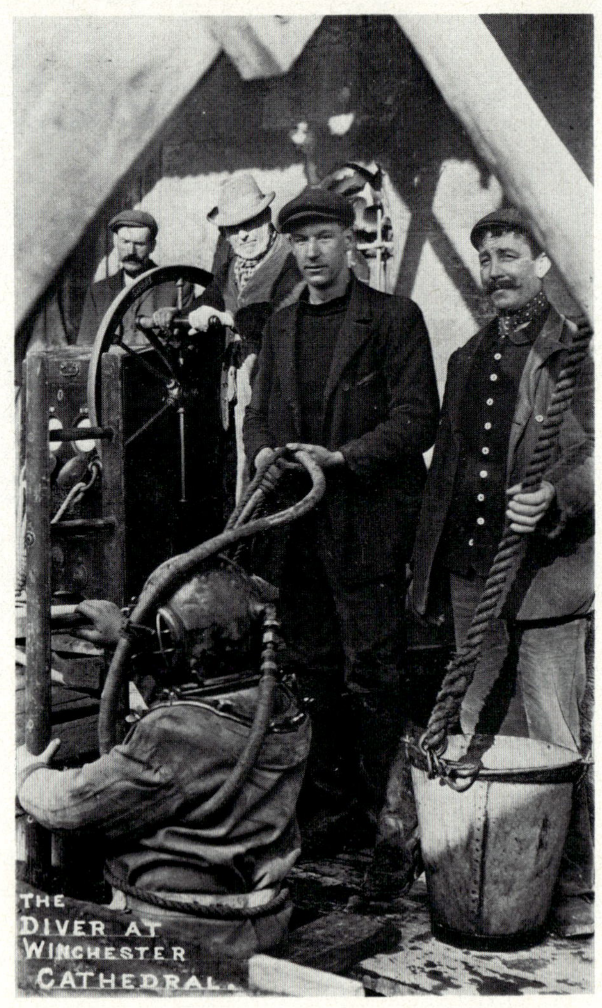

80 (Above) The diver descending to work on the Cathedral foundations. The men on the left are working an air pump.

81 (Above right) 1912. King George V and Queen Mary being driven down Jewry Street to attend the celebrations that marked the completion of the restoration of the Cathedral.

82 (Below right) Hyde St., Winchester looking towards the Worthy Road, c. 1900. On the right is the shop of Mr. Albert Faithfull, the coal merchant.

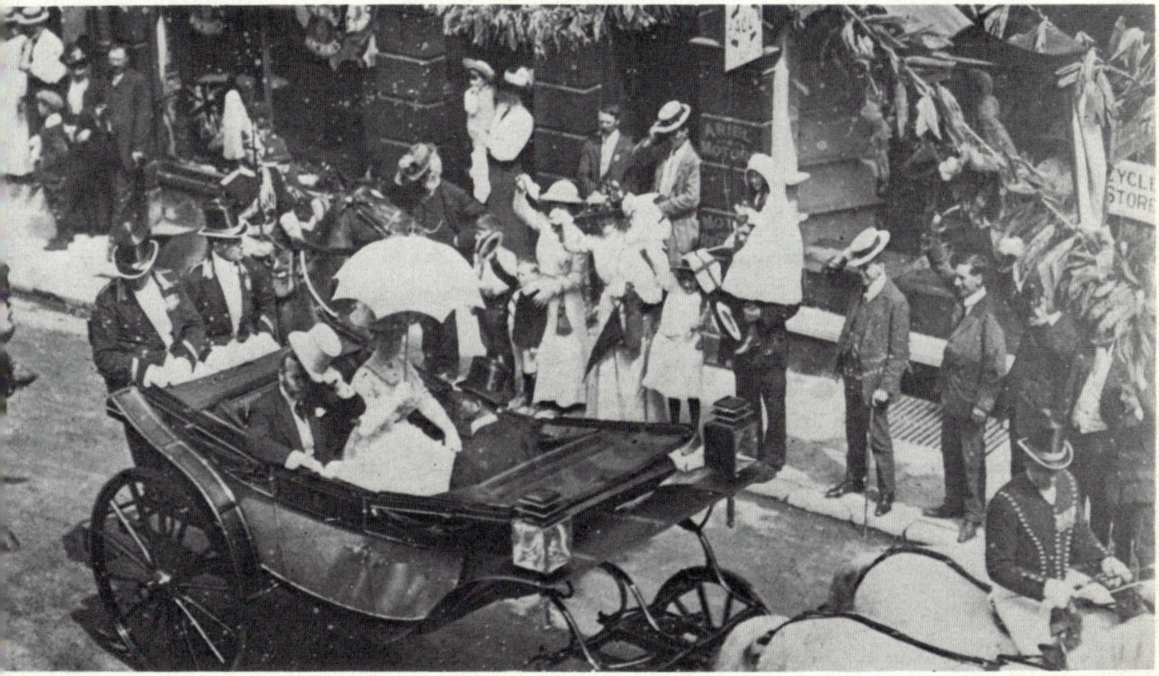

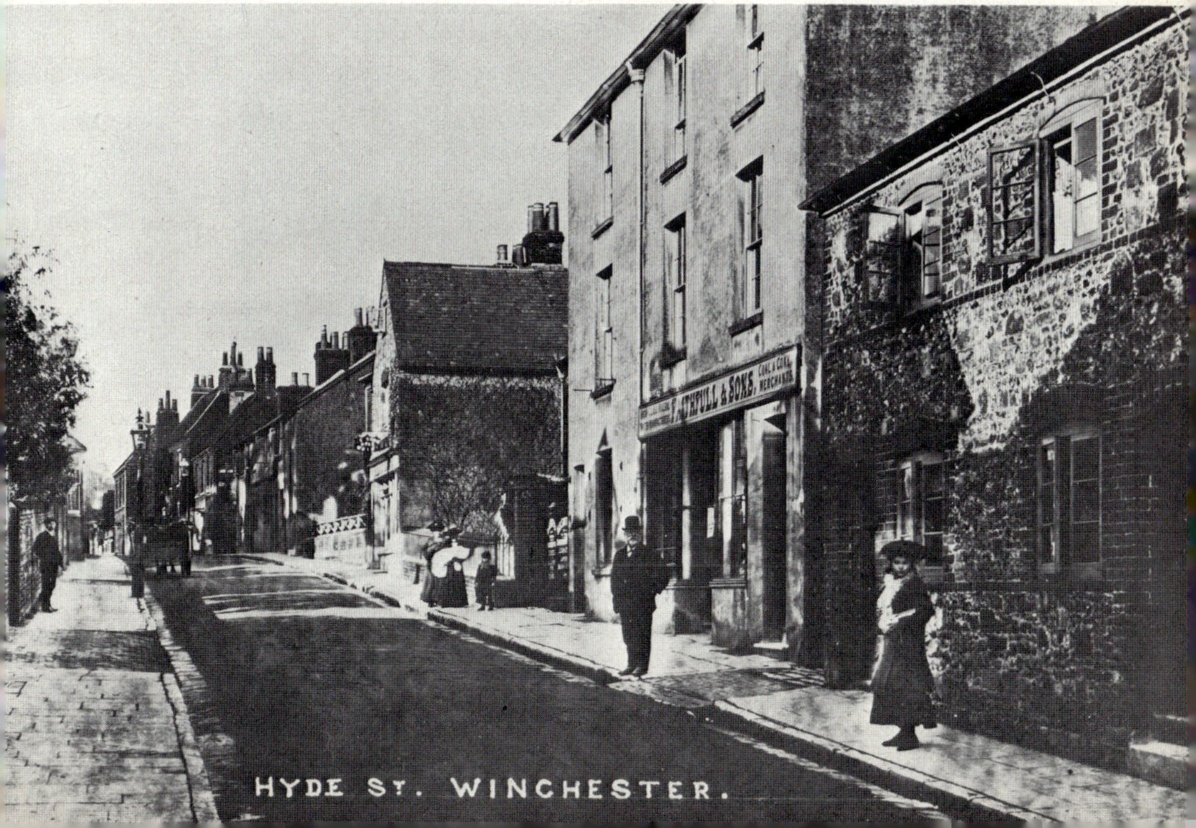

HYDE St. WINCHESTER.

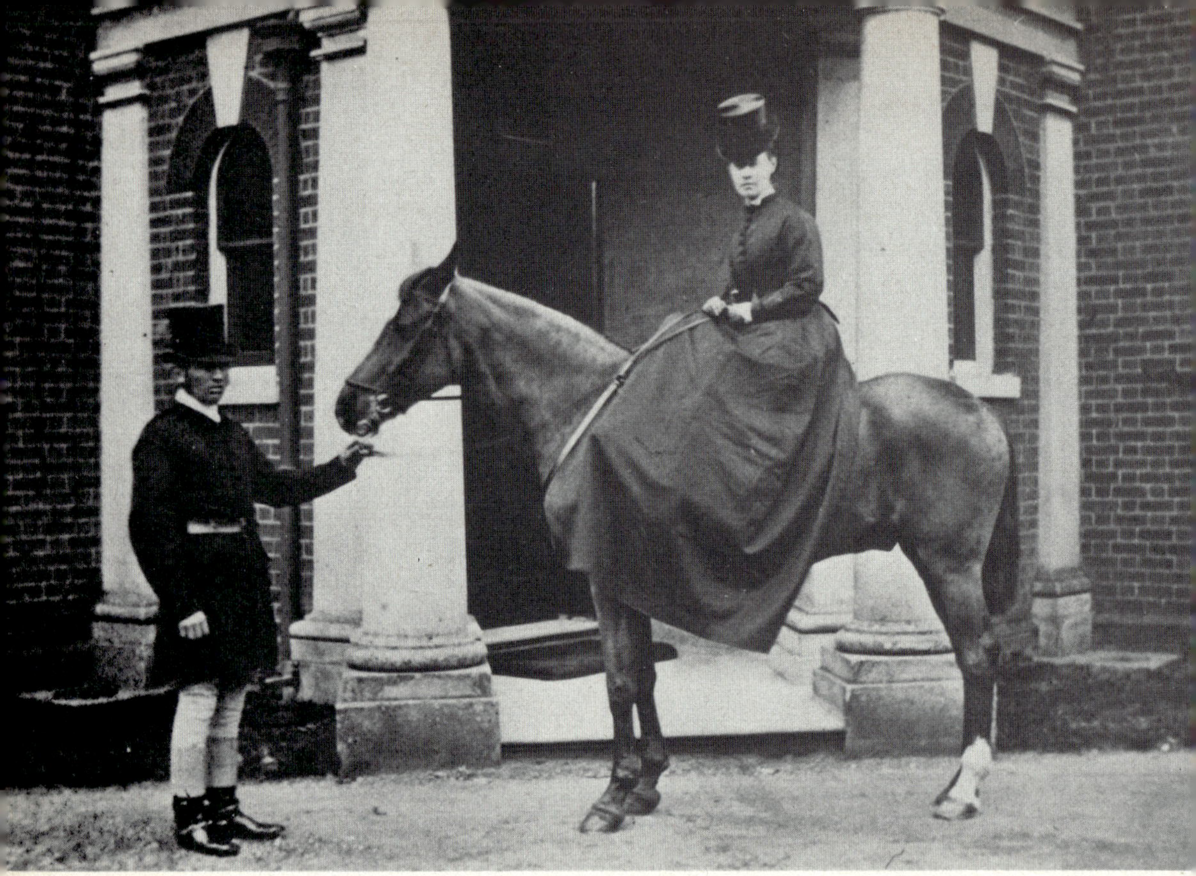

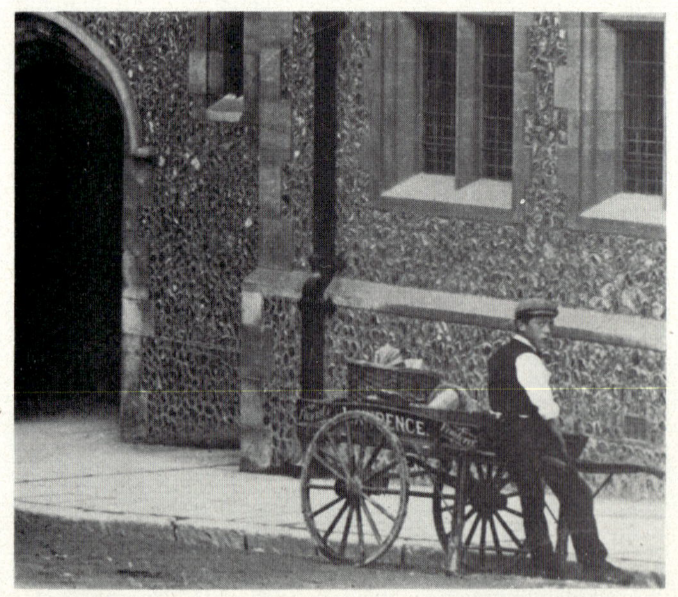

83 (Above left) c 1870. Miss Alice Bowker, daughter of Frederick Bowker, the solicitor who played a major part in the case of the Tichborne Claimant. Miss Bowker was keenly interested in horses and hunting. She was related to Alfred Bowker, the Mayor of Winchester (See plate 77)

84 (Below left) In contrast a delivery boy for Mrs. Lawrence the florist of 20 High Street. The boy is beside the West Gate, c1900.

85 (Below) A gun captured from the Russians during the Crimean War was placed at the junction of High Street and Eastgate Street. It won a place in the affections of Winchester folk and when in 1908 the Mayor decided to tidy up the City by removing the railings around the gun there was a riot. The Gun Riot was led by a Winchester workman called Joe Dumper who can be seen standing on the gun carriage.

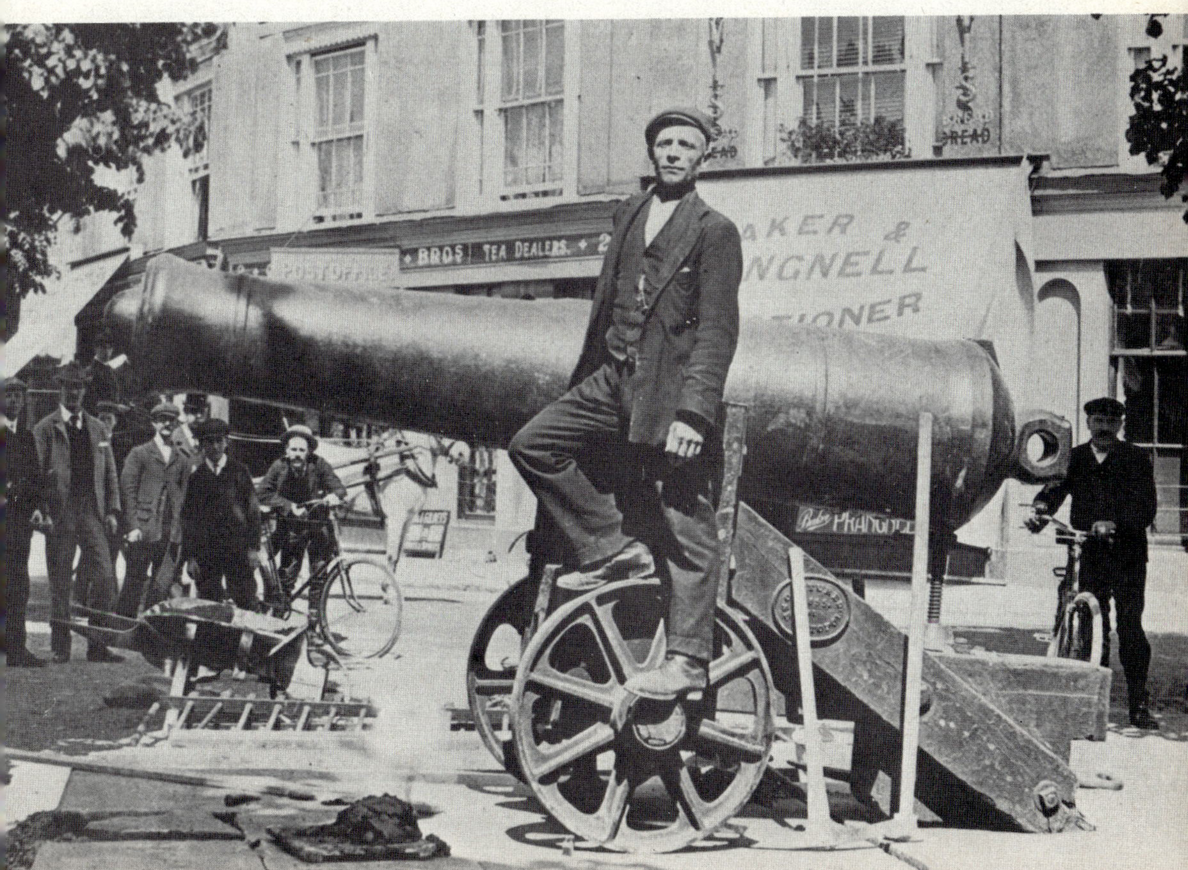

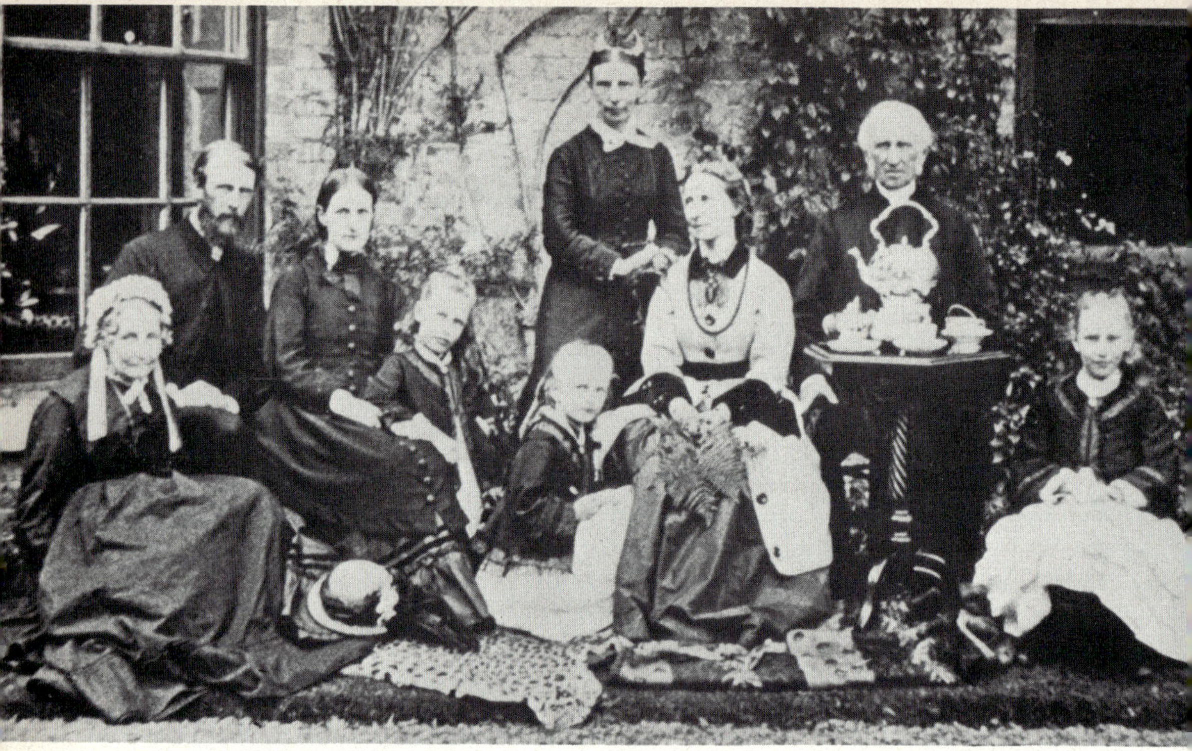

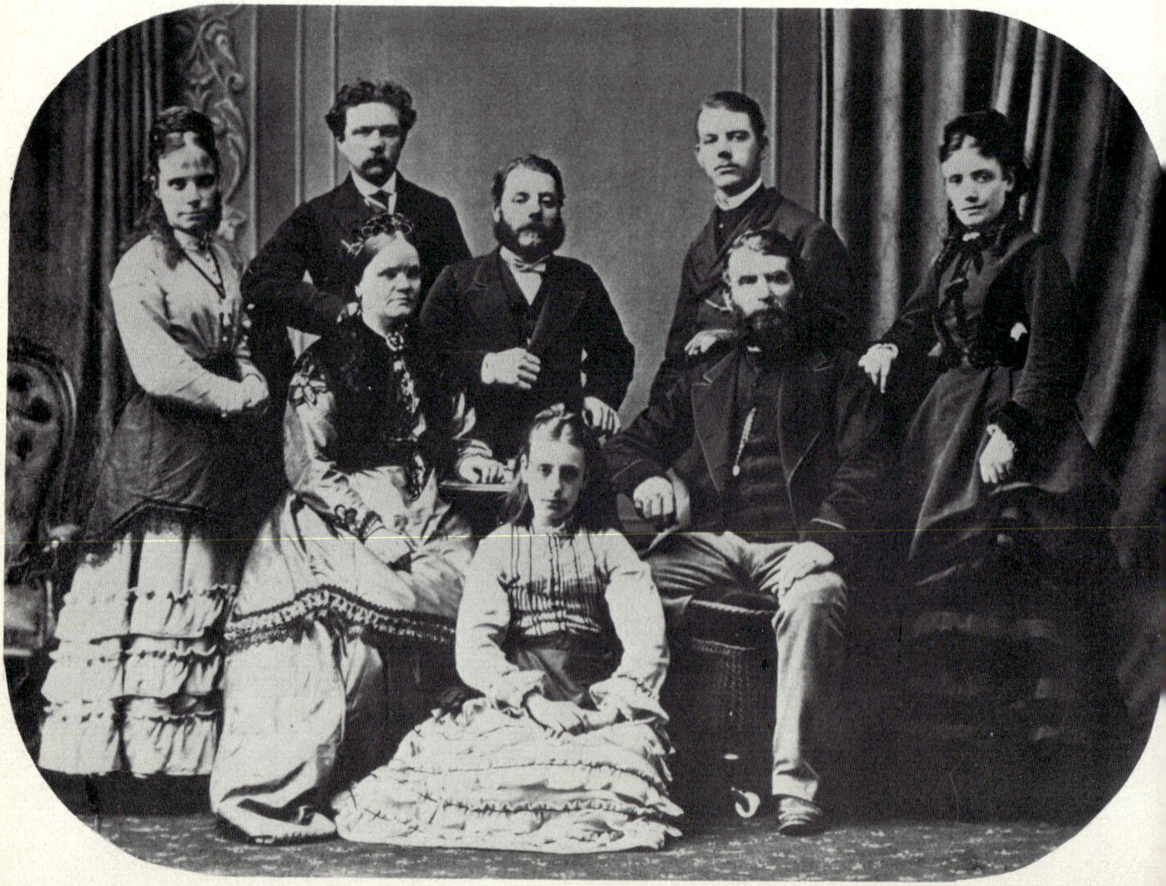

86 (Above left) Archdeacon Philip Jacob and his family taking tea in the garden of their house in the Cathedral Close. c1870.

87 (Below left) c1870. Mr. Josiah George Jones, a music dealer in the High Street, with his family.

88 (Below) The Wheatsheaf Inn at St. Cross c 1865. This has now been replaced by a late Victorian building.

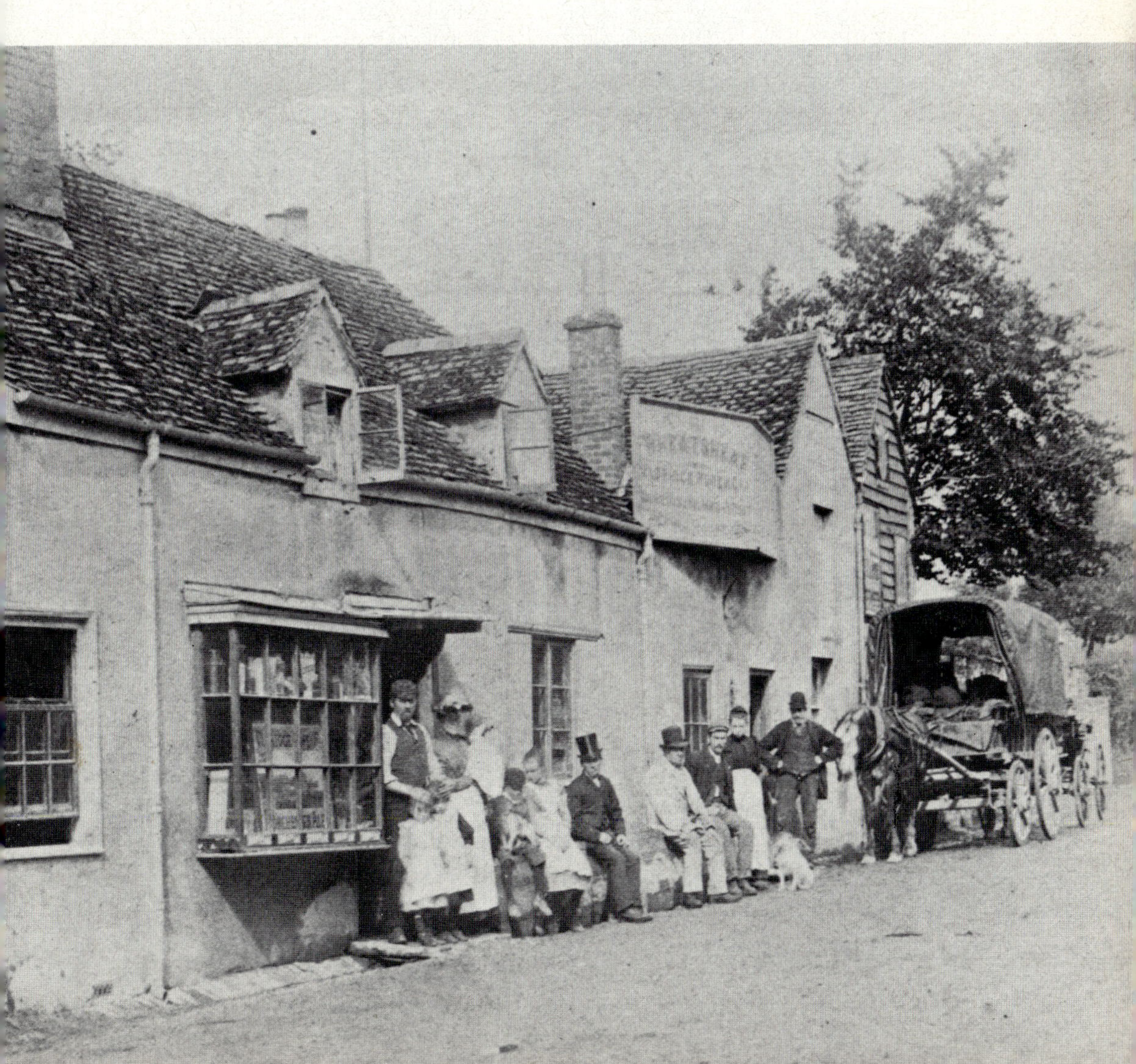

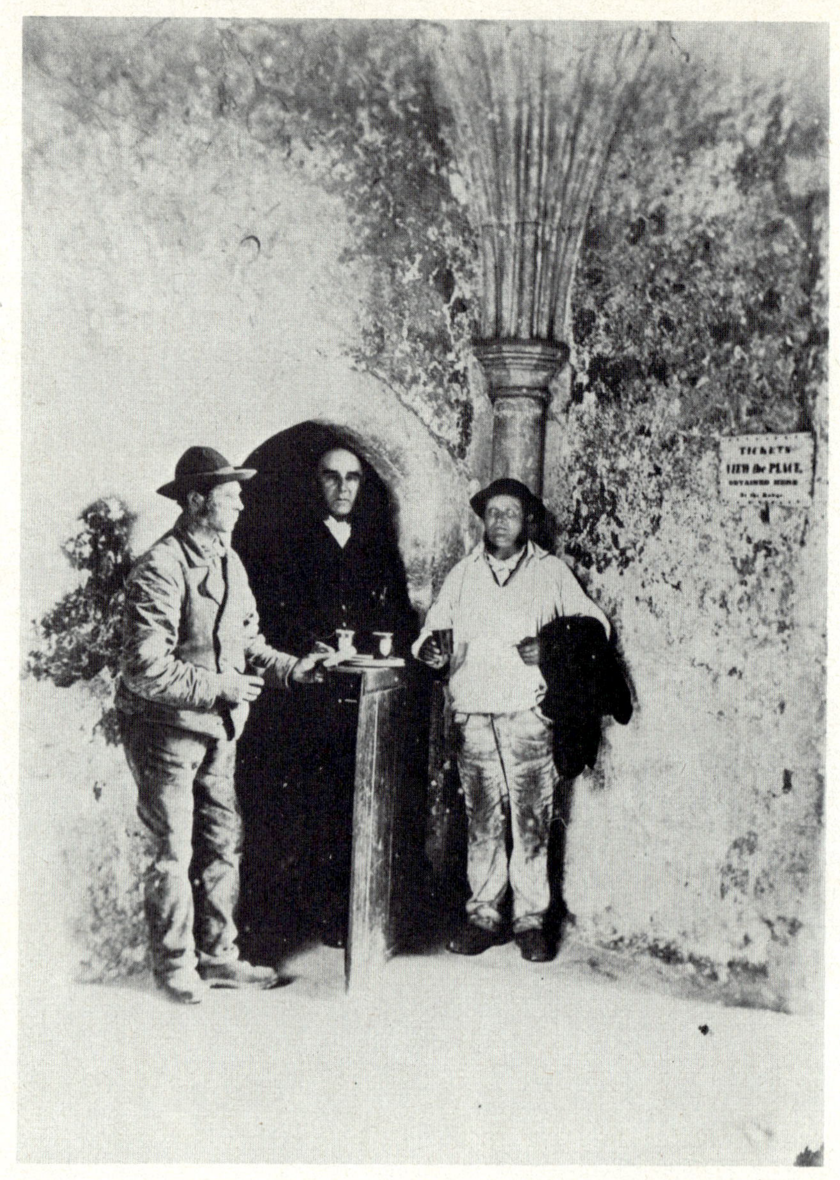

TWO SCENES FROM ST. CROSS HOSPITAL. WINCHESTER.

89 (Above) Two travellers receiving the dole of bread and weak beer. c 1880.

90 (Right) c 1900. Dinner time at St. Cross.

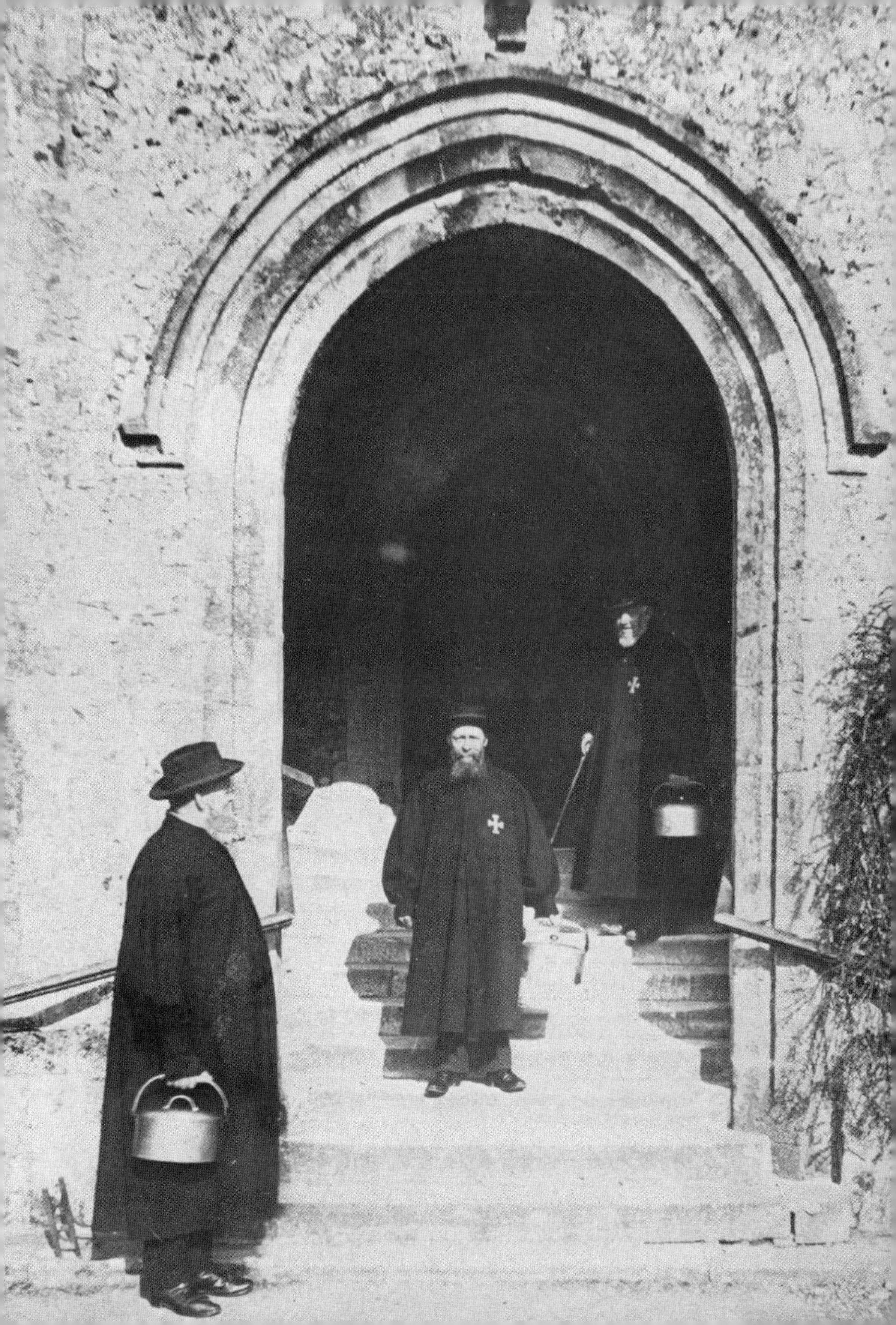

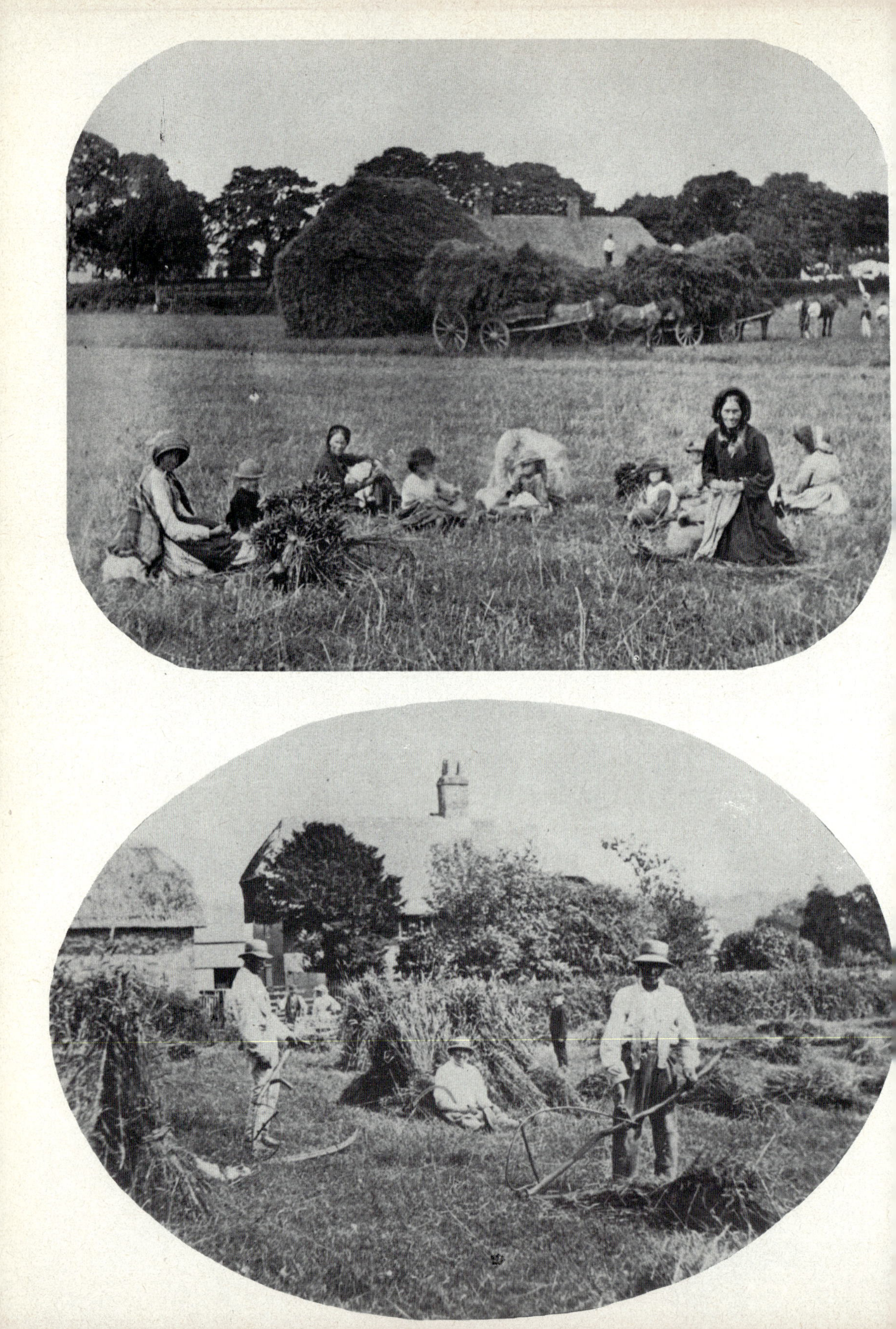

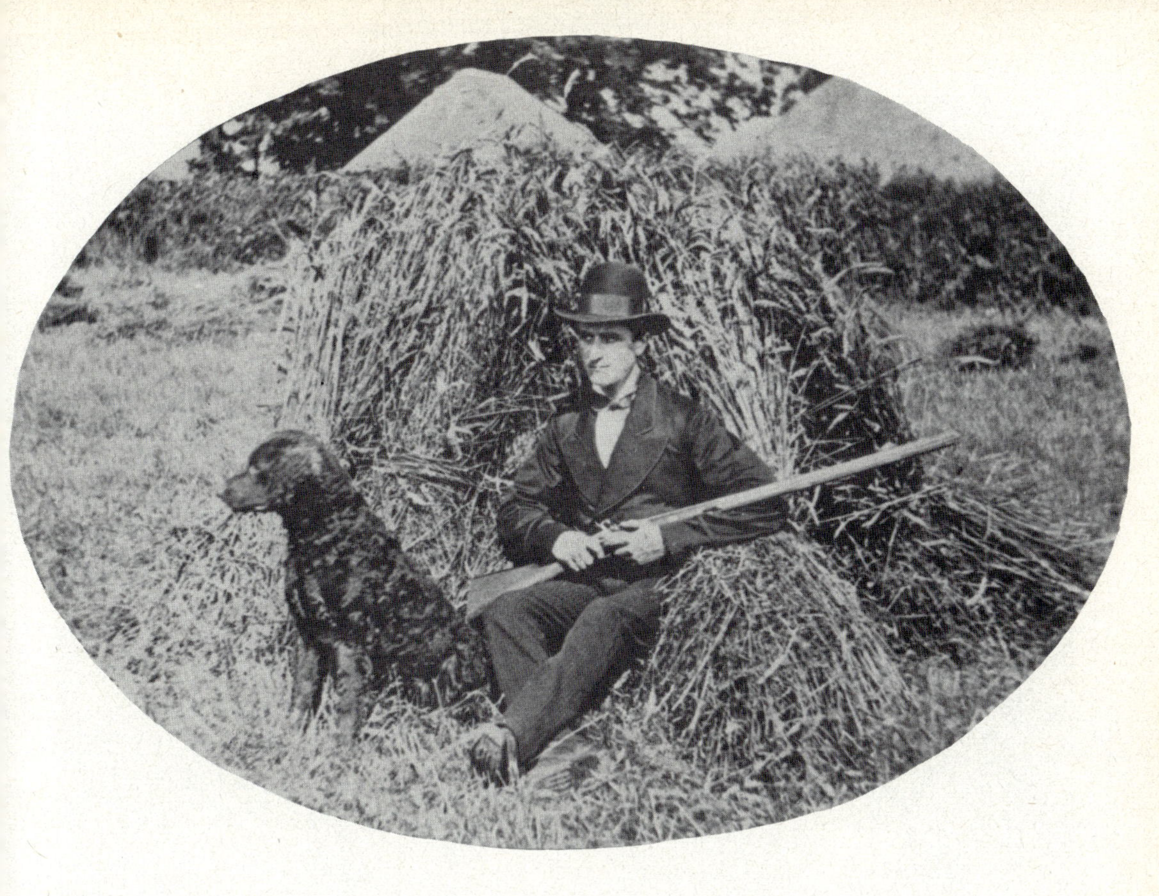

91 (Above left) c 1871. New Down Farm, Micheldever. Just North of the Lunway's Inn on the Winchester–Basingstoke Road. Wives and children of the harvesters rest after gleaning. Their little bundle of wheat is in the left foreground.

92 (Below left) c 1871. Ham's Farm, Bishopstoke. Just north of Eastleigh, beside the River Itchen. Labourers cutting wheat with scythes. The bow on the scythe draws the cut wheat away from the blade.

93 (Above) c 1871. Ham's Farm, Bishopstoke. The man leaning against the stook with the hammer gun is probably the farmer's son. He hopes to shoot rabbits that bolt from the corn as it is cut.

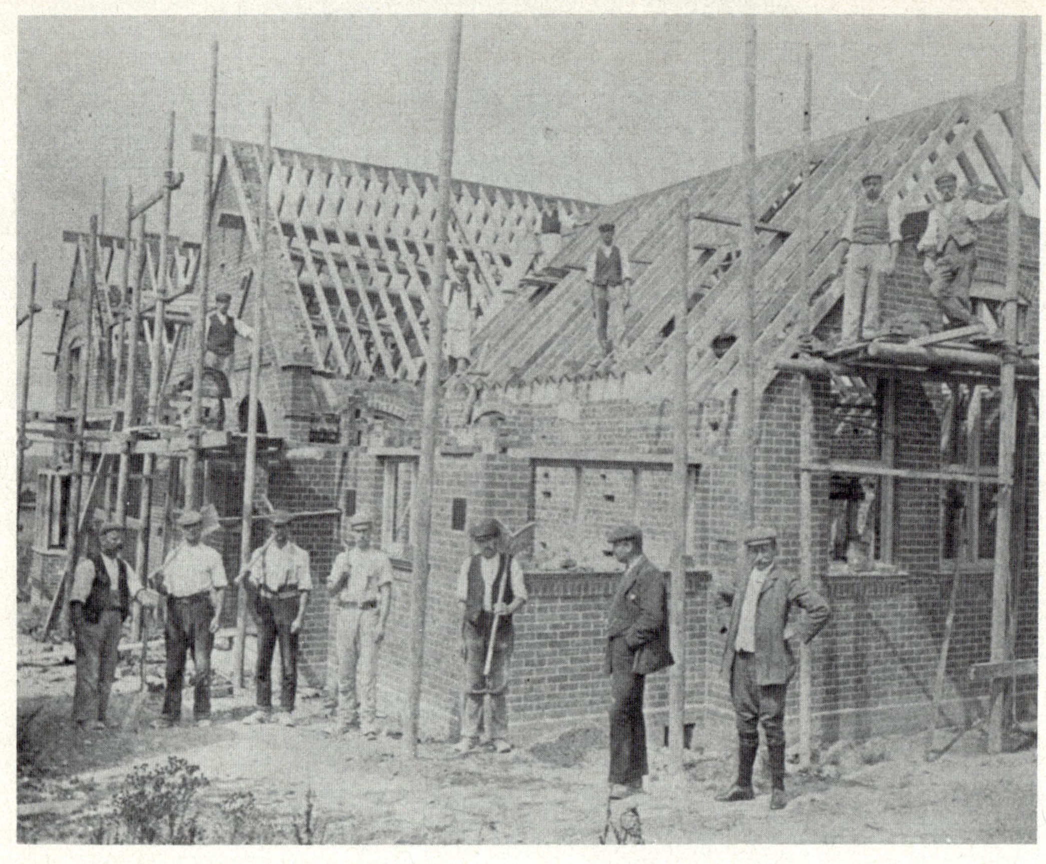

94 (Above) Building Beauworth elementary school in 1913. At that time the adjacent Preshaw and Longwood Estates employed many people. Now that farming is highly mechanised and a large indoor staff too expensive, families have left the area and the school has been closed.

95 (Right) The Shepherd, Mr. Messenger of Littleton Farm, August 1900. His sheepfolds can be seen in the middle distance.

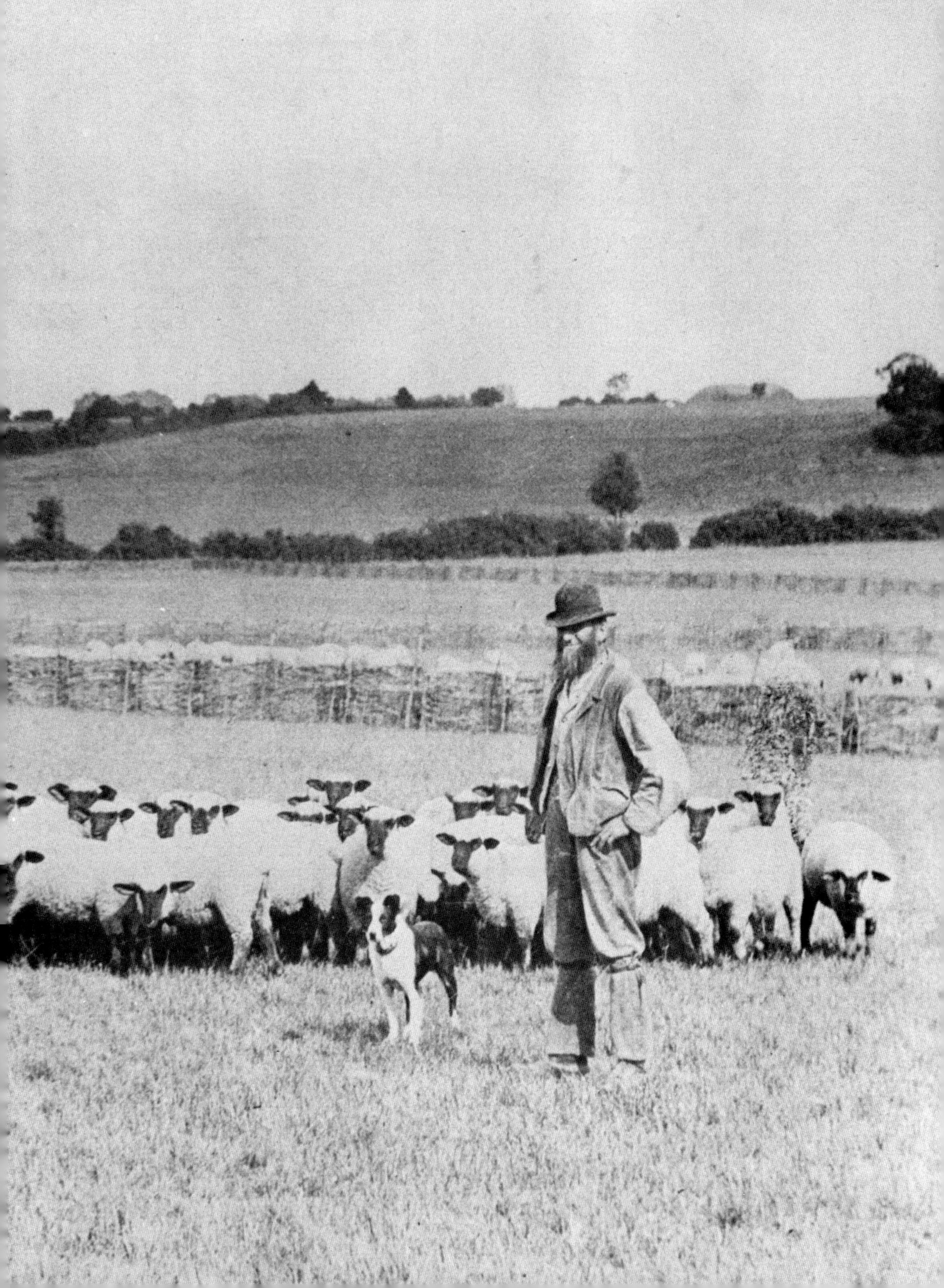

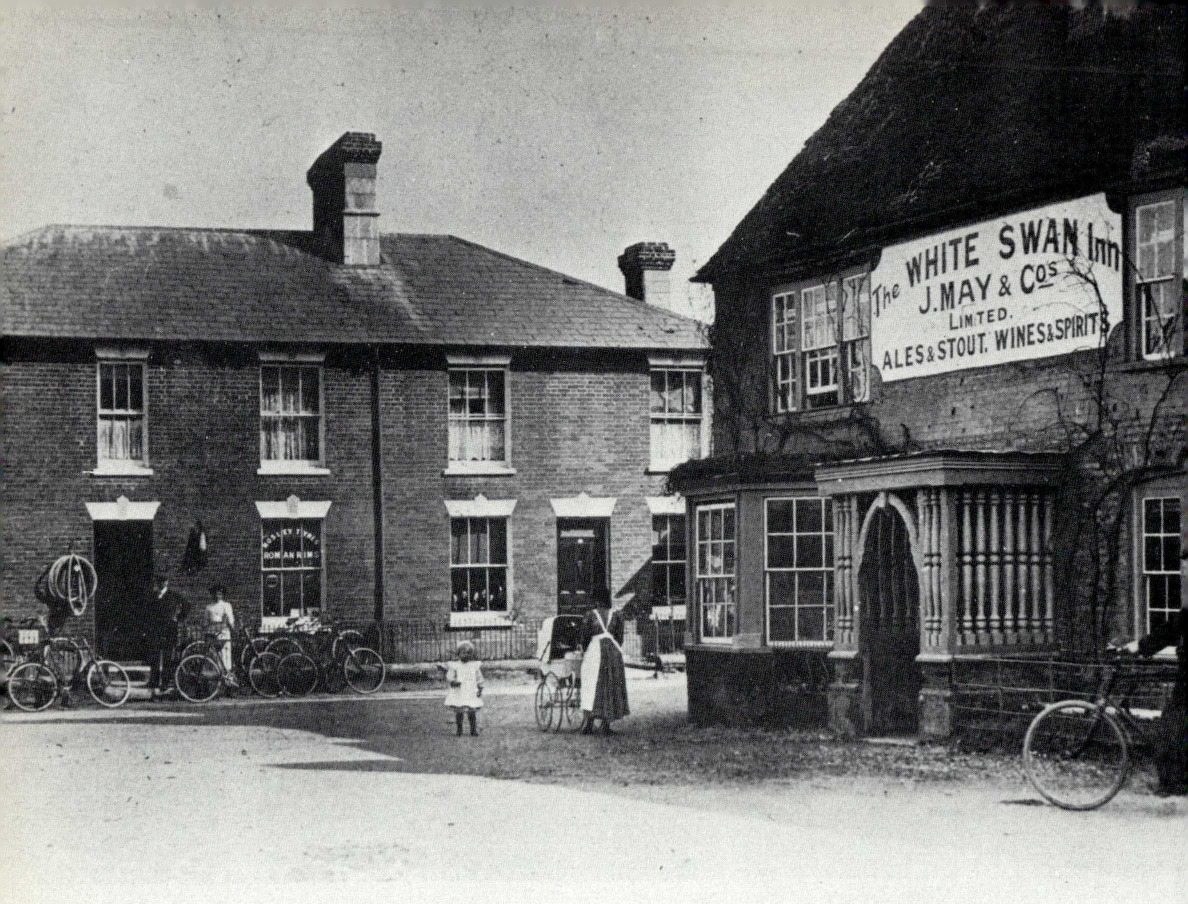

96 (Above) The Square at Sutton Scotney c 1905.

97 (Above right) The forge at Otterbourne c 1910. (Now the Old Forge Restaurant)

98 (Below right) At the bottom of Otterbourne Hill, looking north c 1905. This scene has been transformed by the building of a new road in 1957.

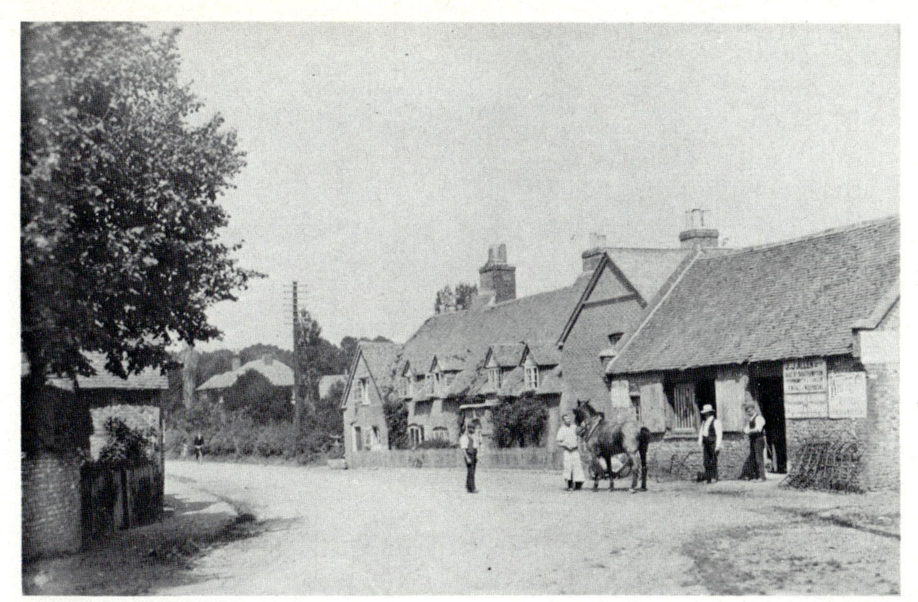

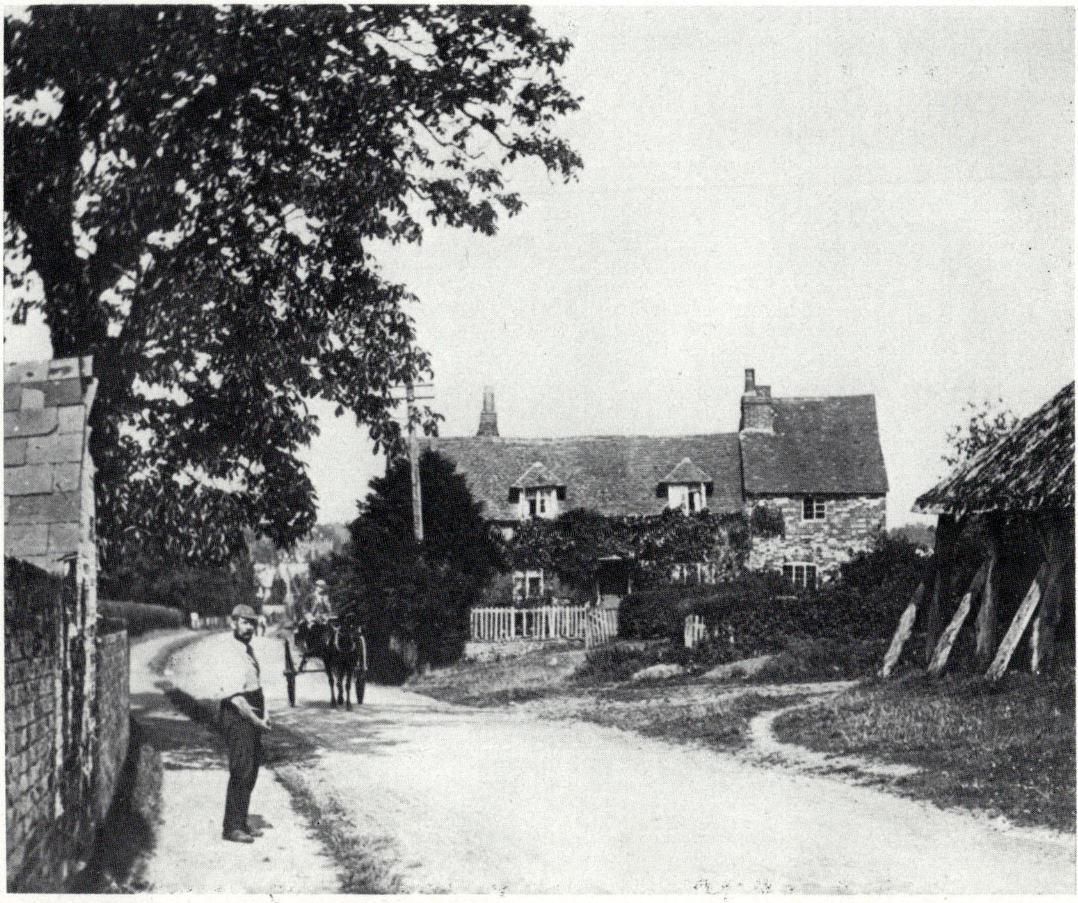

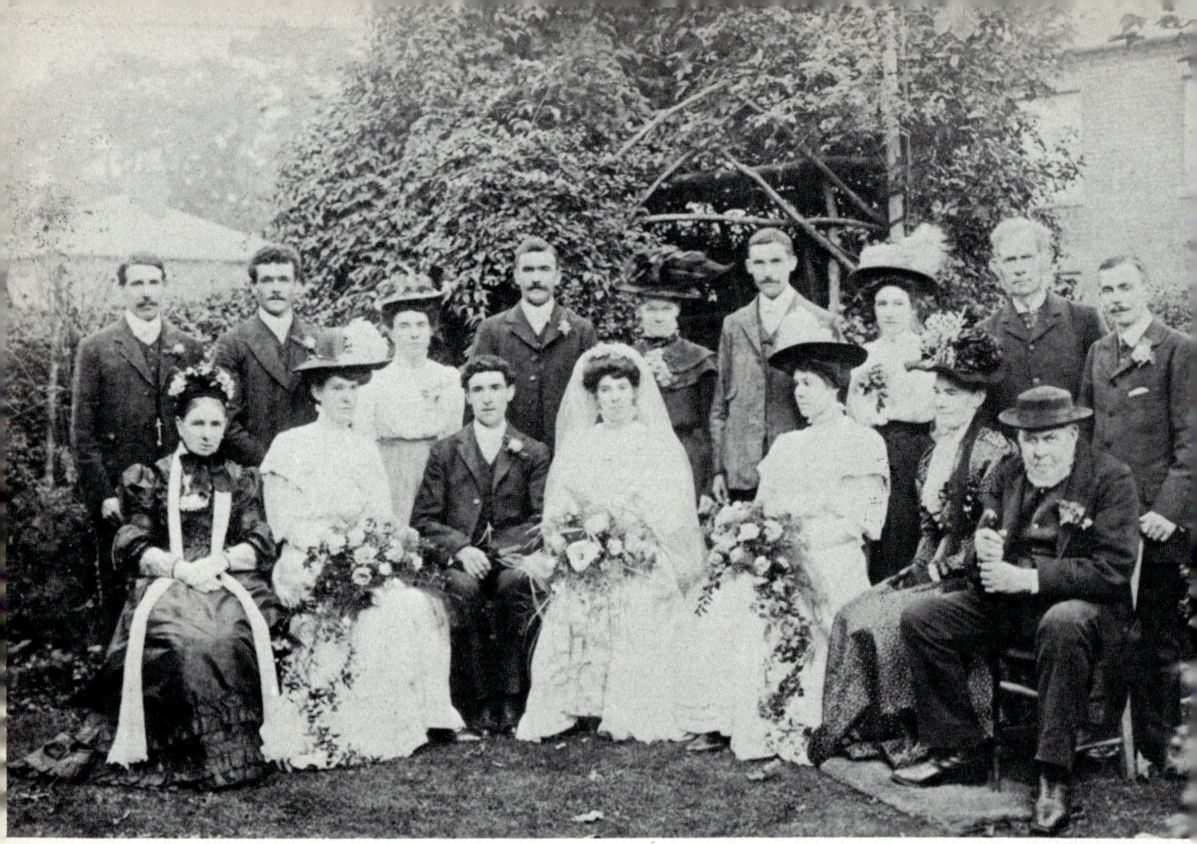

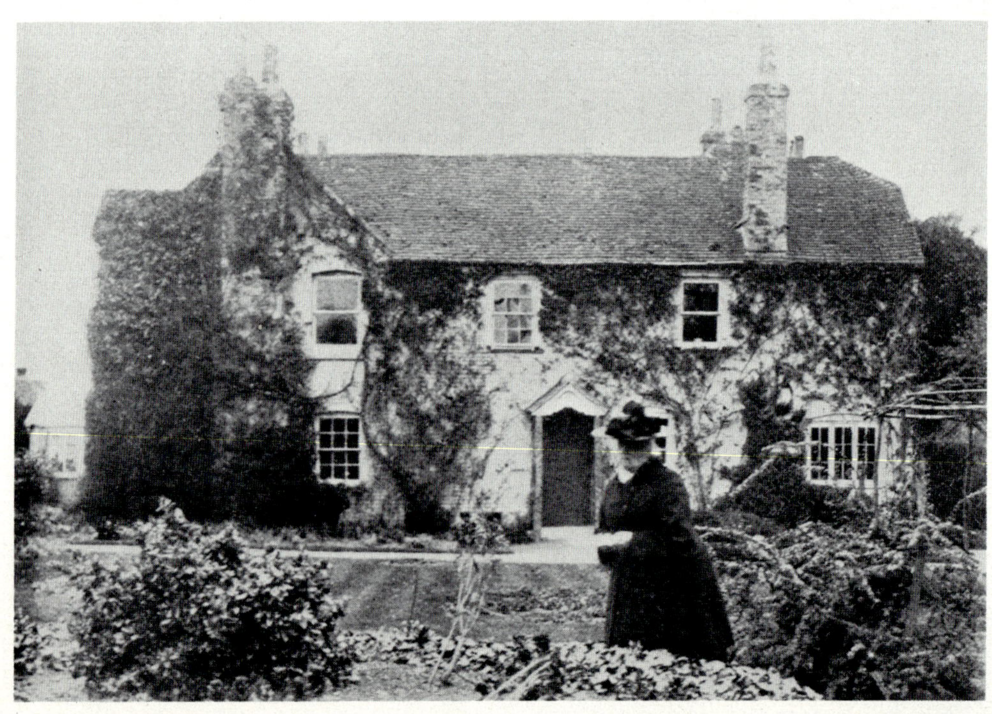

99 (Above left) A wedding group at Rose Cottage Otterbourne on October 8th. 1908. The bride was Miss S. M. Ray and the groom Mr. E. T. Soffe, a gardener at Cranbury. The bride's father Mr. C. Ray stands second from the right. He was Charlotte Yonge's gardener and a man of considerable importance in the village.

100 (Below left) Charlotte Yonge, the writer, in the garden of her house Elderfield at Otterbourne c 1898.

101 (Below) c 1920. On the right is Mr. Jewell the dairy farmer of Kiln Farm, Otterbourne, supervising the carting of hay. Mr. Jewell also had a milk-round, selling his milk direct to the public.

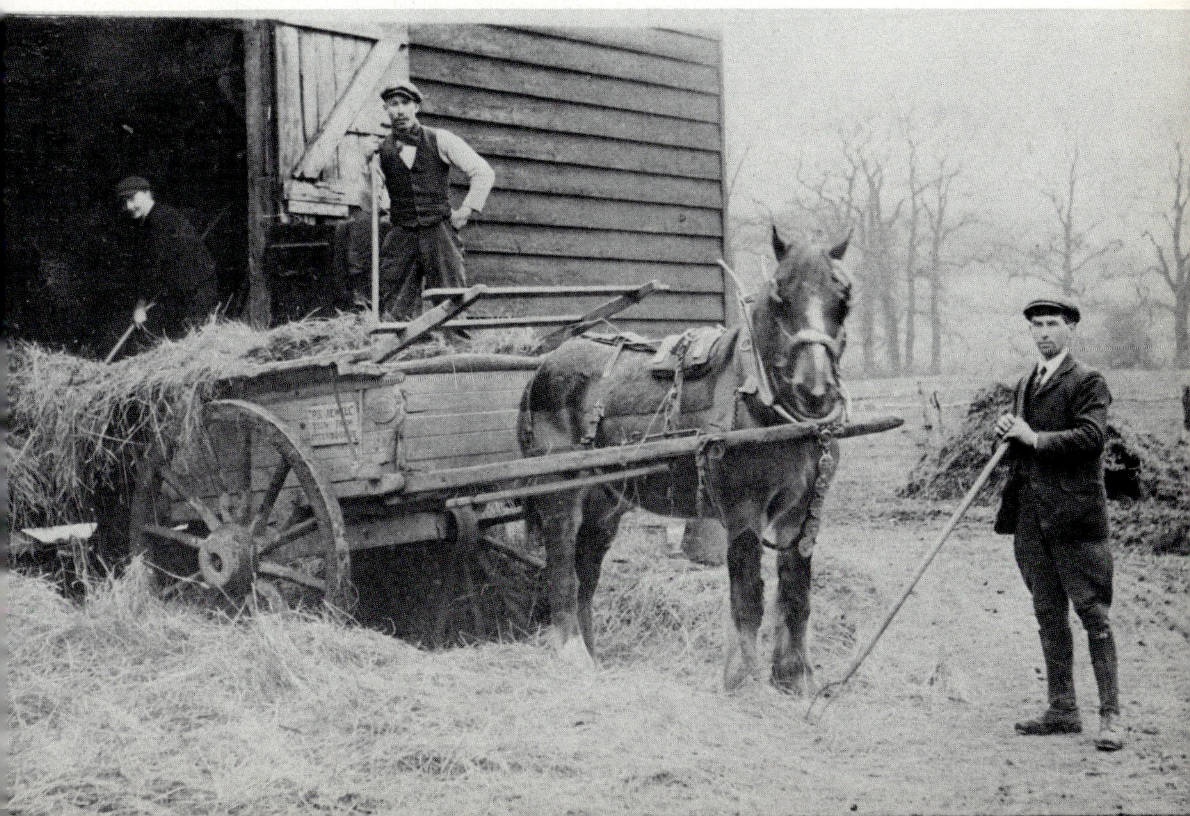

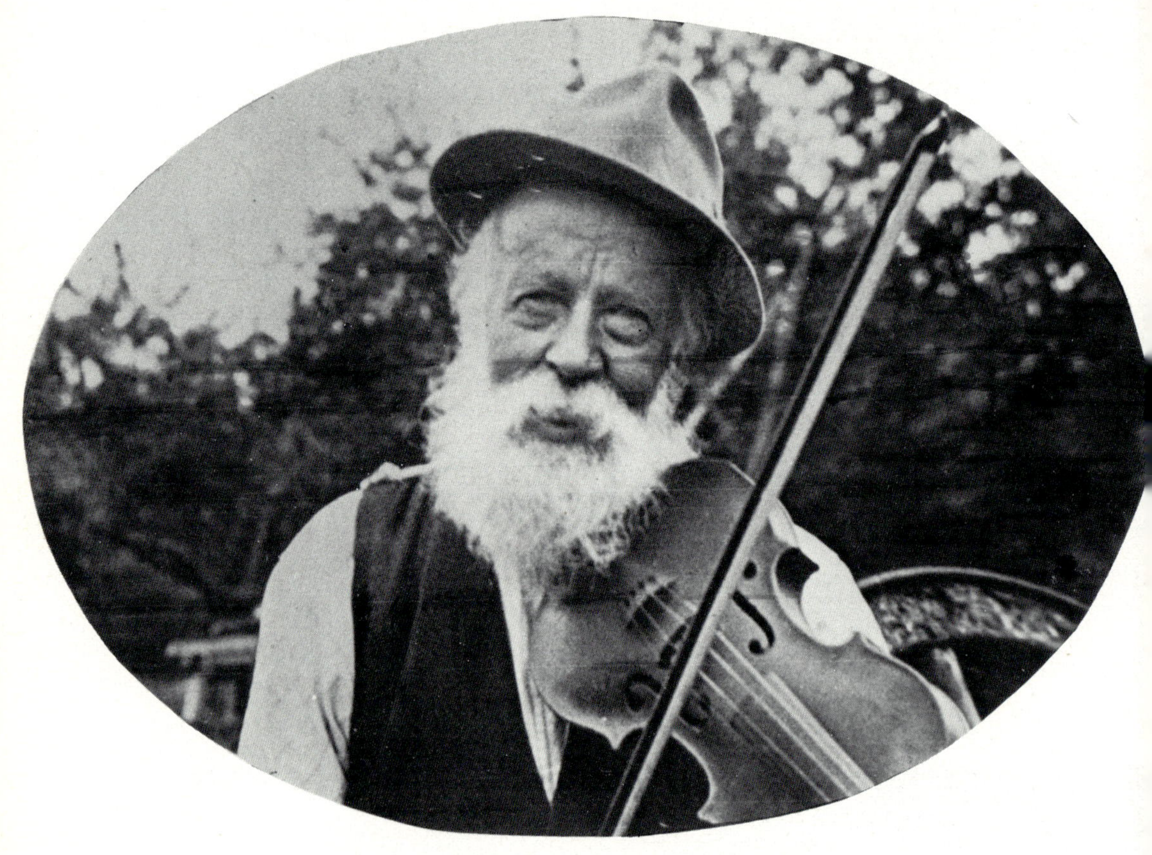

102 (Above) 23rd. November is the Feast of St. Clement, patron saint of blacksmiths. On this day "Clem Feast" used to be held at the Bugle Inn, Twyford with Mr. Thomas Young in the chair and with Mr. Carter or Mr. Froome (both blacksmiths) as vice-chairmen. Mr. Walter Hawkins (above) of Colden Common usually attended the feasts to entertain the assembled company with his fiddle.

103 (Right) Mr. William Carter (1856–1936) the Twyford blacksmith, c. 1920. He was son and grandson of blacksmiths in Twyford and their old forge still stands beside the main road near the Phoenix Inn car park.

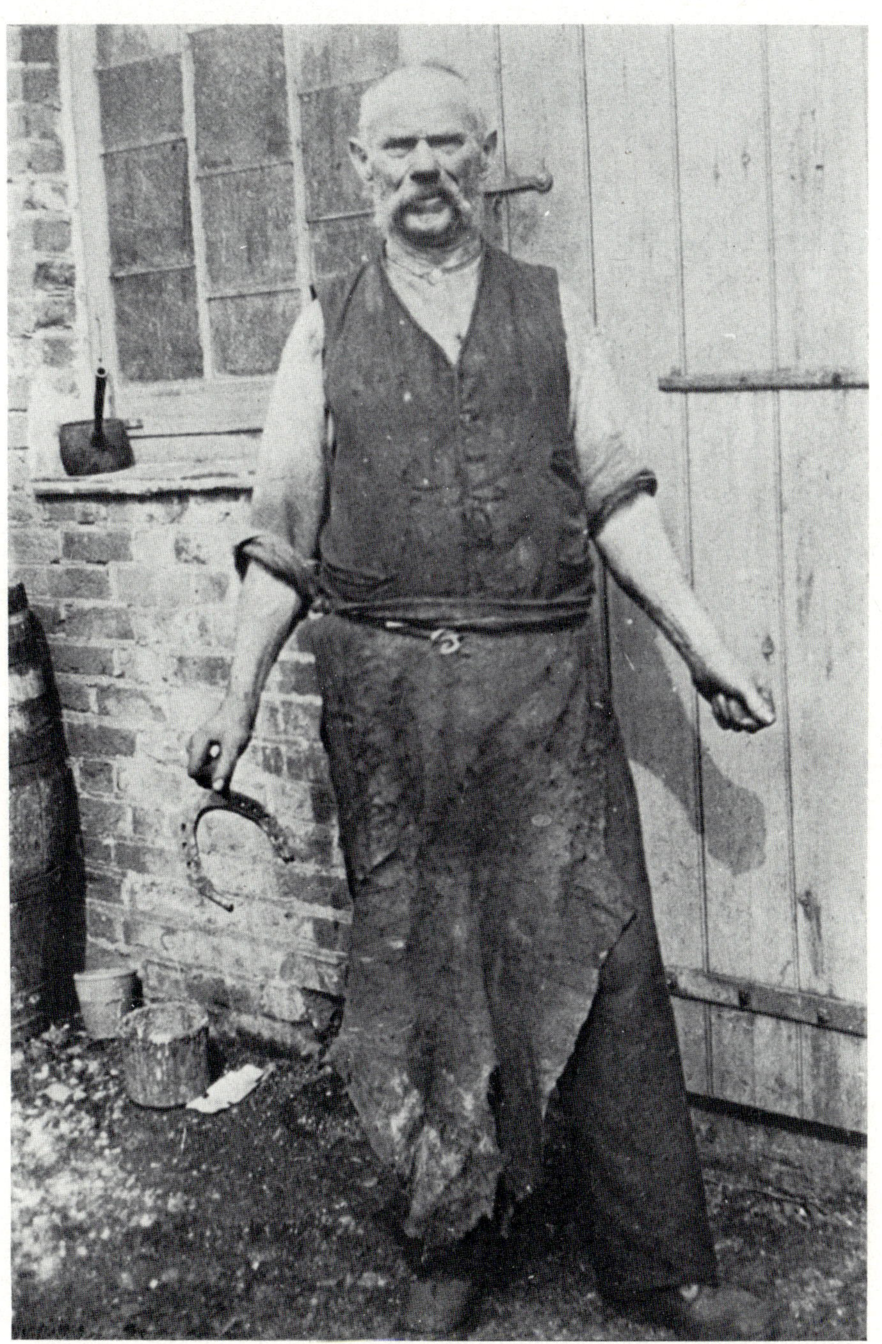

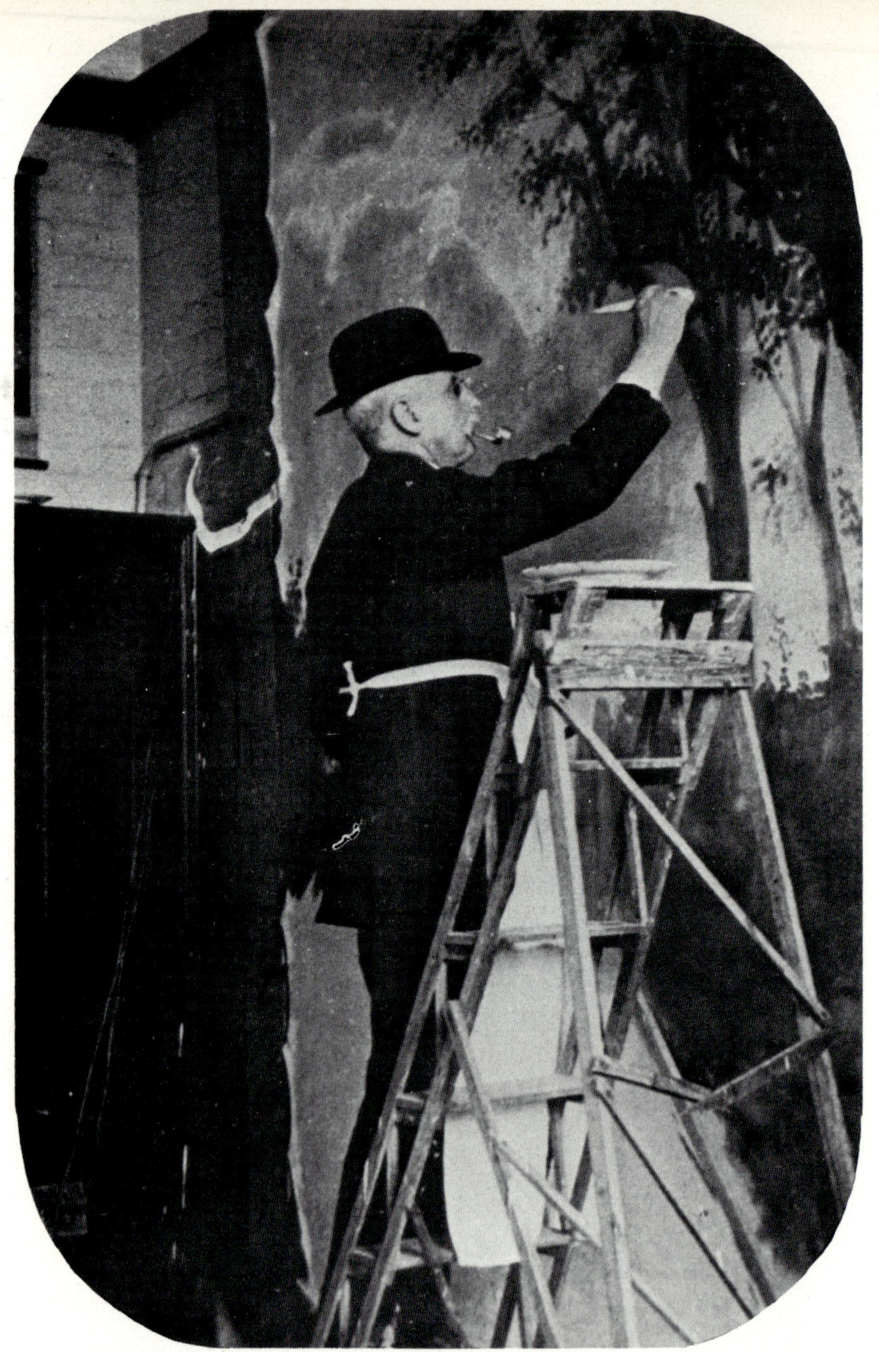

104 (Above) Mr. Edward Gilbert, Headmaster of Twyford Elementary School for 44 years until his retirement in 1919. He formed a school orchestra, a brass band and a village orchestra. He was organist and choir master at the church. He ran coal and clothing clubs. He established a reading room in the school premises. Another hobby was painting and here he is painting the drop curtain in the Parish Hall.

105 (Right) Mr. Gilbert's school at Twyford c 1905. At that time boys and girls were severely segregated. They entered the school by separate doors and here the boys may be seen in their playground.

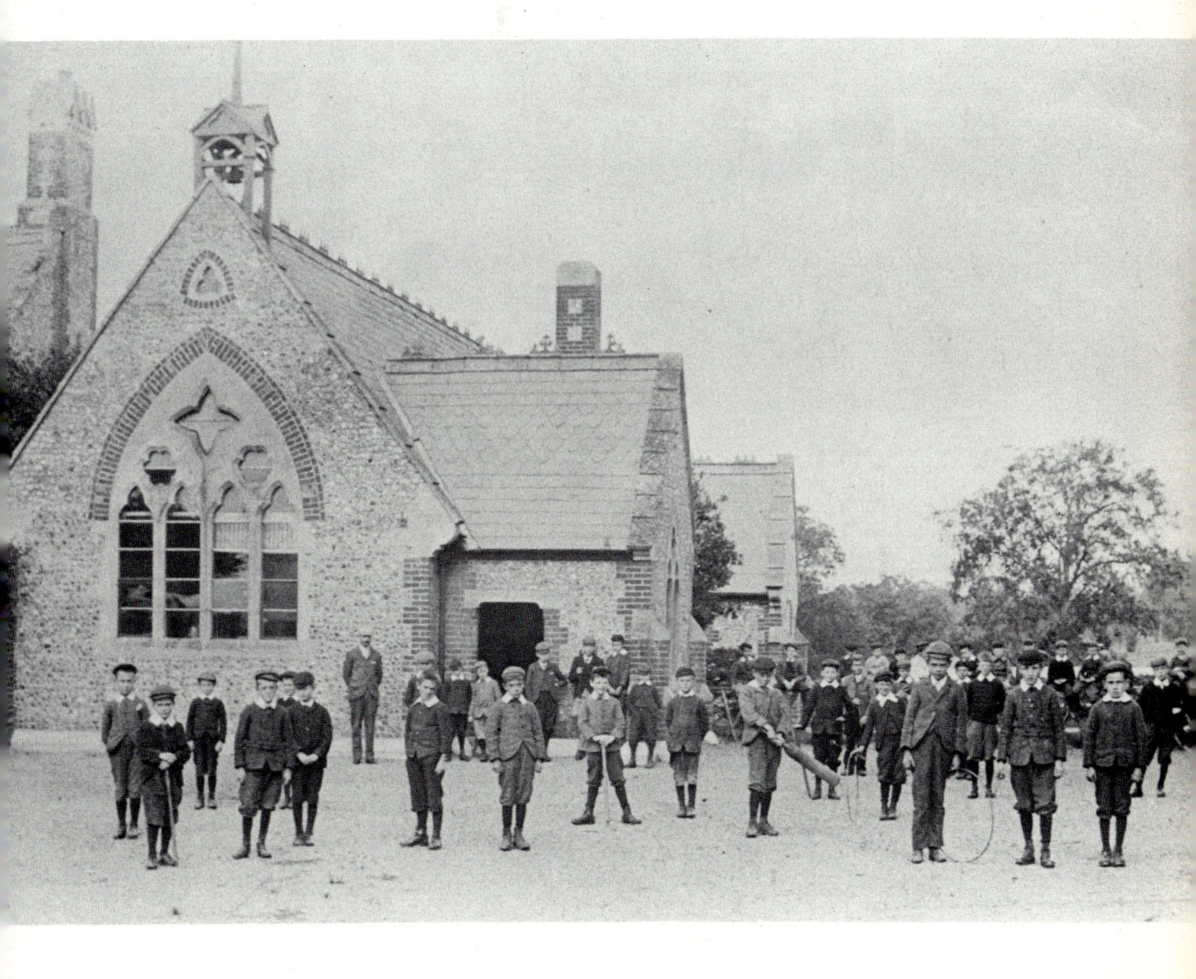

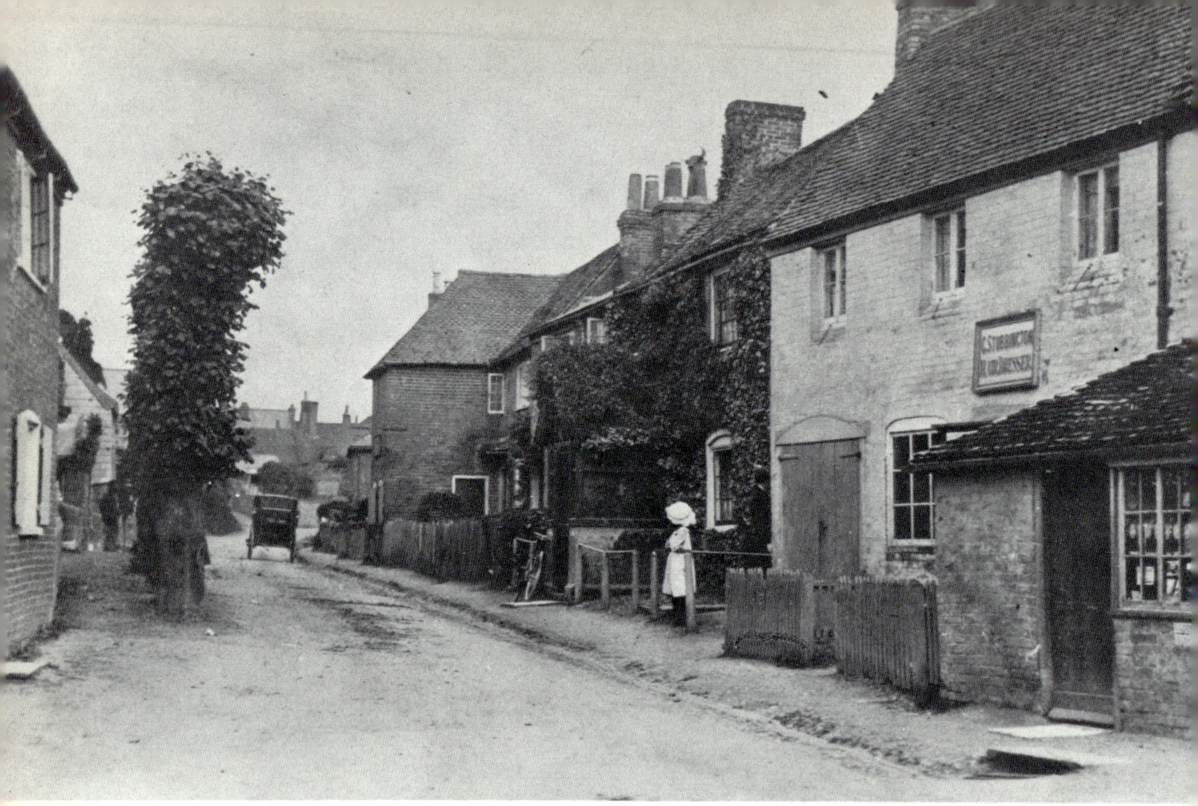

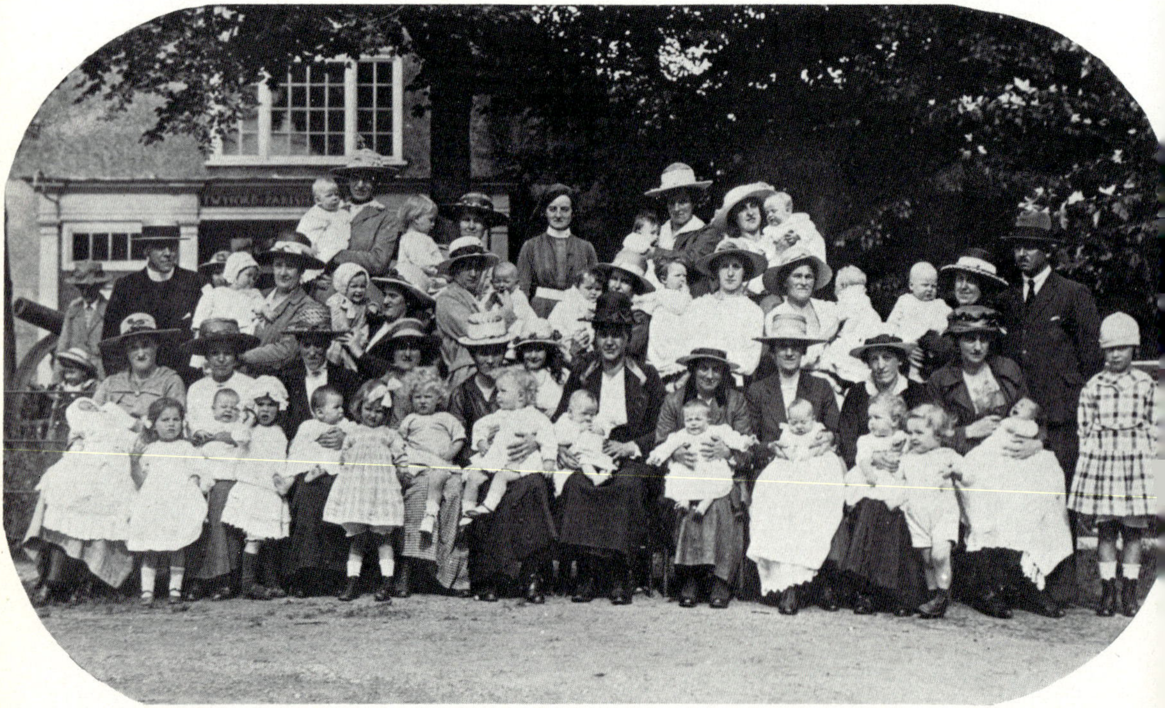

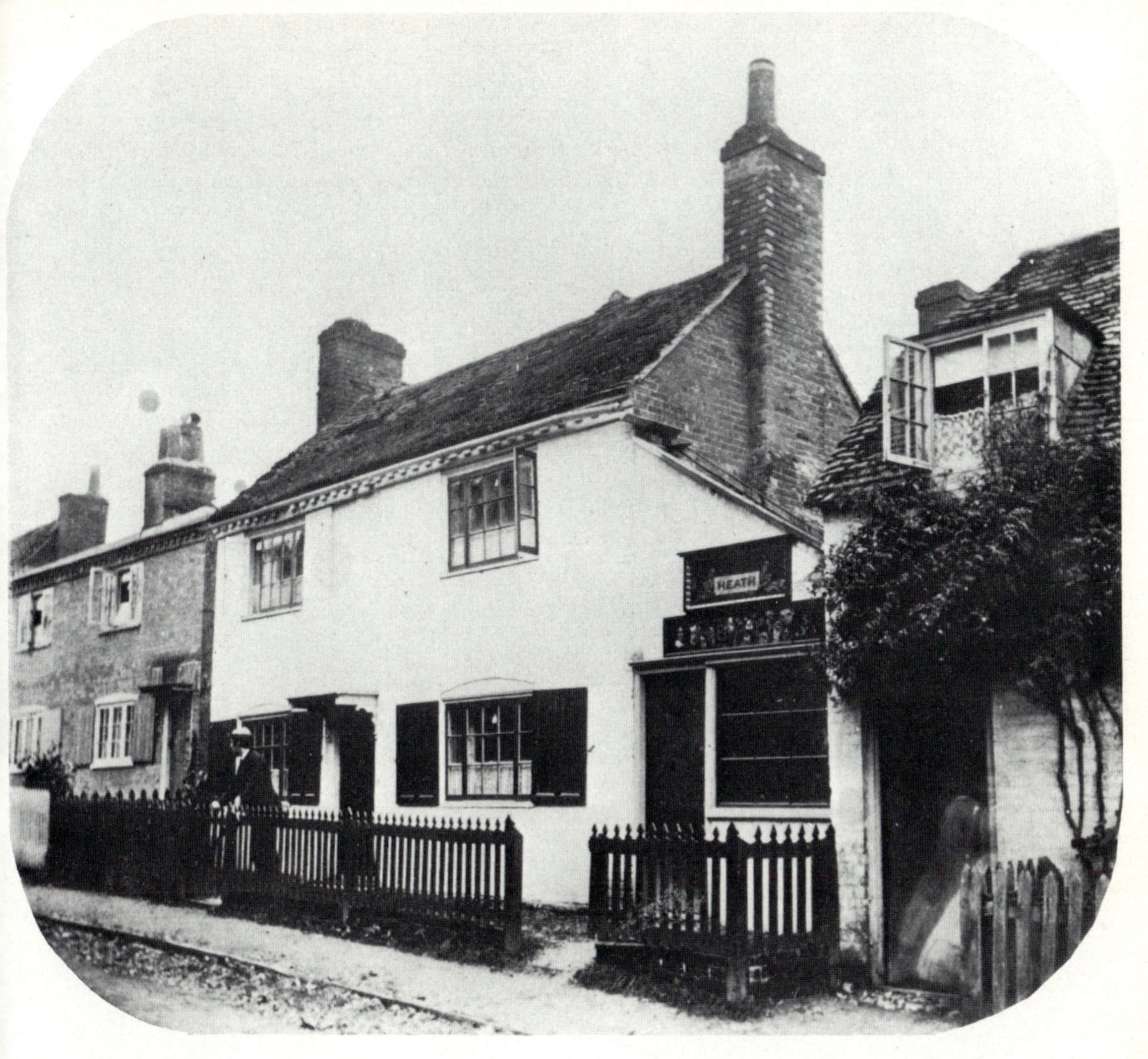

106 (Above left) Queen Street Twyford c1906. The shop on the right belonged to C. Stubbington, hairdresser.

107 (Below left) A baby show in front of Twyford Parish Hall 1919. Standing on the left is the Rev. Harold Morris, in the middle at the back is Nurse Arnold and on the right is Dr. Marsden Roberts.

108 (Above) c 1870. The shop of Mr. Heath the cabinet maker and photographer of Queen Street, Twyford.

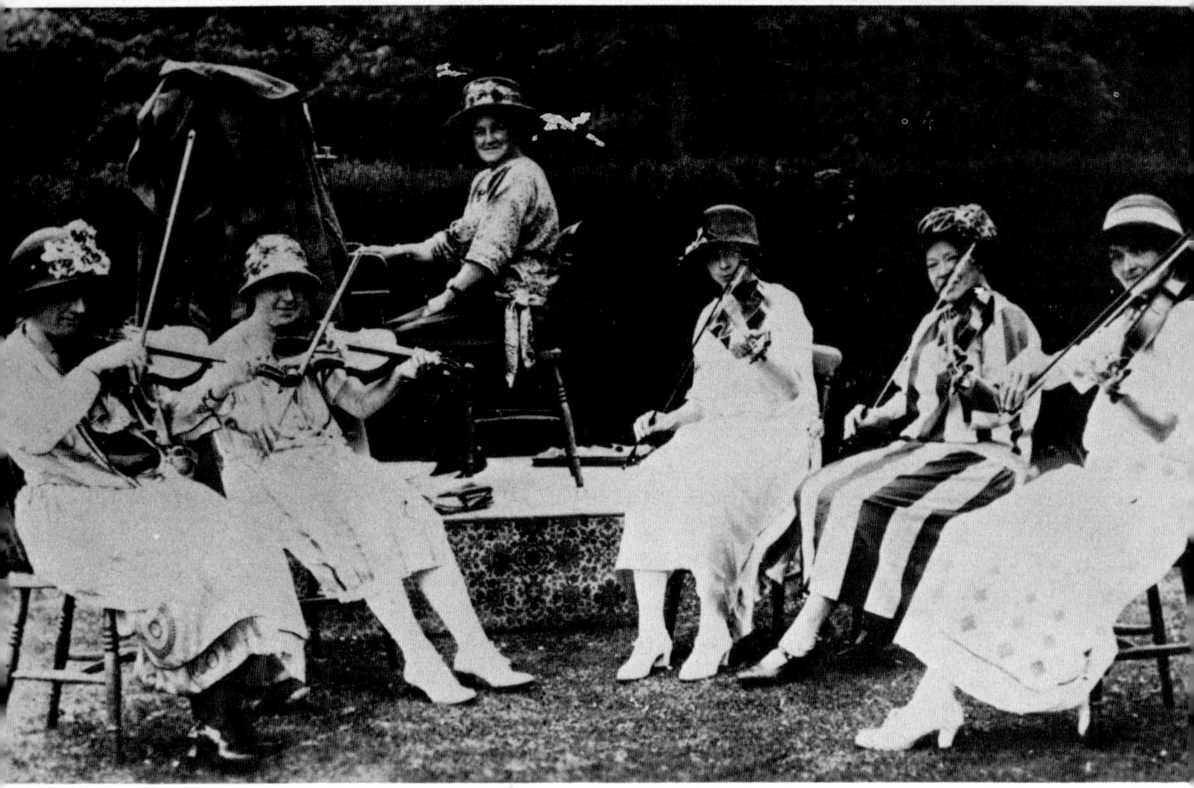

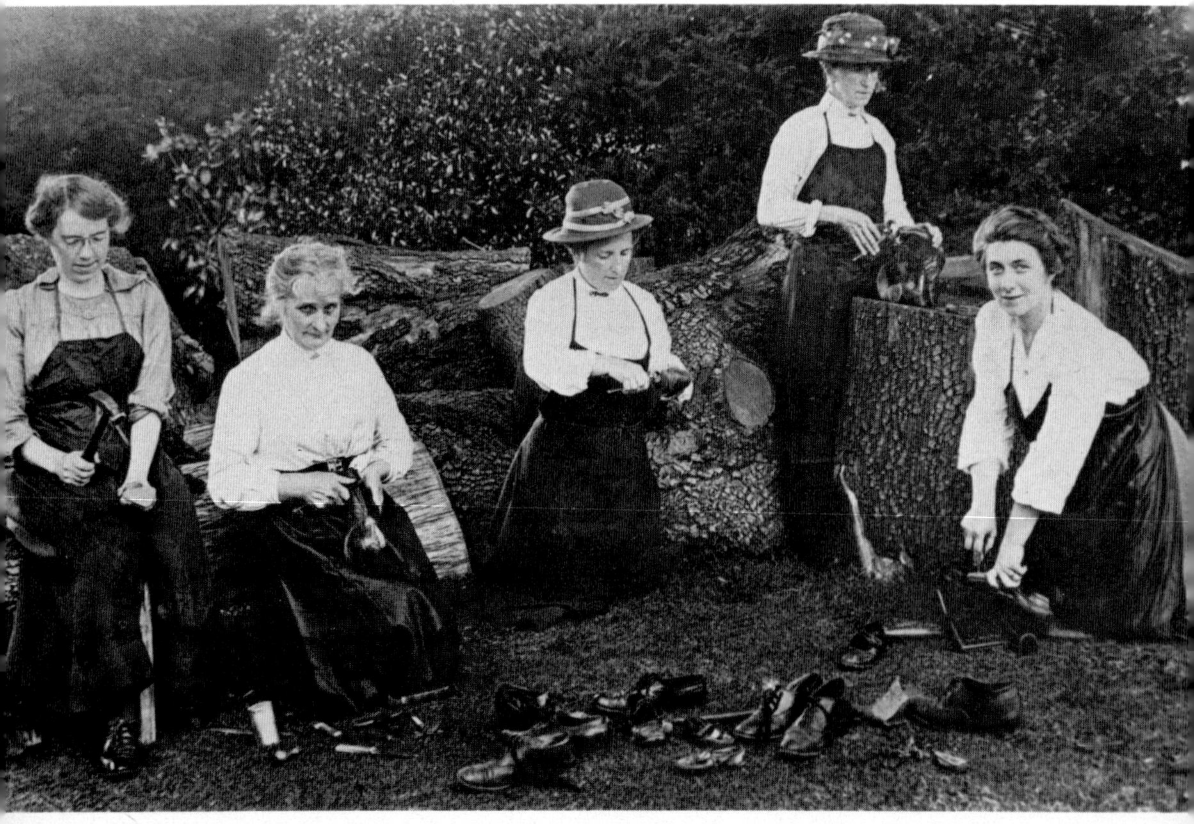

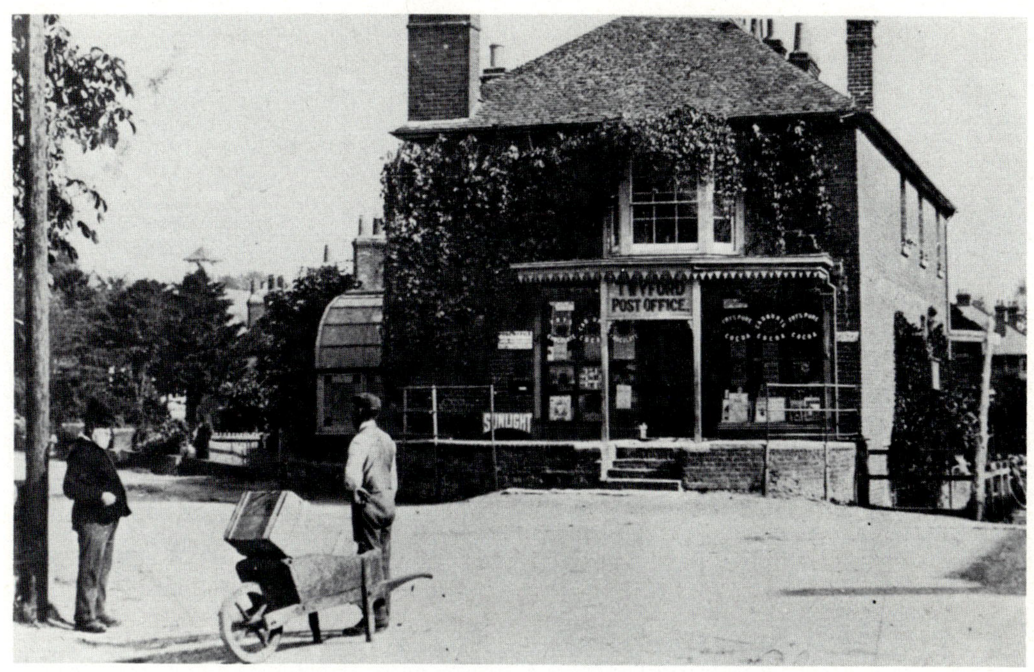

109 (Above left) Twyford Women's Institute Orchestra c 1920. From the left the musicians are: Miss Campbell; Miss Scone; Mrs. Samways; Mrs. Grover and Mrs. Longman.

110 (Below left) Twyford W.I. Members mending shoes in 1917, when the Great War was occupying male shoemakers. From the left. Miss Parey, Mrs. Meath, Mrs. Foard, Mrs. Hickman and Mrs. Stubbington.

111 (Above) Twyford Post Office c 1900.

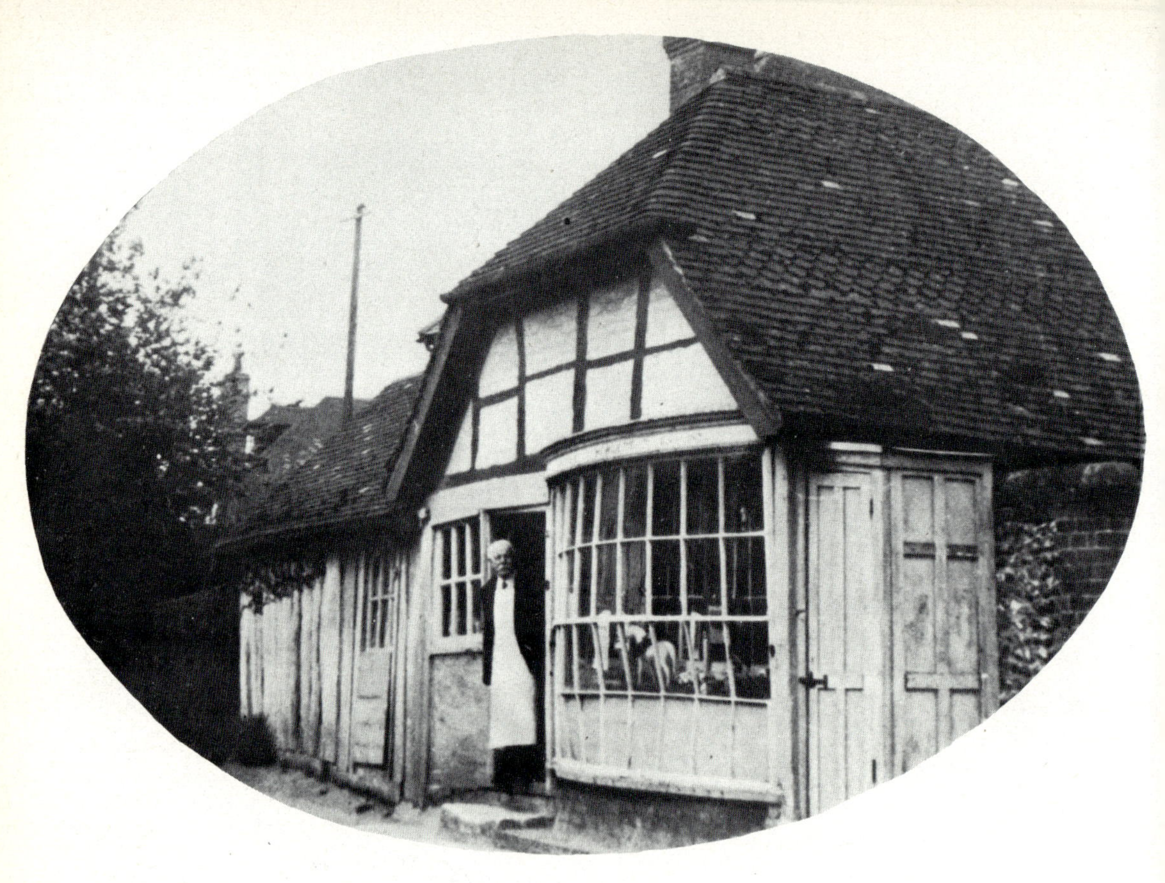

112 (Above) Mr. Hewlett, the saddler, standing at the door of his shop in Twyford c 1920. The model horse that can be seen in the window had a sample saddle on it and was much coveted by small children.

113 (Right) Mr. Froome, the blacksmith (see plate 102) at his forge in Church Lane, Twyford, c 1900. In this picture he is shrinking an iron tyre onto a cart wheel. The forge has been demolished.

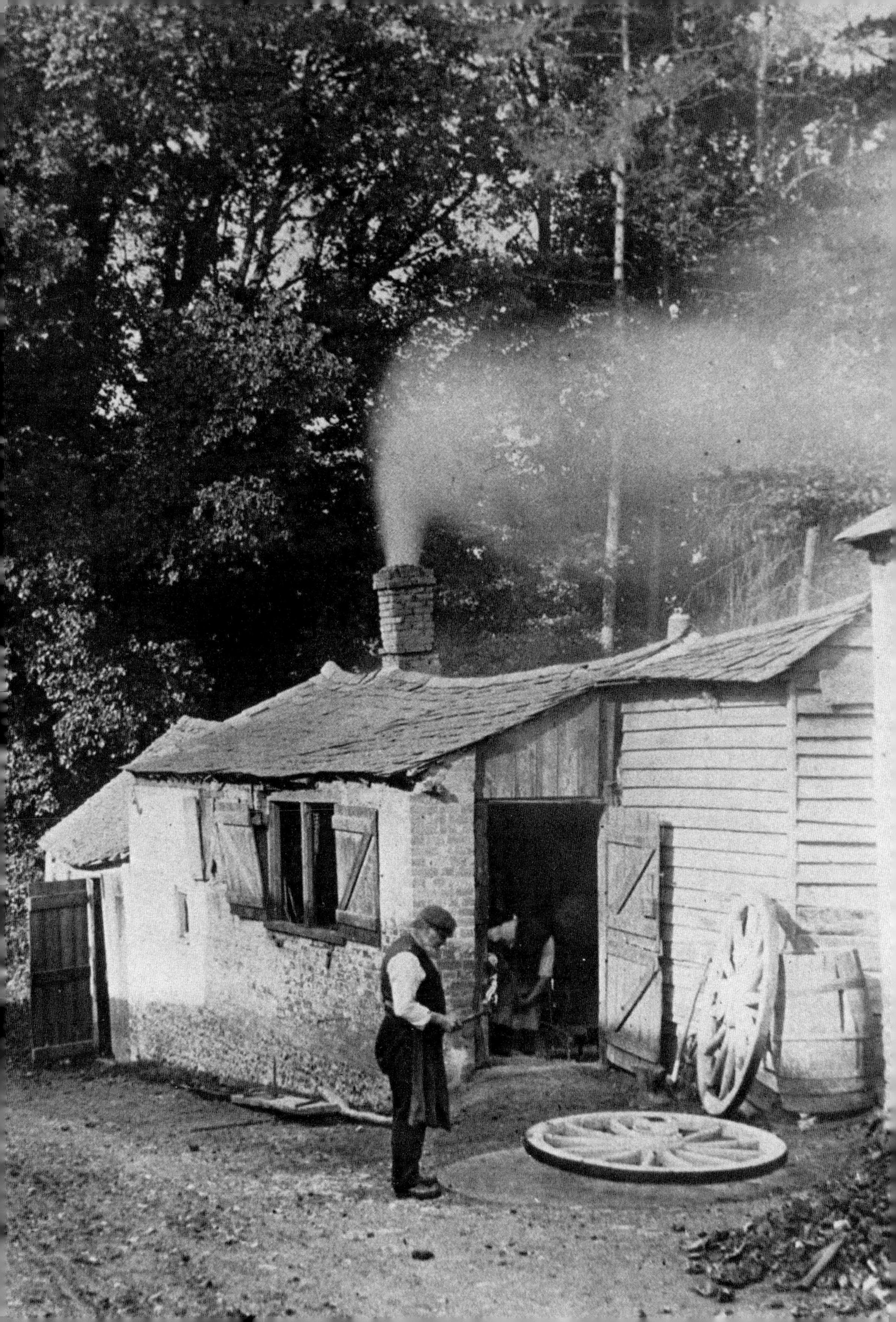

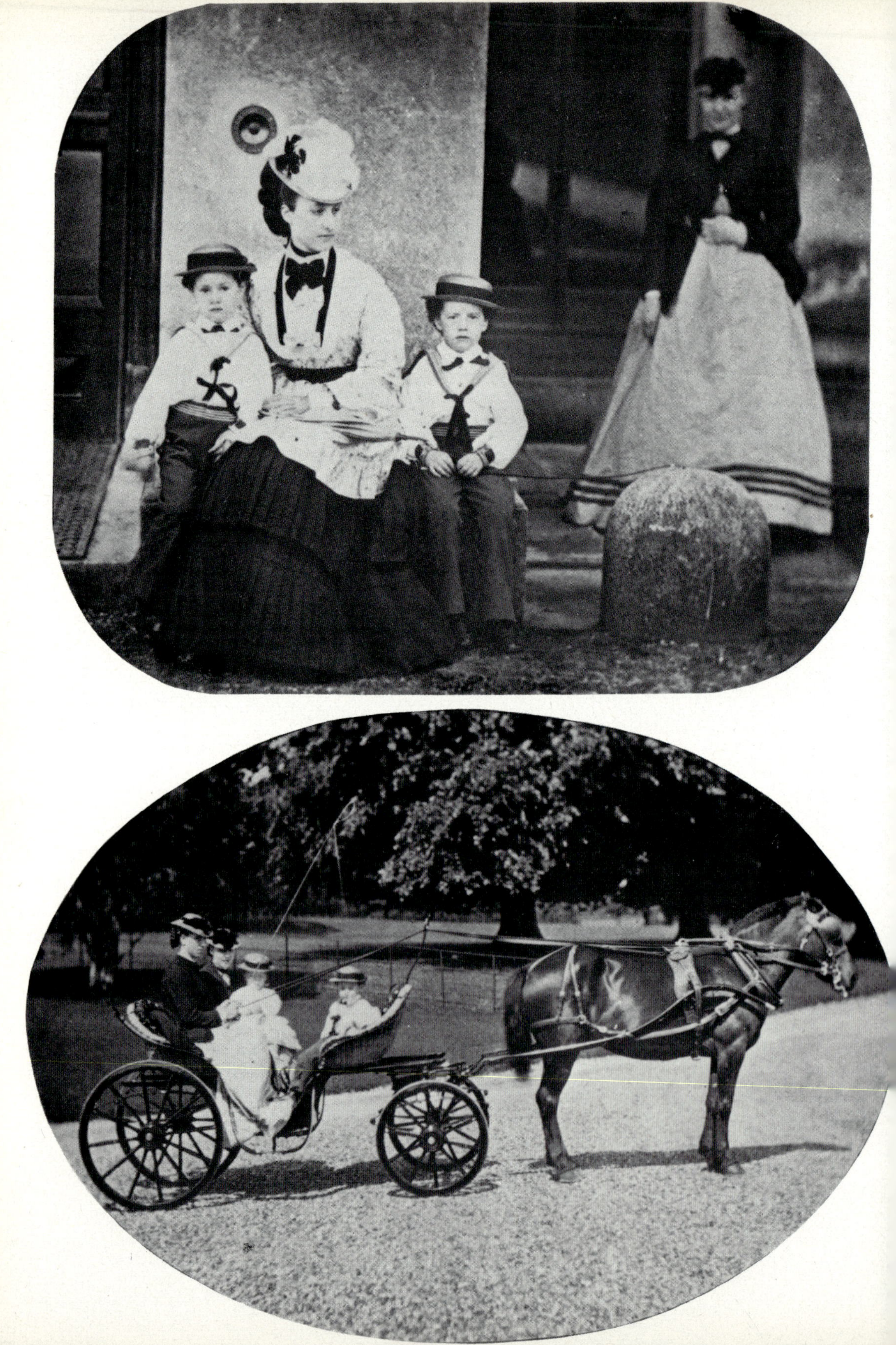

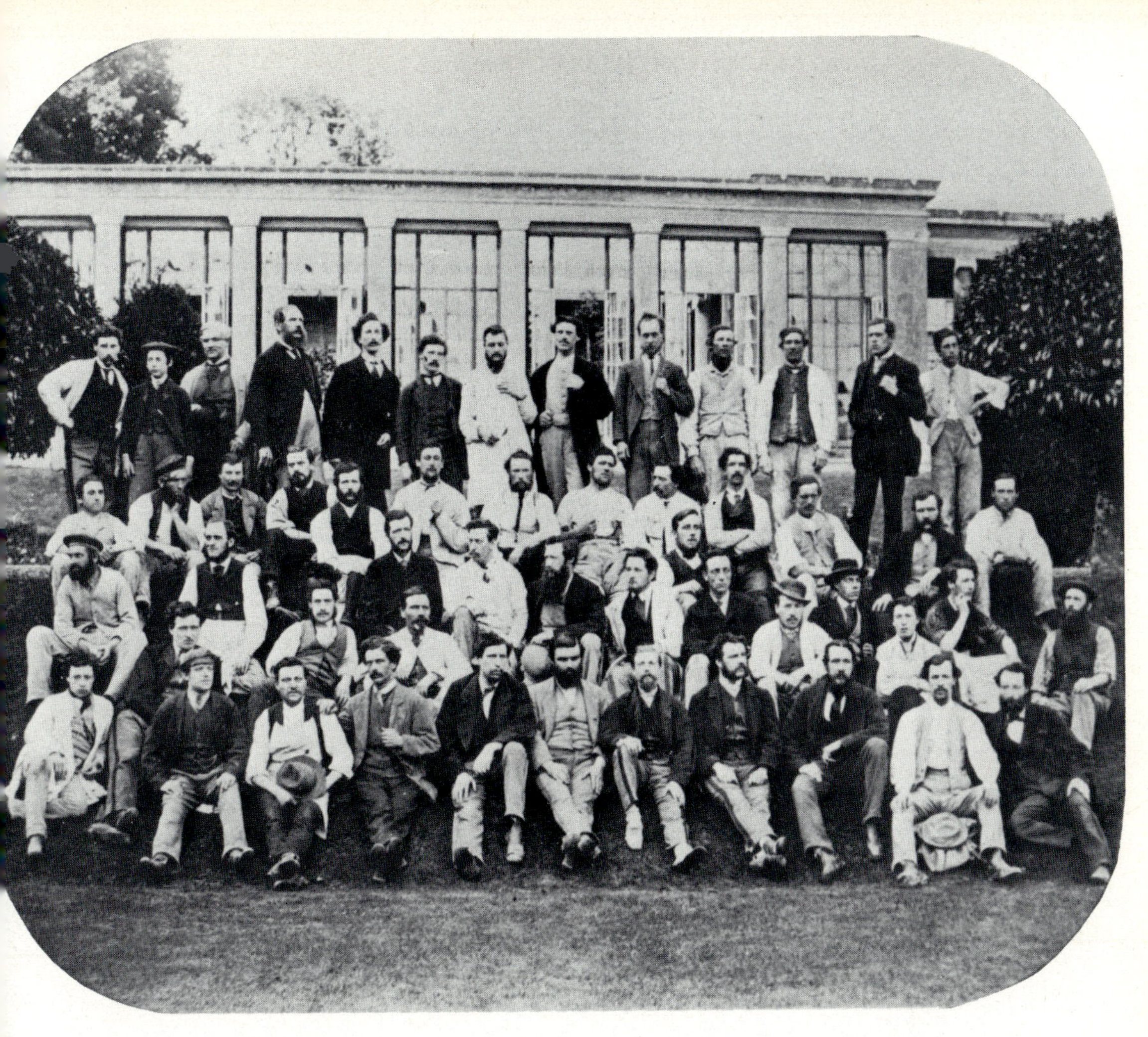

114 (Above left) The Grange, Northington 1871. The 4th Lady Ashburton with her sons Francis (left) and Frederick. Their nanny stands discreetly in the background.

115 (Below left) The Grange 1871. Lady Ashburton, her two sons and her sister the Hon. Teresa Digby in a pony trap in the grounds.

116 (Above) August 1870. Estate workmen in front of the Orangery at the Grange.

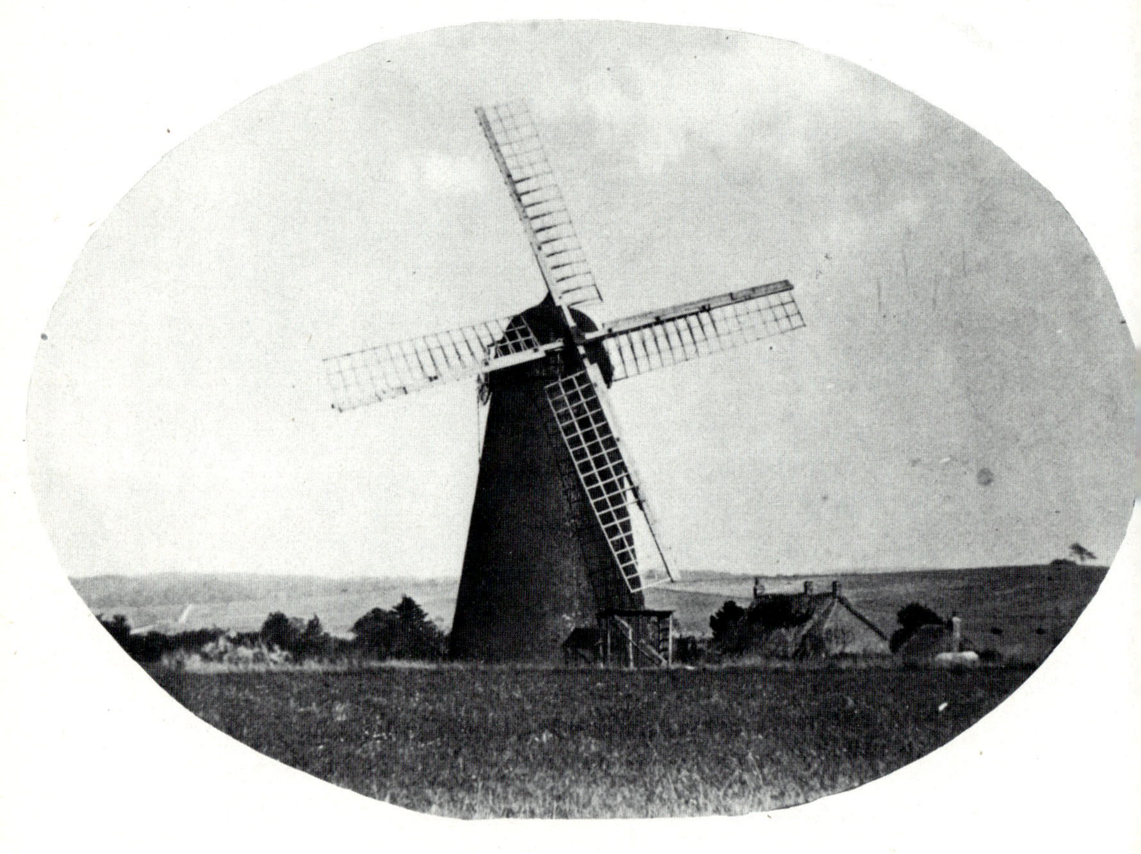

117 (Above) Owslebury Windmill. c 1870. According to a letter in the Hampshire Independent of February 1890 it was the last working corn windmill in Hampshire. By 1900 it was derelict and it has now been demolished.

118 (Right) Owslebury wind pump c1900. It was built about 1870 to supersede the old treadmill above the well at the Chestnuts, Owslebury. The wind pump could raise sufficient water to supply three taps in the village.

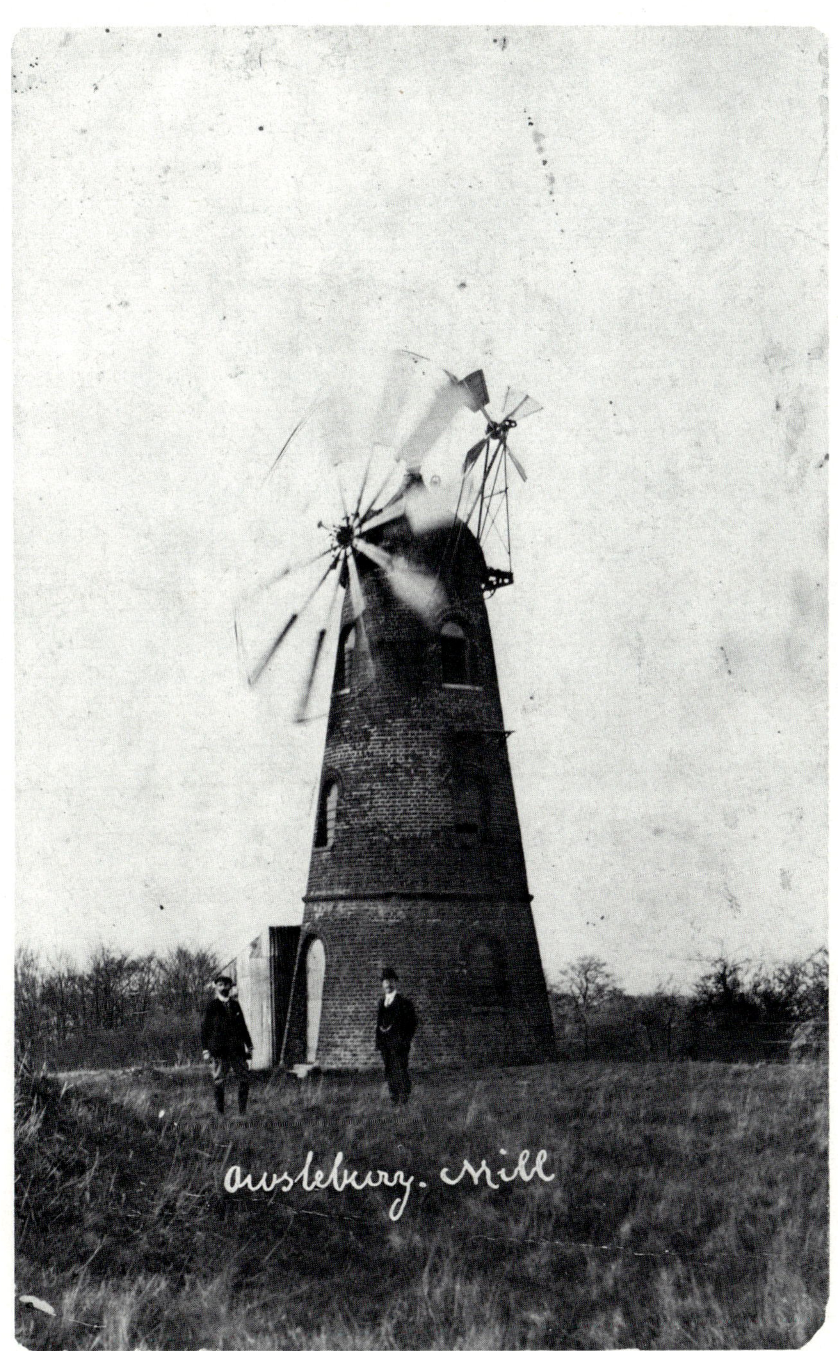
Owslebury. Mill

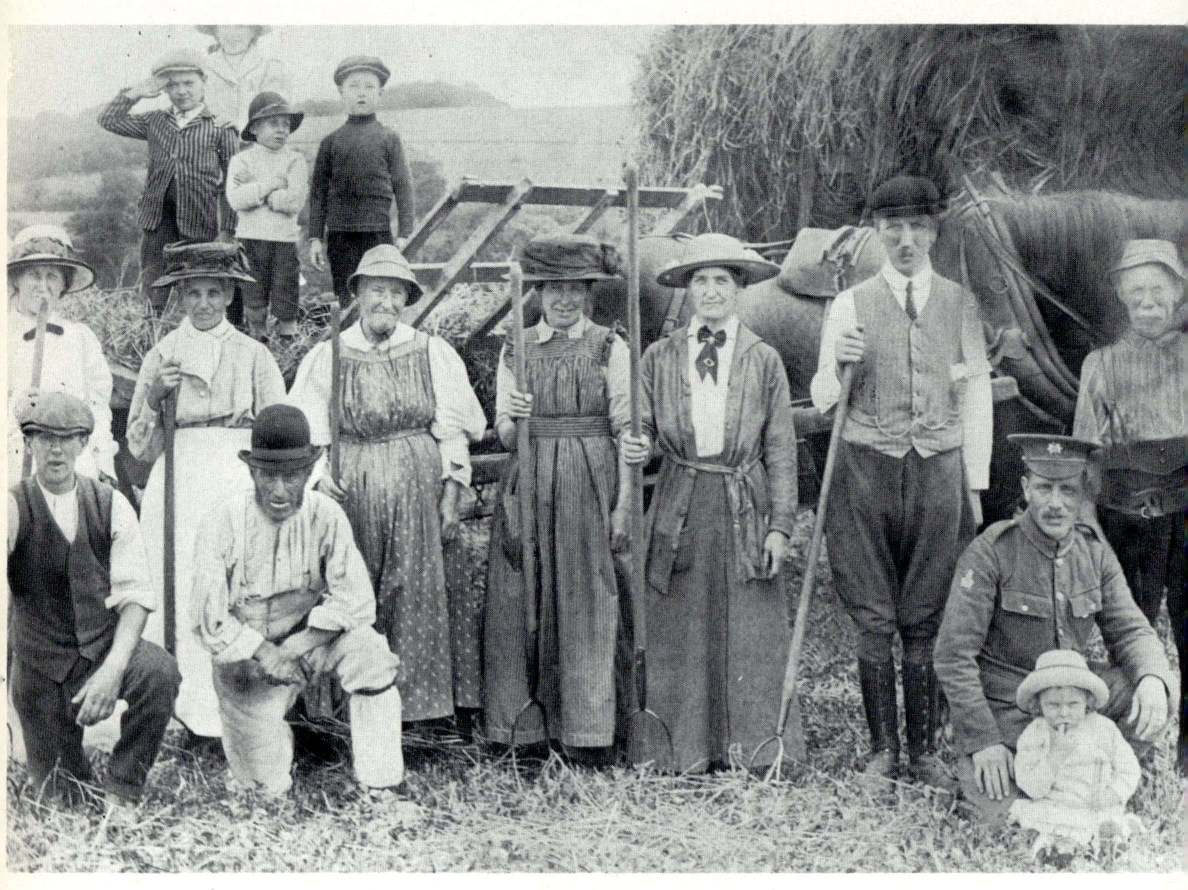

119 (Above) Mr. Frank Coredery, farmer at Morestead Manor Farm, with his helpers at haymaking time. On the far left is Mrs. Maud Bradley a shepherd's wife. Note the high proportion of women, children and old men. This, together with the young soldier and the little boy's military salute, suggests that the photograph was taken during the Great War.

120 (Above right) The younger children at Owslebury elementary school c 1895. On the right is Mr. King, the schoolmaster and on the left is his daughter who taught the younger children.

121 (Below right) Owslebury cricket team outside their thatched pavilion in 1920. The team included a farmer, a policeman, a carpenter, a schoolmaster and a rabbit catcher. Sitting on the extreme right is Mr. E. Harfield an outstanding village cricketer who scored 139 not out in 50 minutes in 1924 at the County Ground Southampton.

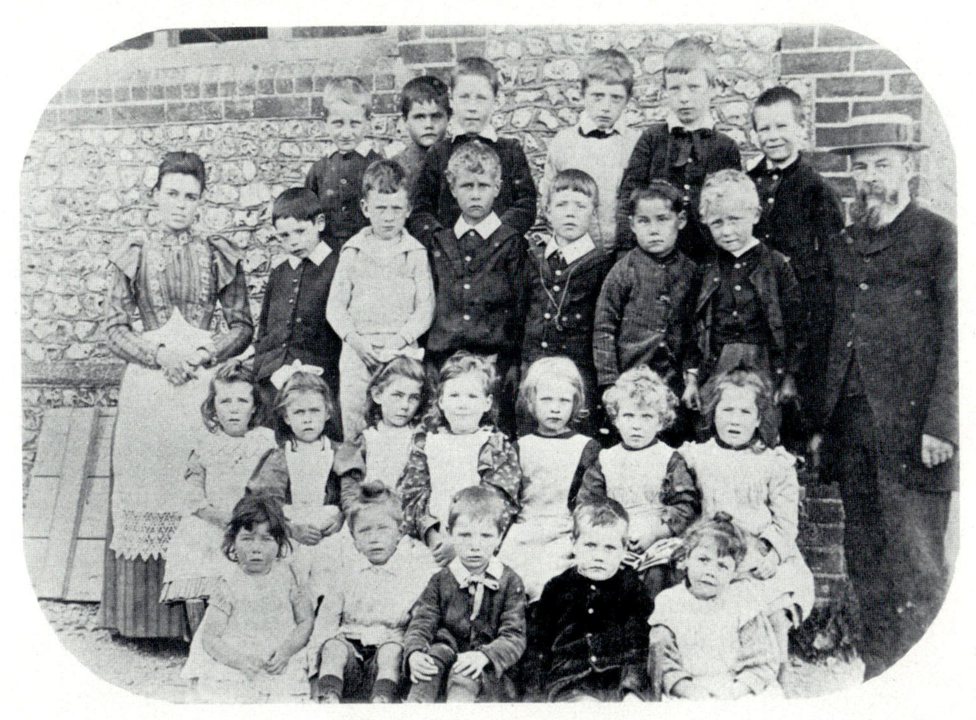

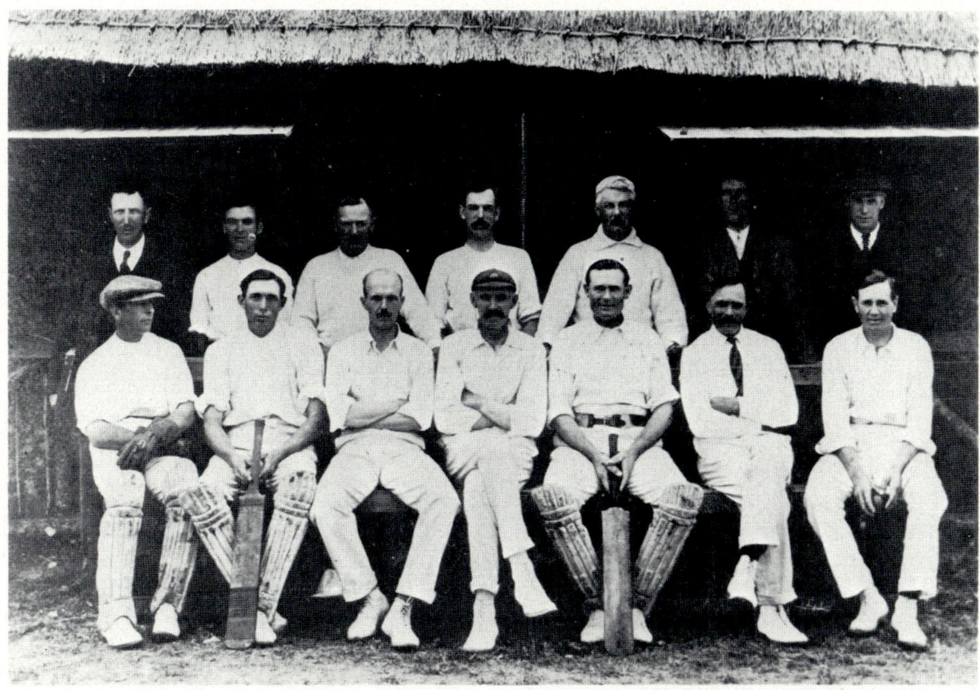

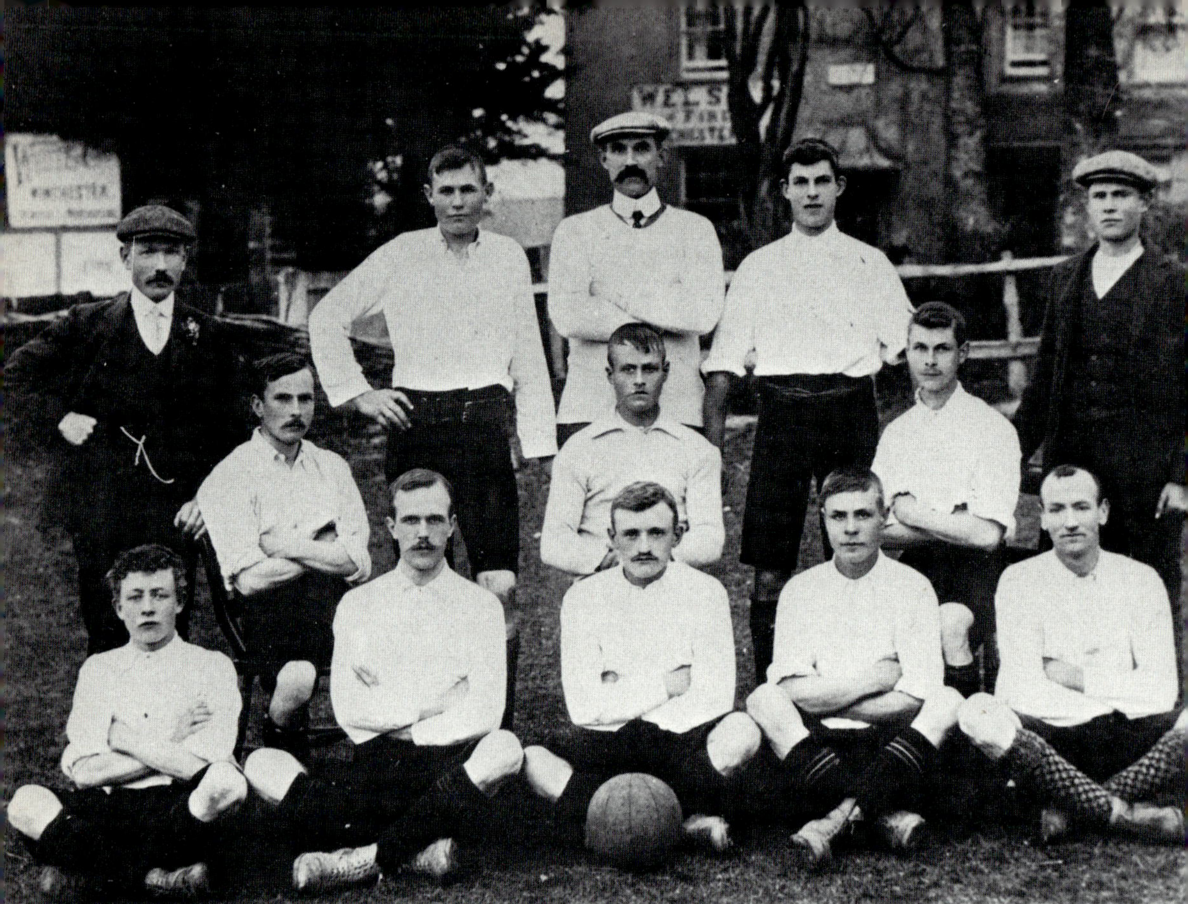

122 (Above) Owslebury football team (c 1908) outside the Cricketer's Inn, which was their clubhouse.

123 (Above right) The King's Head Inn at Hursley. c1865.

124 (Below right) Dr. Livingston and his wife outside their house, 79, Hursley. c1900. Their coachman is Mr. William Jones (See plate 27) who later established a bus company.

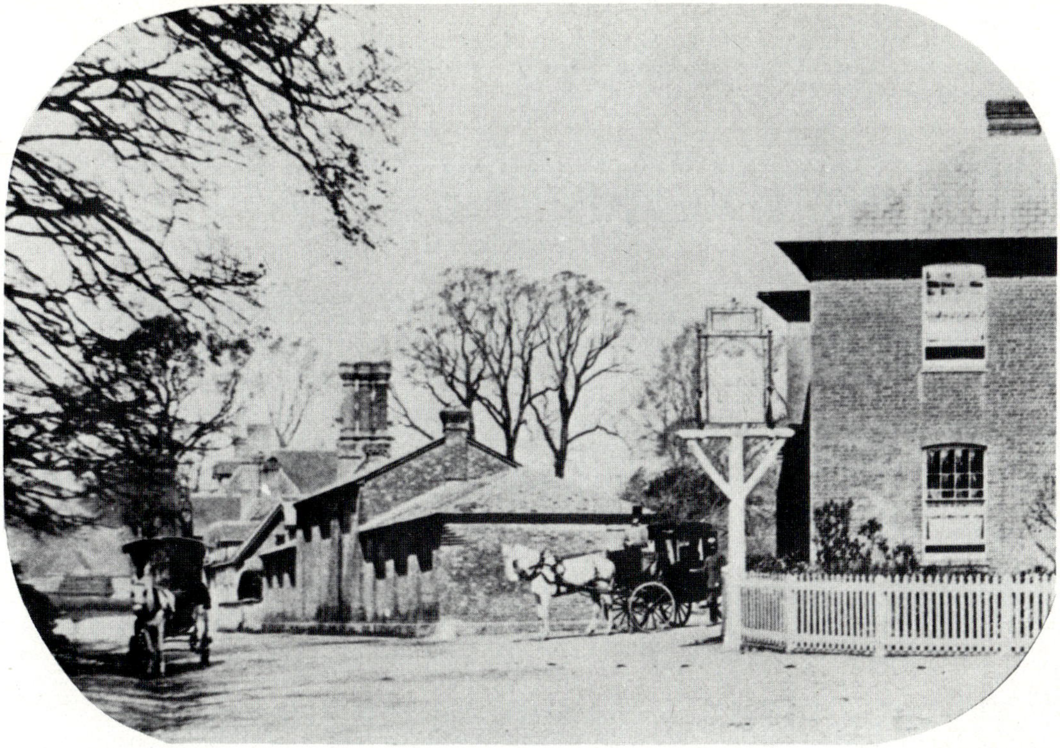

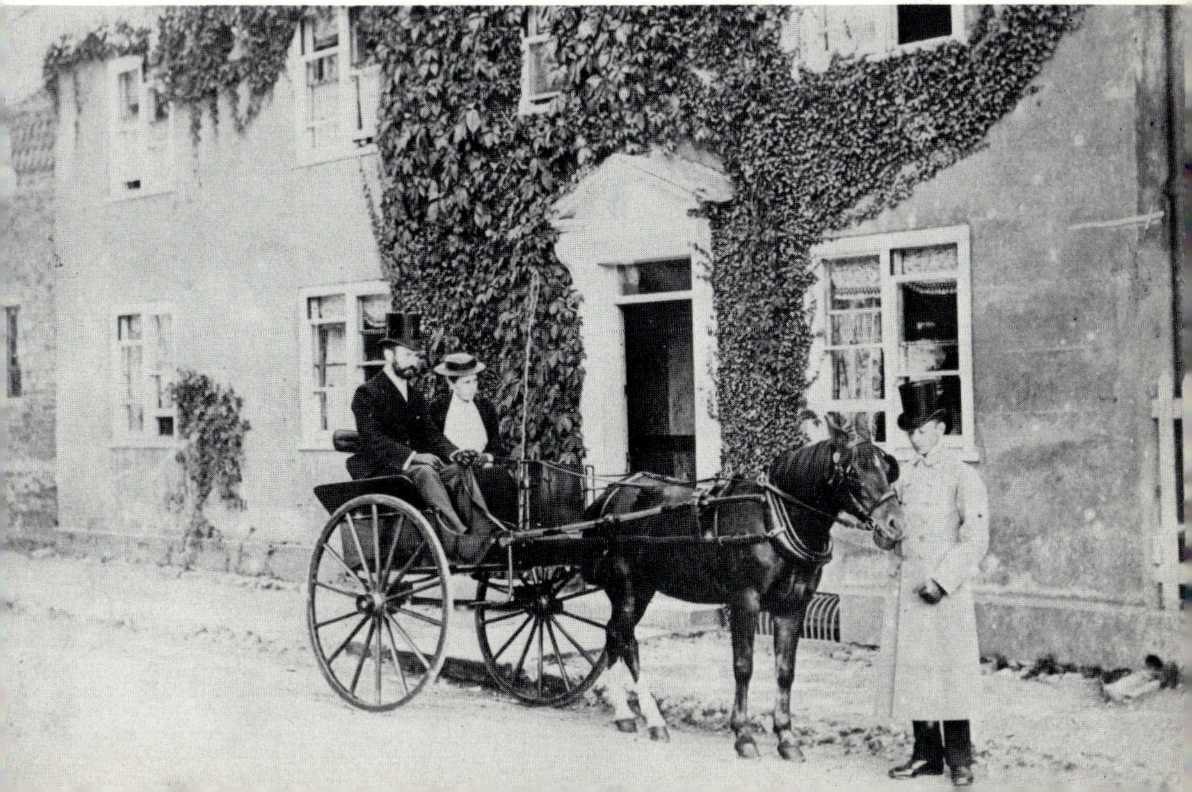

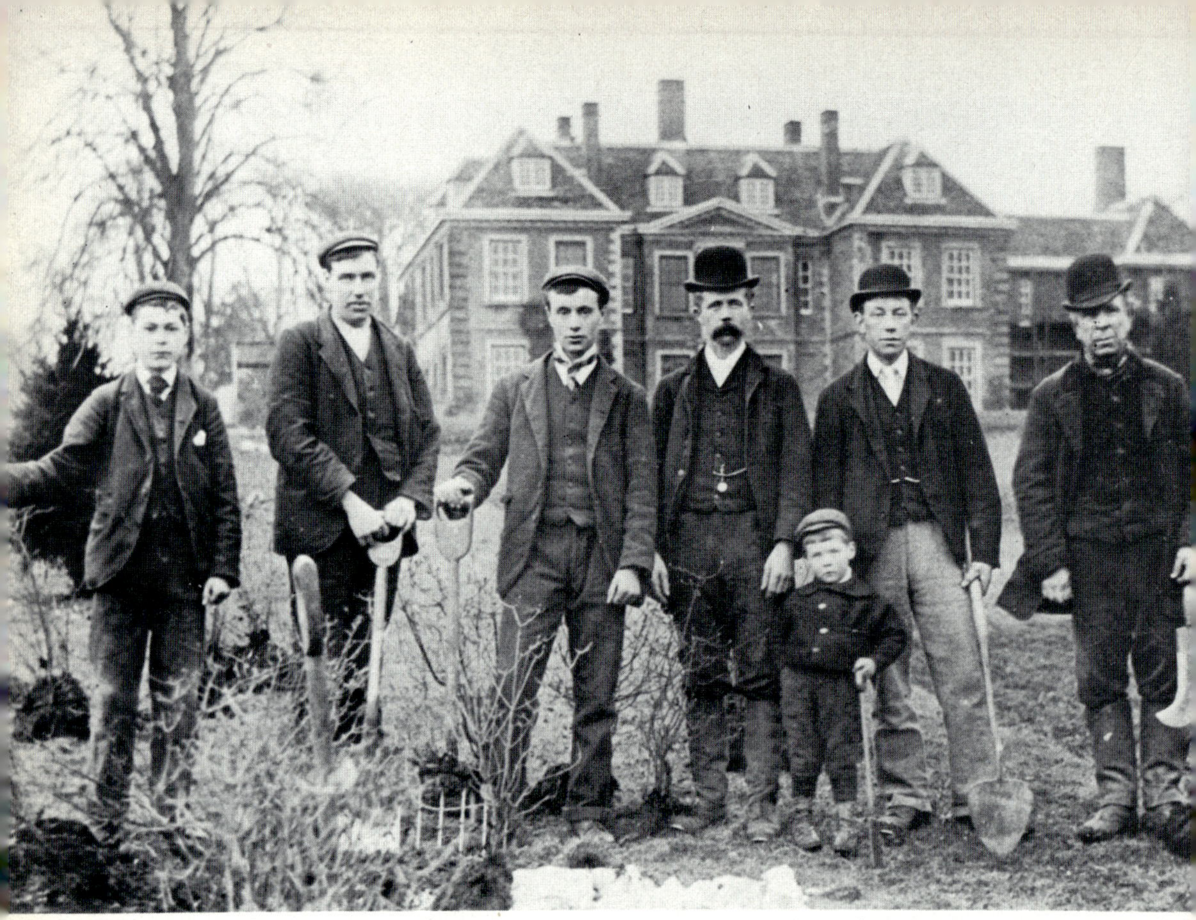

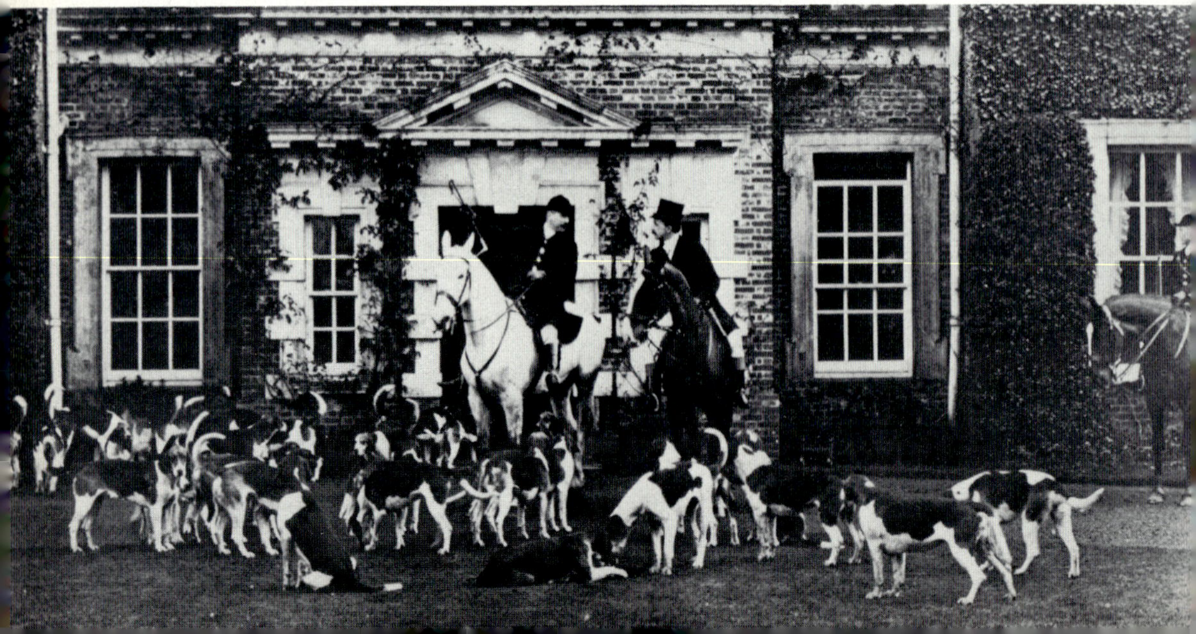

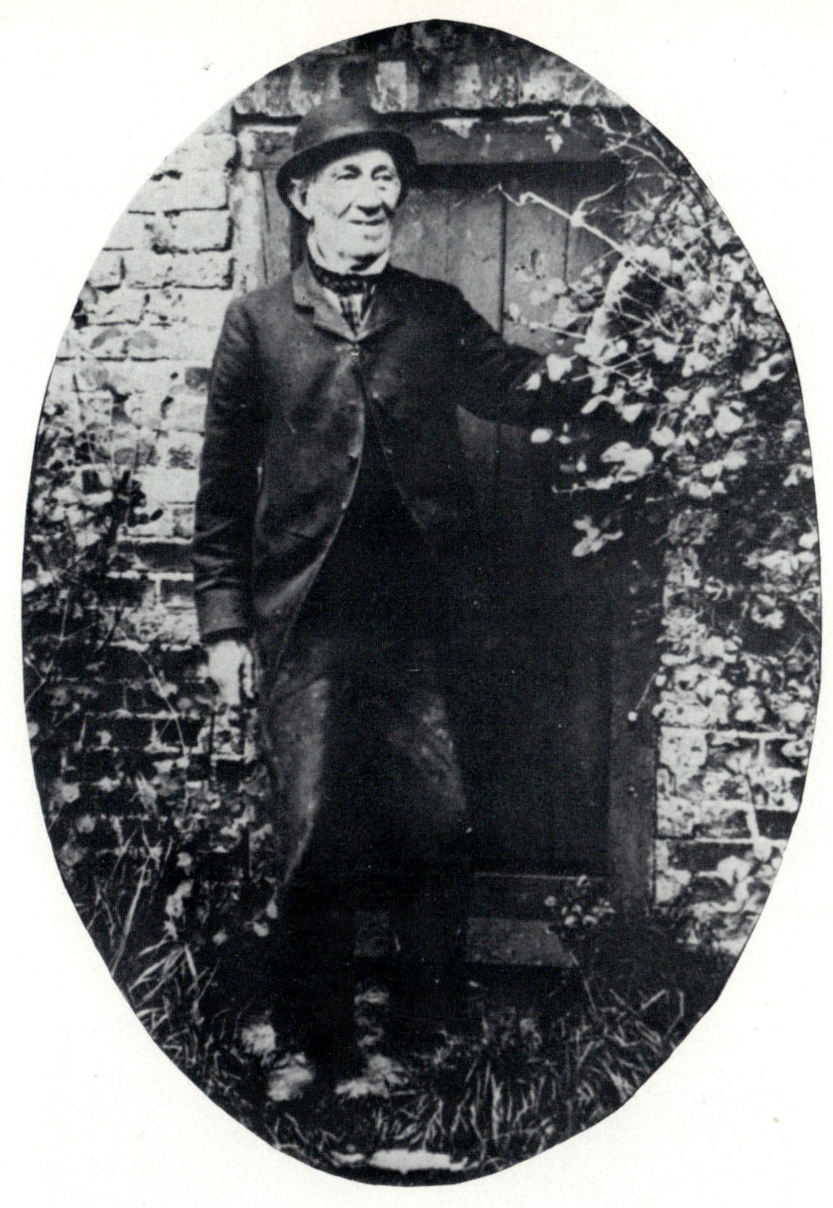

125 (Above left) Gardeners at Lainston House, c 1905.

126 (Below left) Mr. Bostock (in the top hat) outside his home at Lainston House. He was Master of the Hursley Hunt. c 1905.

127 (Above) Robert Goater c 1895. He was parish clerk of Sparsholt for over fifty years.

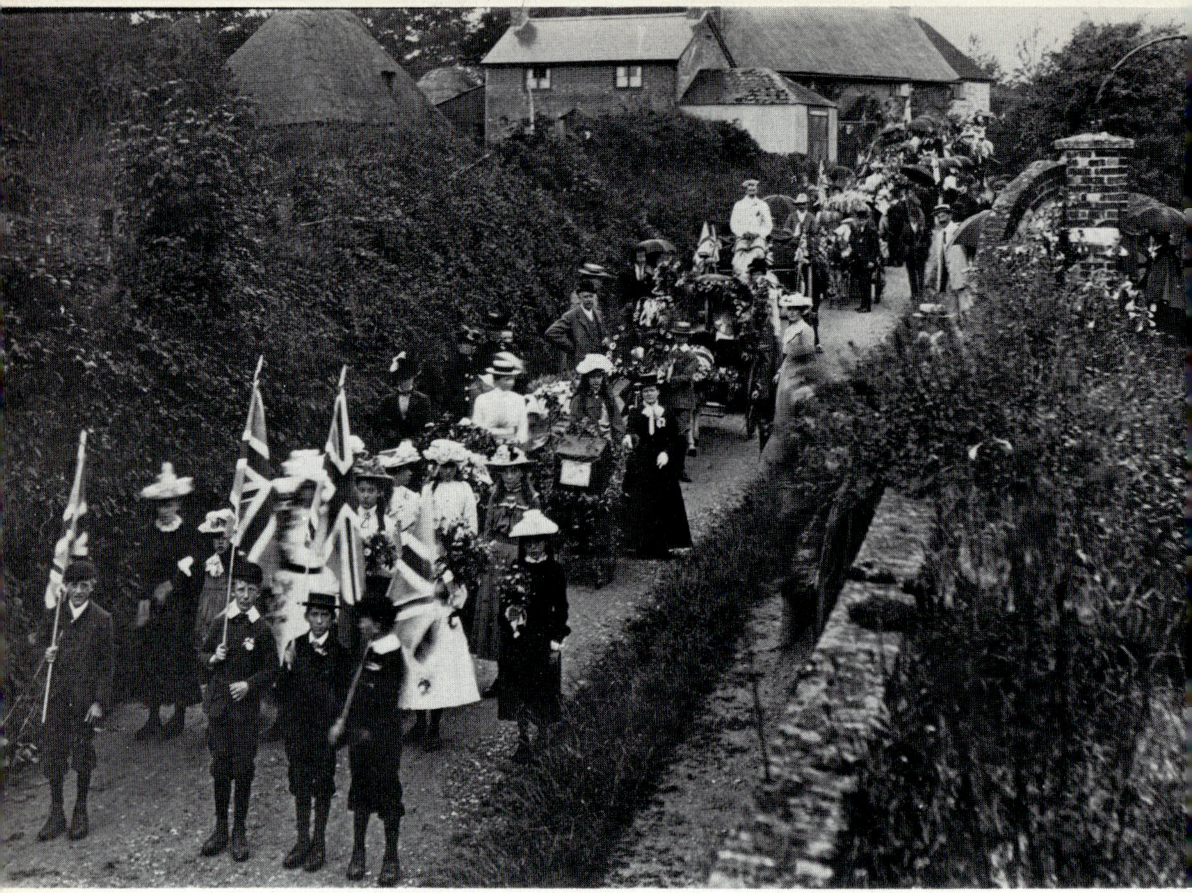

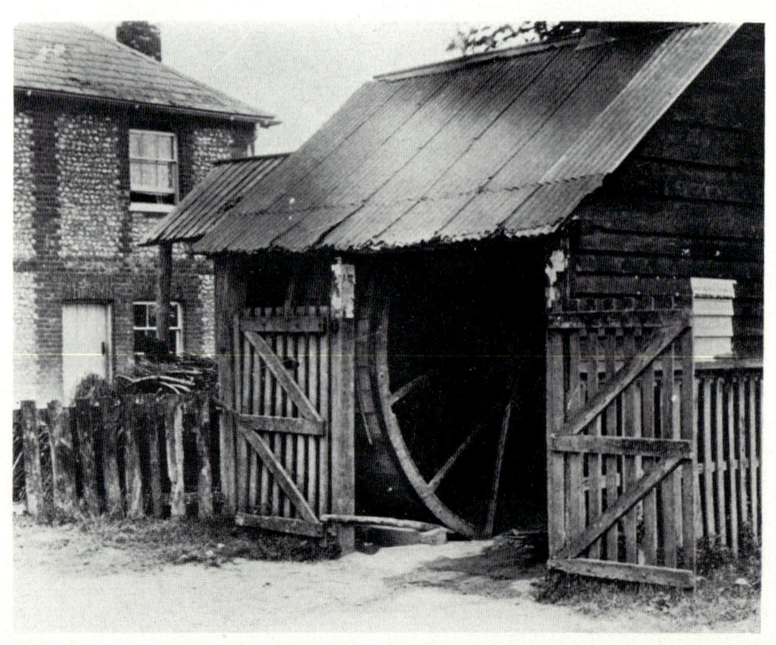

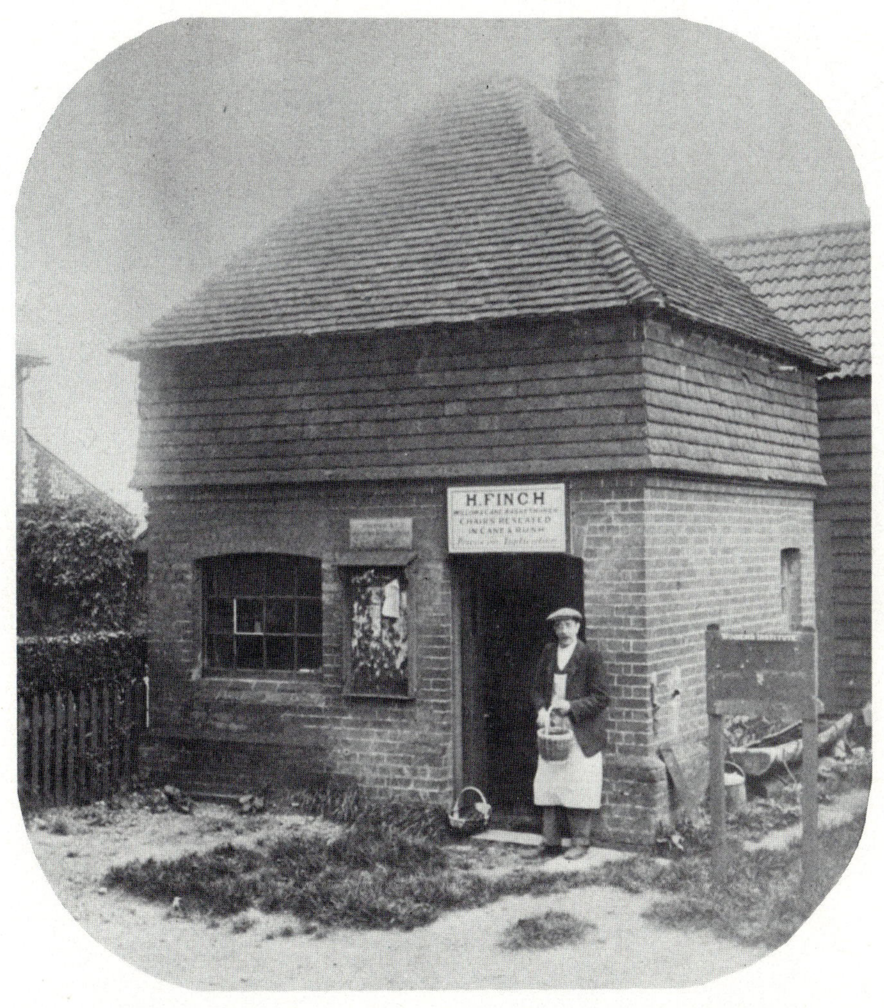

128 (Above left) 1897. The procession to celebrate Queen Victoria's Diamond Jubilee pauses outside Sparsholt Church. On one of the carts is Mr. T. S. Goater, wearing his white baker's coat and hat.

129 (Below left) The old treadmill beside Sparsholt Post Office. One or two people walked inside the wheel to bring up a large barrel-shaped bucket of water, c 1895.

130 (Above) In 1897, the old wheel was replaced by the pump-house. When water was piped to the village, the pump-house was used as a workshop by Mr. Finch the blind basket maker. c 1935.

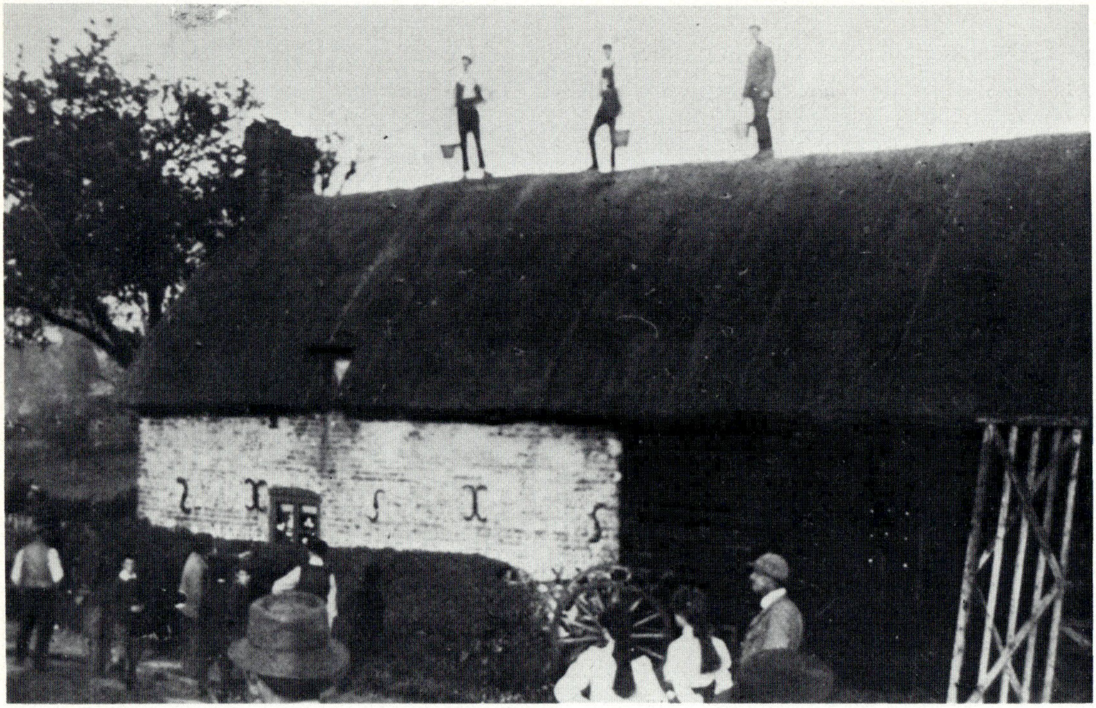

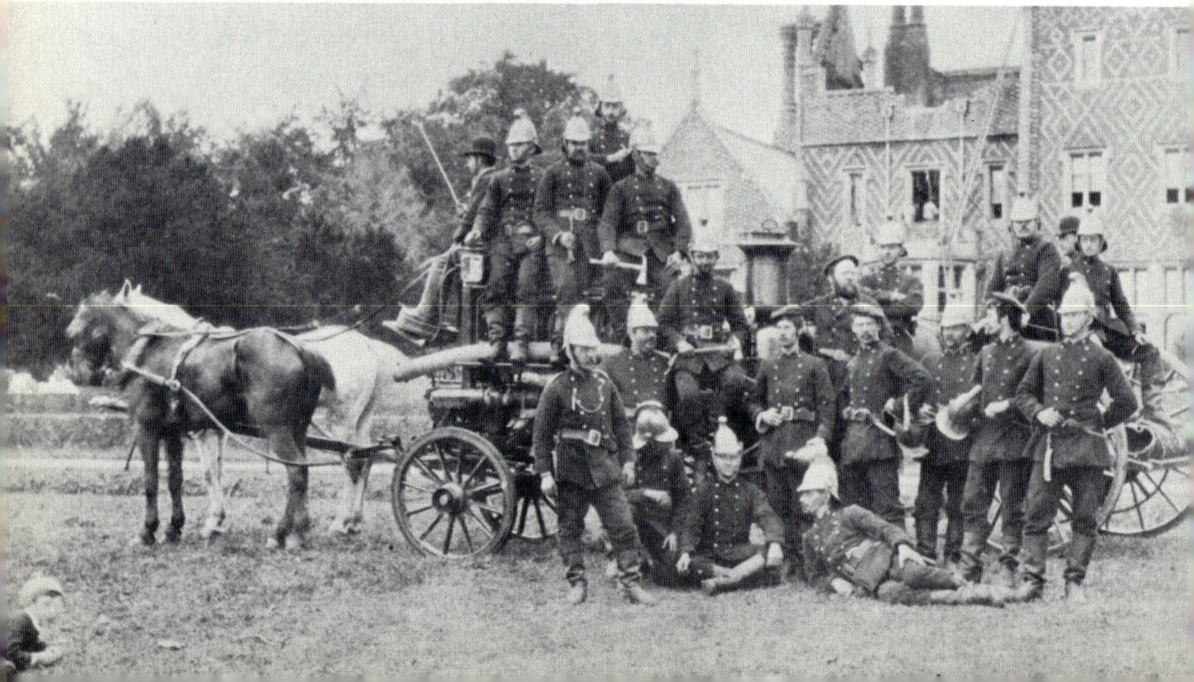

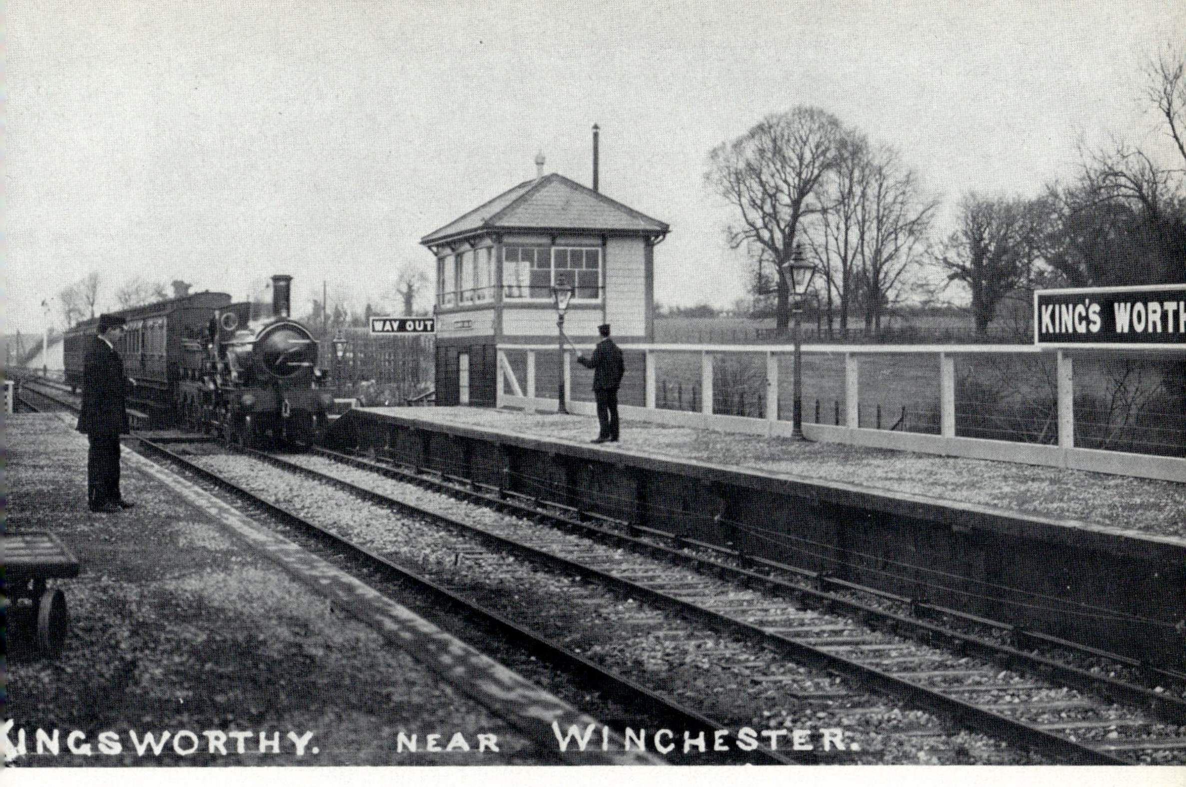

131 (Above left) Dean, near Sparsholt, 1910. An old-fashioned method of fire-fighting. Men are standing on a thatched barn holding buckets of water. A nearby building is on fire and they are ready to douse the flames should a spark set the straw alight. The field gate on the right has been used as a make-shift ladder.

132 (Below left) More sophisticated methods were used at a fire in Mr. Coteworth's house at Abbot's Worthy House. The Winchester Fire Brigade c 1895.

133 (Above) The opening day at King's Worthy Station, February 1909. On the left is Mr. Chapman the Station Master.

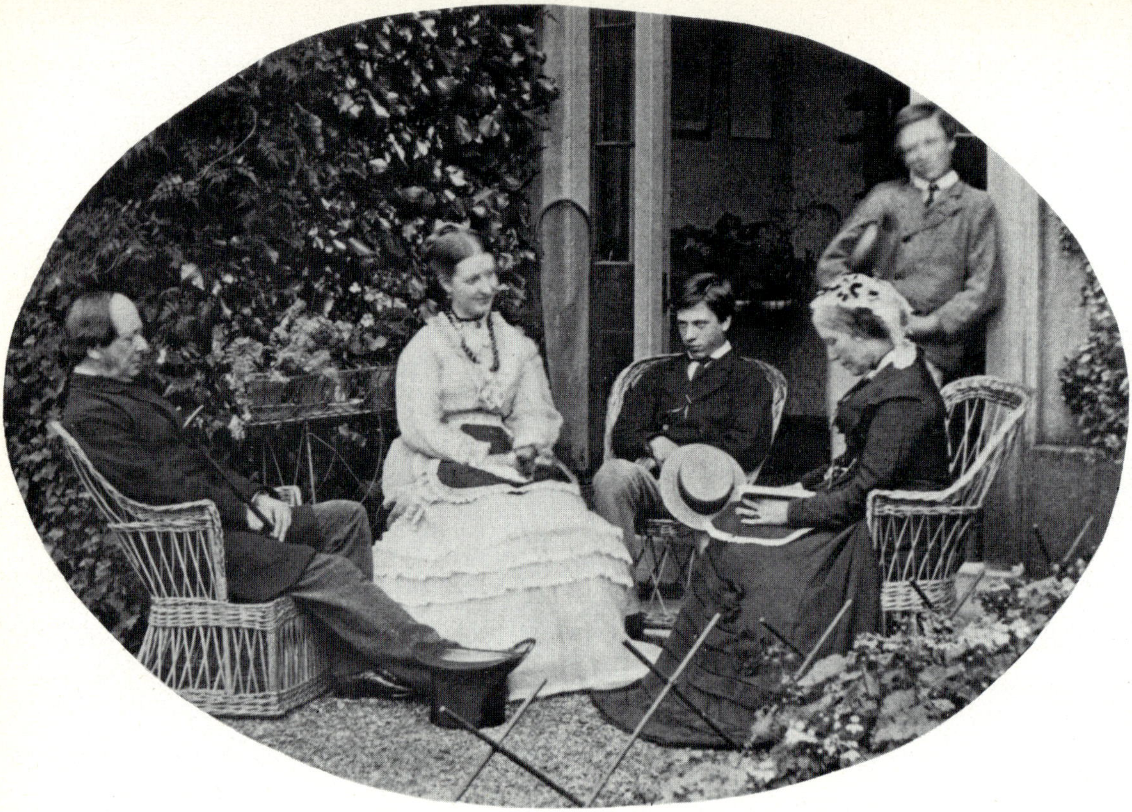

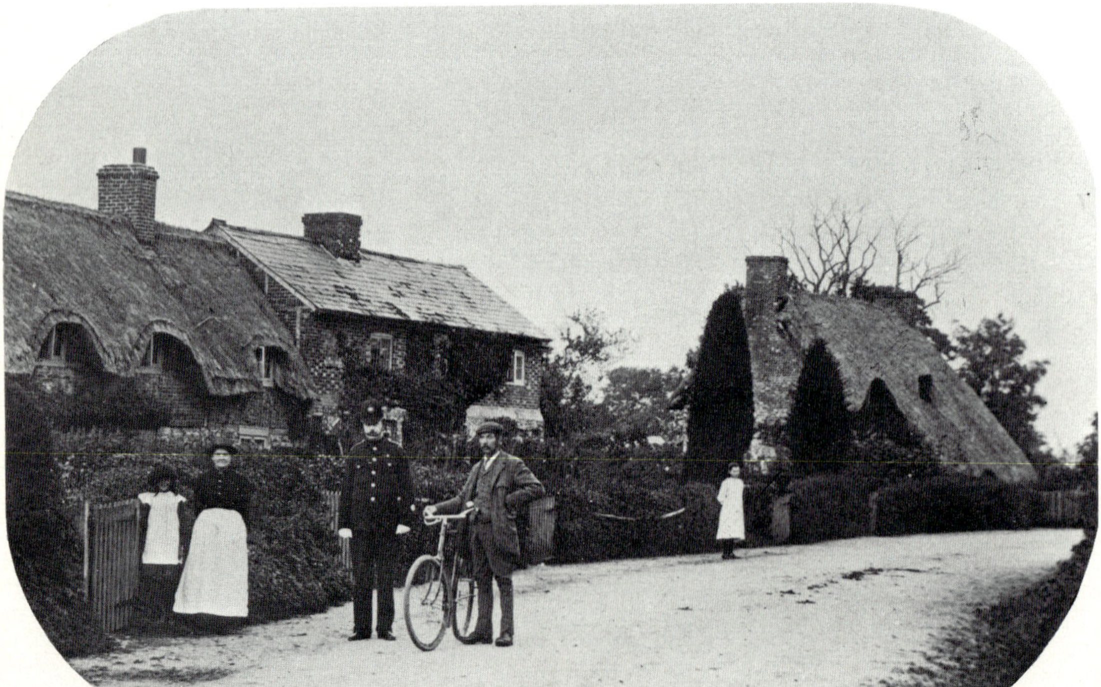

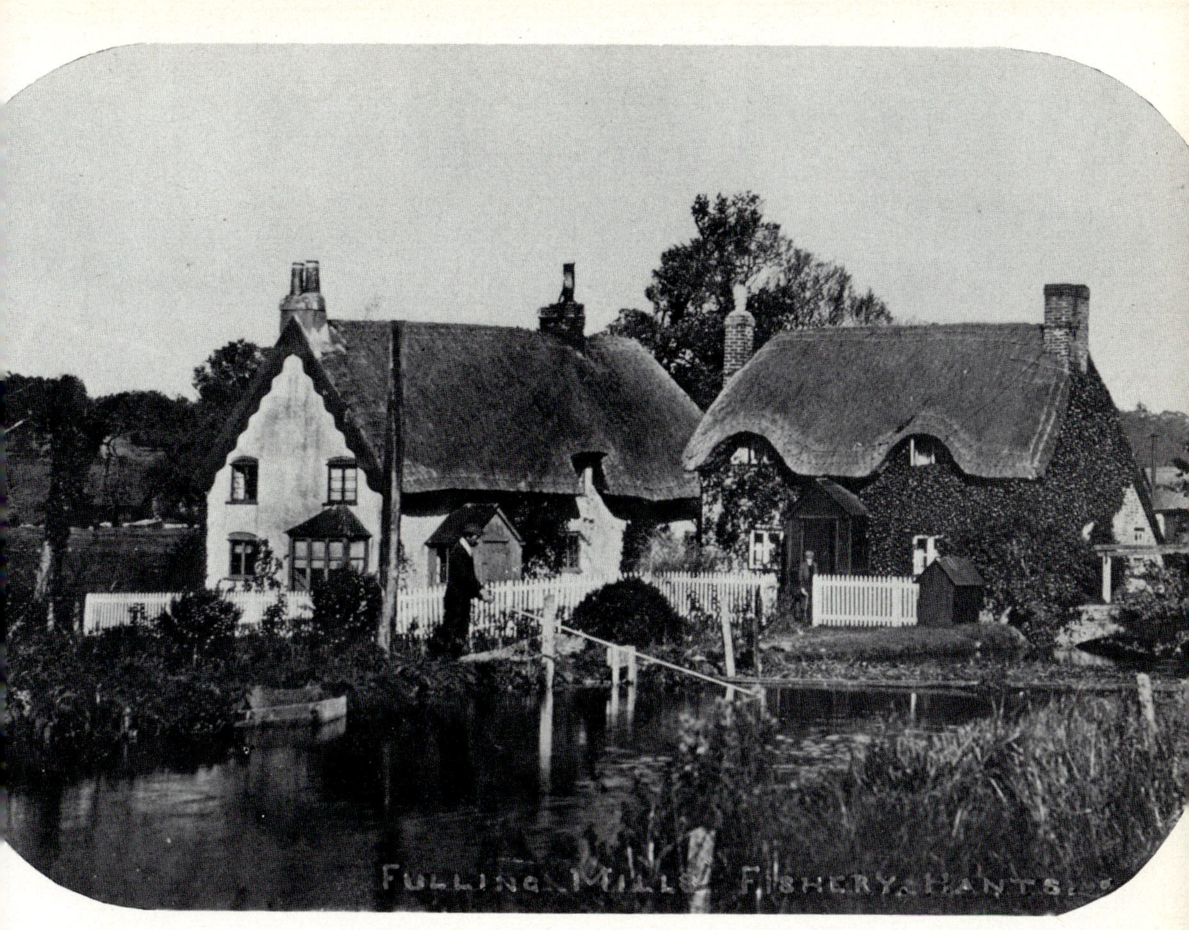

134 (Above left) The Rev. and Lady Eleanor Wodehouse at Easton Rectory, c 1870.

135 (Below left) c 1909. At Easton on the road leading towards Avington, P. C. Day talks to Mrs. Smith, wife of a gardener at Chilland, and to a gamekeeper from Avington Lodge.

136 (Above) c 1905. The old fulling mills between Easton and King's Worthy. At this time a water keeper lived in the right hand house and the other was let to fishermen.

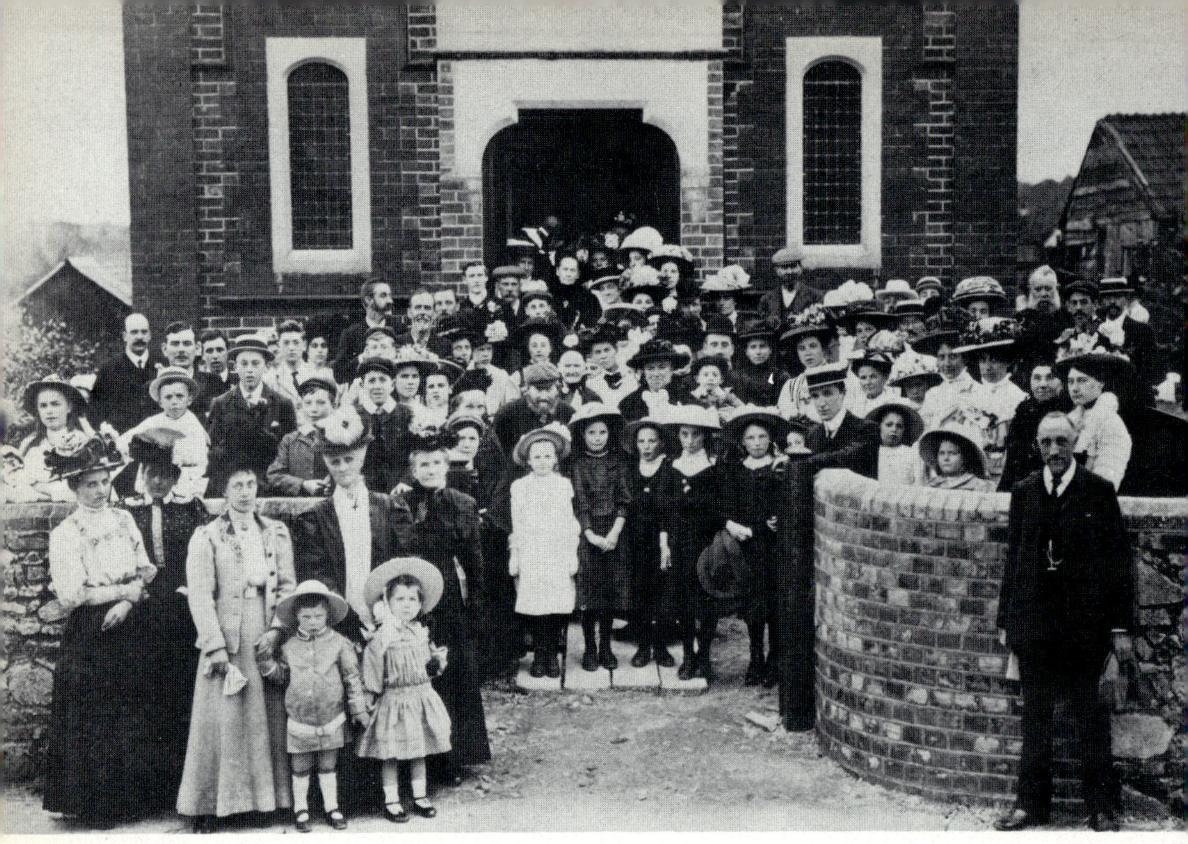

137 (Above) Easton Primitive Methodist Chapel; the opening ceremony 1909. In front of the wall on the right is Mr. Weeks who built the chapel. The balding man on the left at the back is Rev. Scott the minister.

138 (Above right) c 1899. Packing trout at the fish farm at Lower Chilland near Matryr Worthy.

139 (Below right) The same trout farm c 1905. The men are netting 8 inch trout to be despatched to other waters.

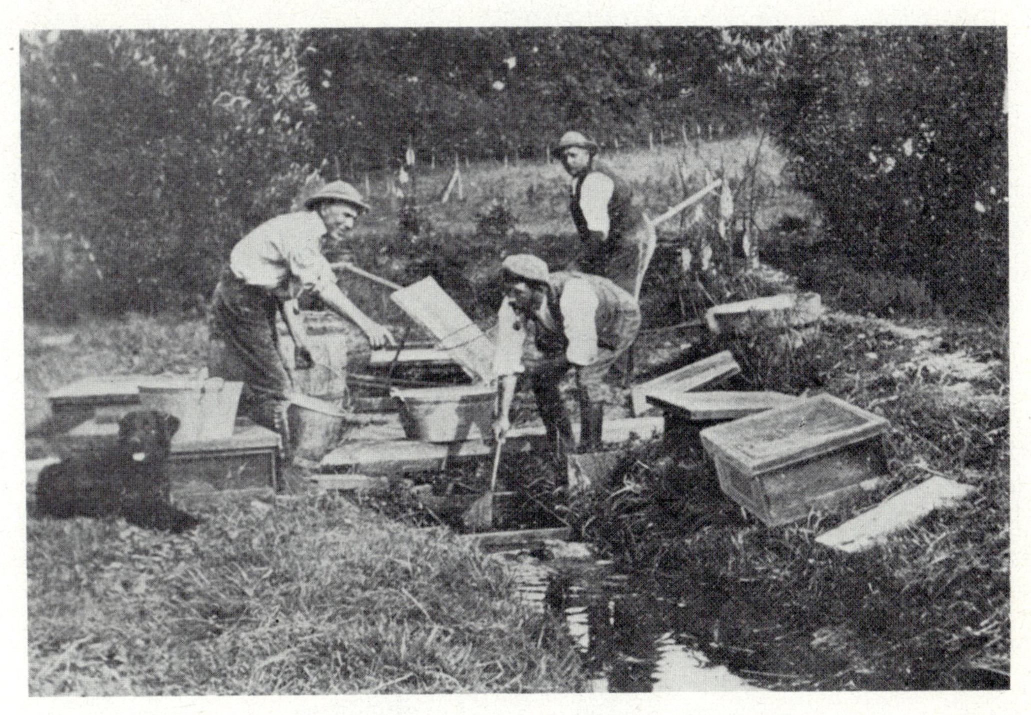

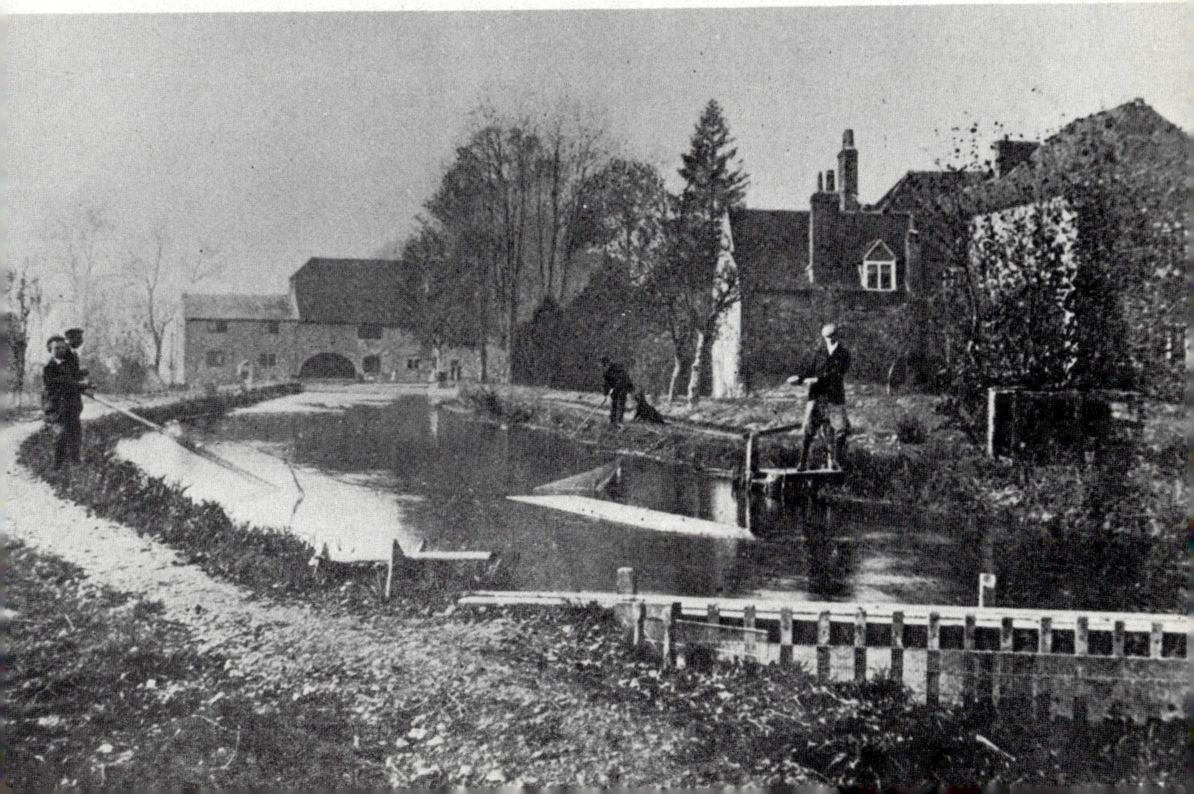

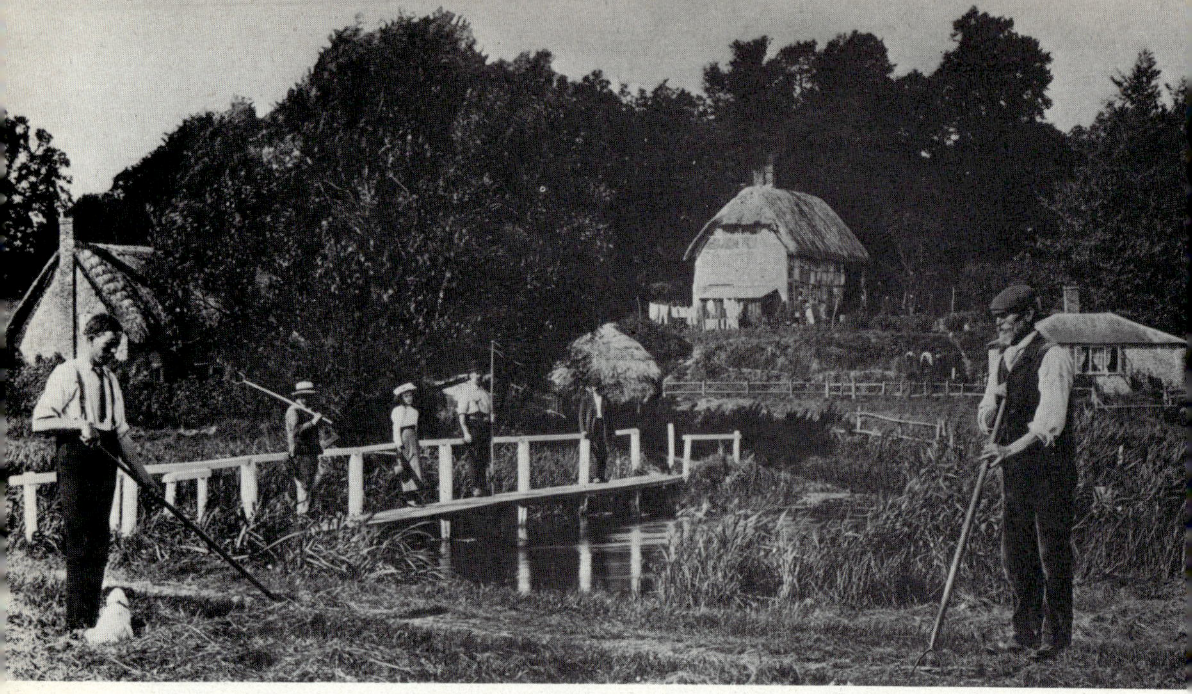

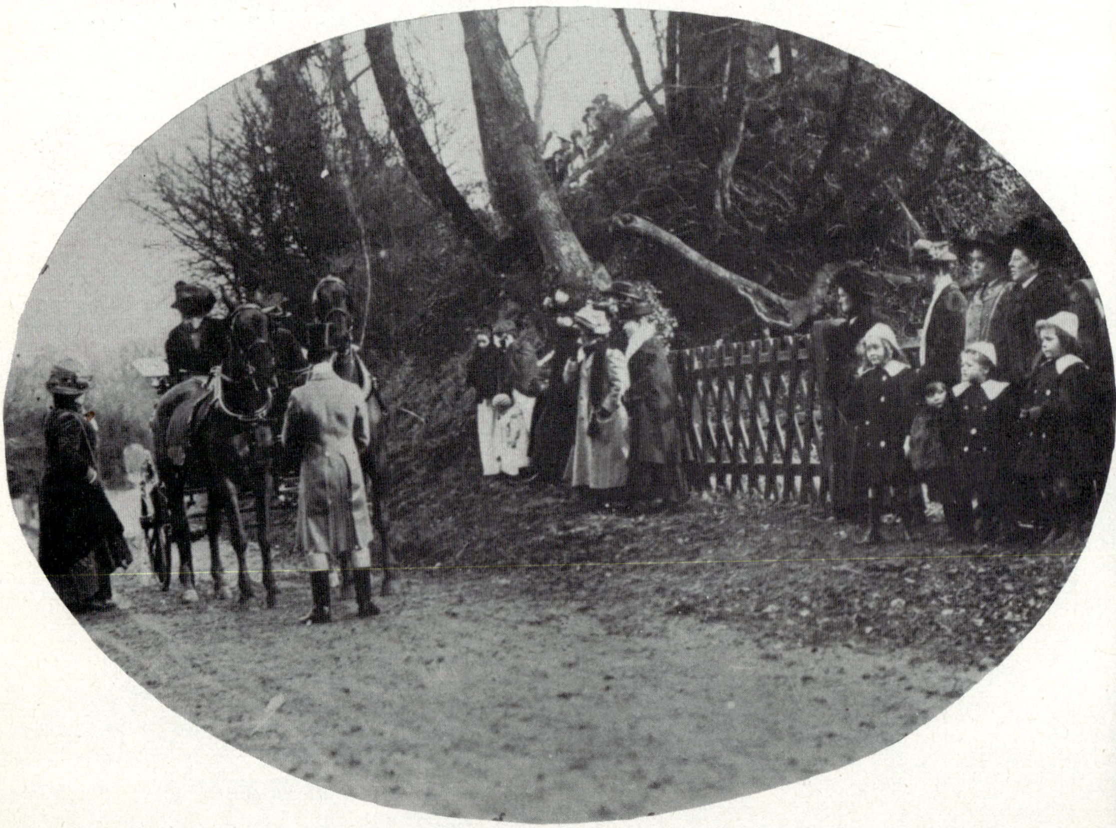

140 (Above left) Haymaking beside the River Itchen at Martyr Worthy c1910. On the left is Mr. Collard who kept the Chestnut Horse Inn at Easton. He also kept horses and hired out a wagonette.

141 (Below left) Ladies in a carriage from Dymoke House, Easton arriving for a meet of the H. H. at Avington Dairy. c 1908.

142 (Below) Itchen Stoke c 1910. The men in the wagon are probably on a club outing.

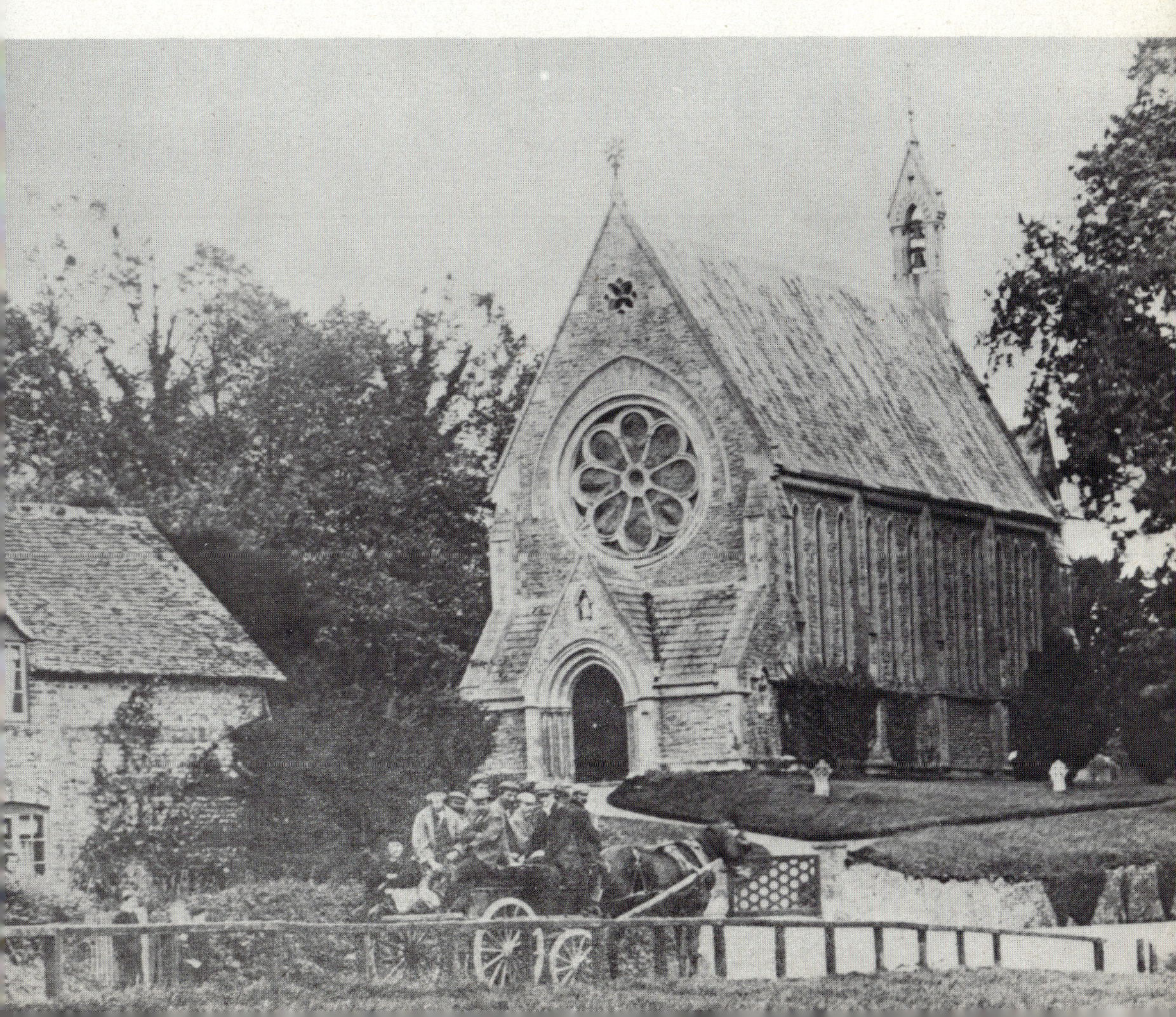

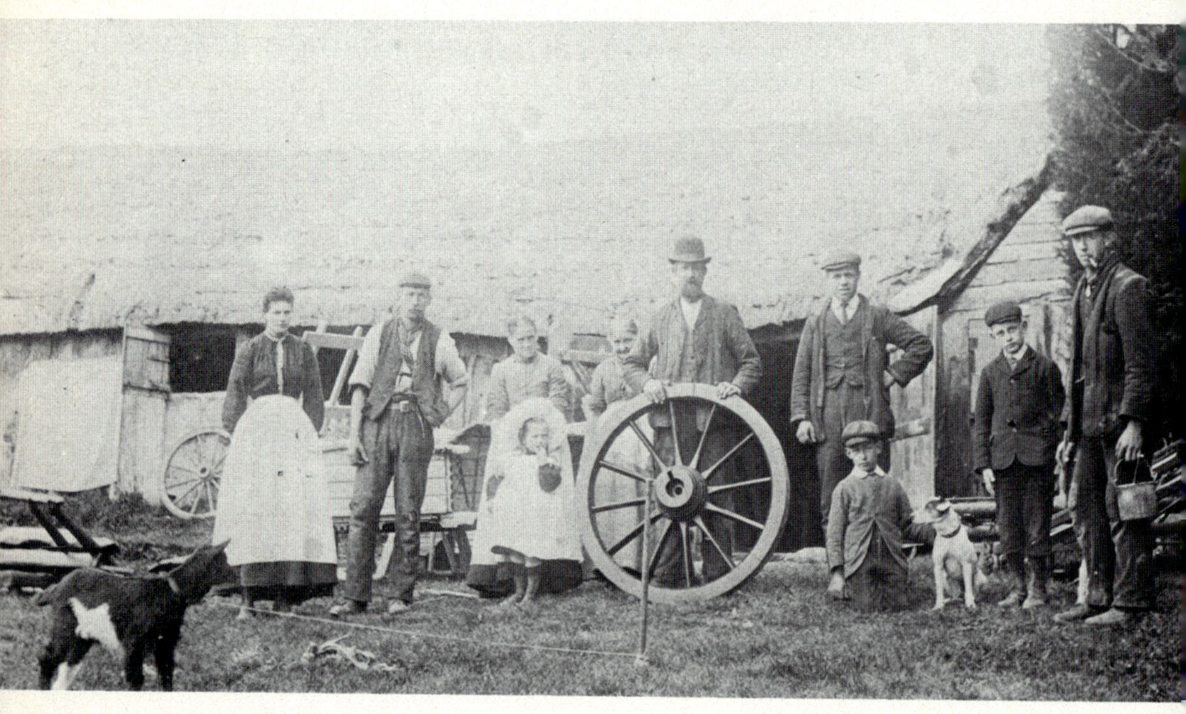

143 (Above) Mr. James Knight with a wheel at his wheelwright's shop at Woodmancote Lane, Brown Candover, c 1900. It was a family business, all but two of the people in this picture being related to Mr. Knight.

144 (Right) c. 1910. Mr. George "Daddy" Richardson (1835–1911). He was a professional tramp in the Shawford, Compton and Twyford area. He slept on Shawford Down except when the weather was very severe, then he slept in a barn. He breakfasted every morning at Compton Manor where he was fed on one condition – that he sang the verse of a hymn.

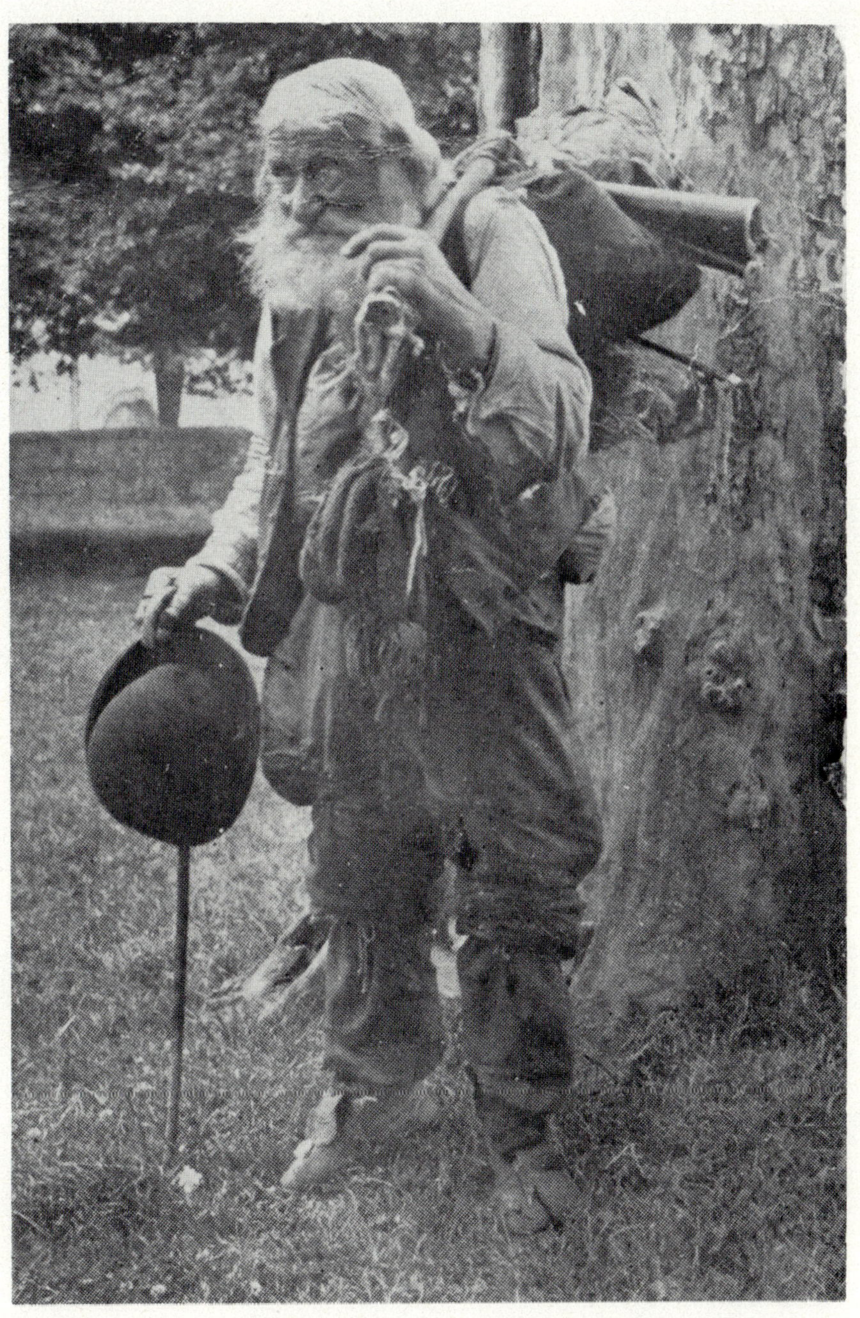

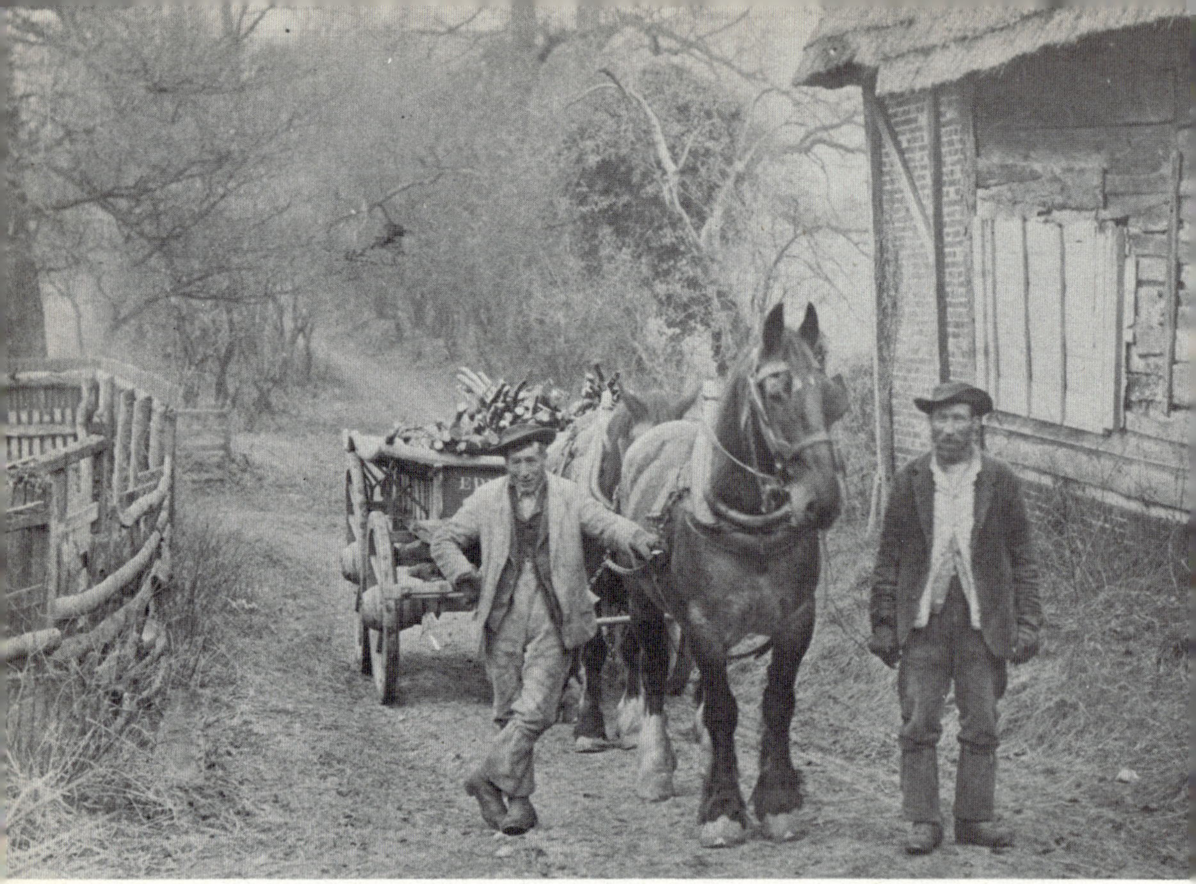

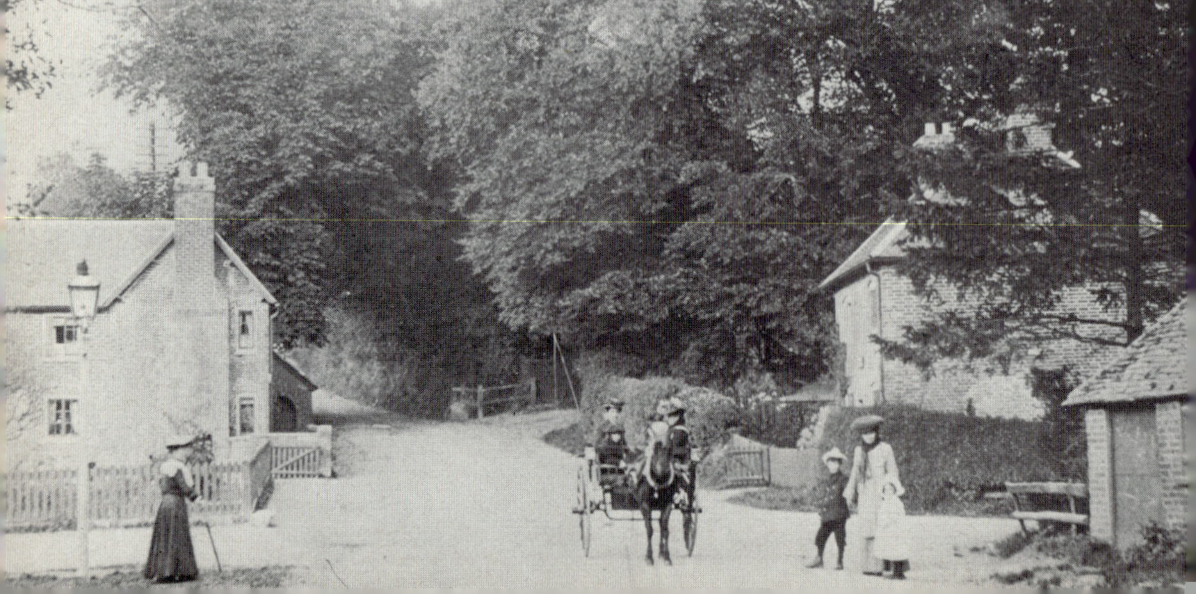

145 (Above left) Carman's Lane, Compton 1902. On the left is Mr. Wallis, head carter for Mr. Edward Lyne at Compton Farm. He is probably carting shaws or stakes for sheep hurdles. On the right is Walter Hickman.

146 (Below left) Compton cross roads looking north towards Winchester. 1908. On the right is the old forge, destroyed by a car in the 1920's.

147 (Below) Compton. 1905. Mr. Charlie Hillier the thatcher pointing spars.

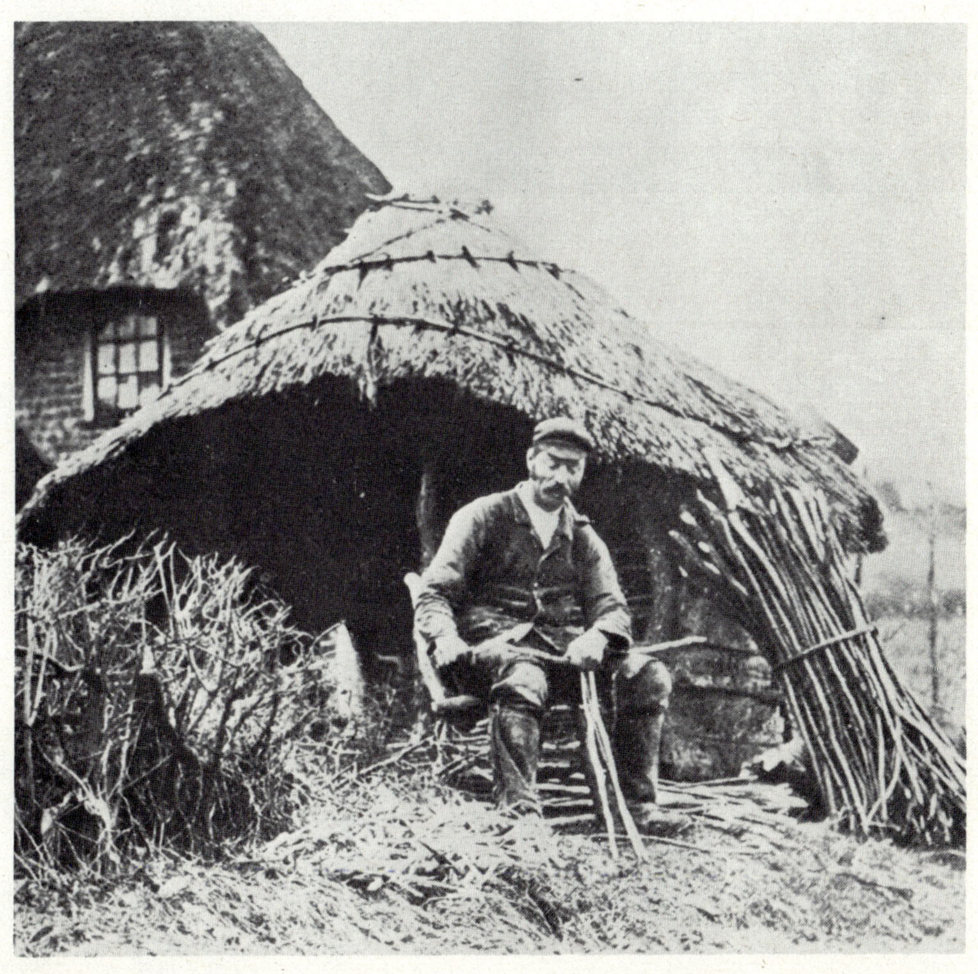

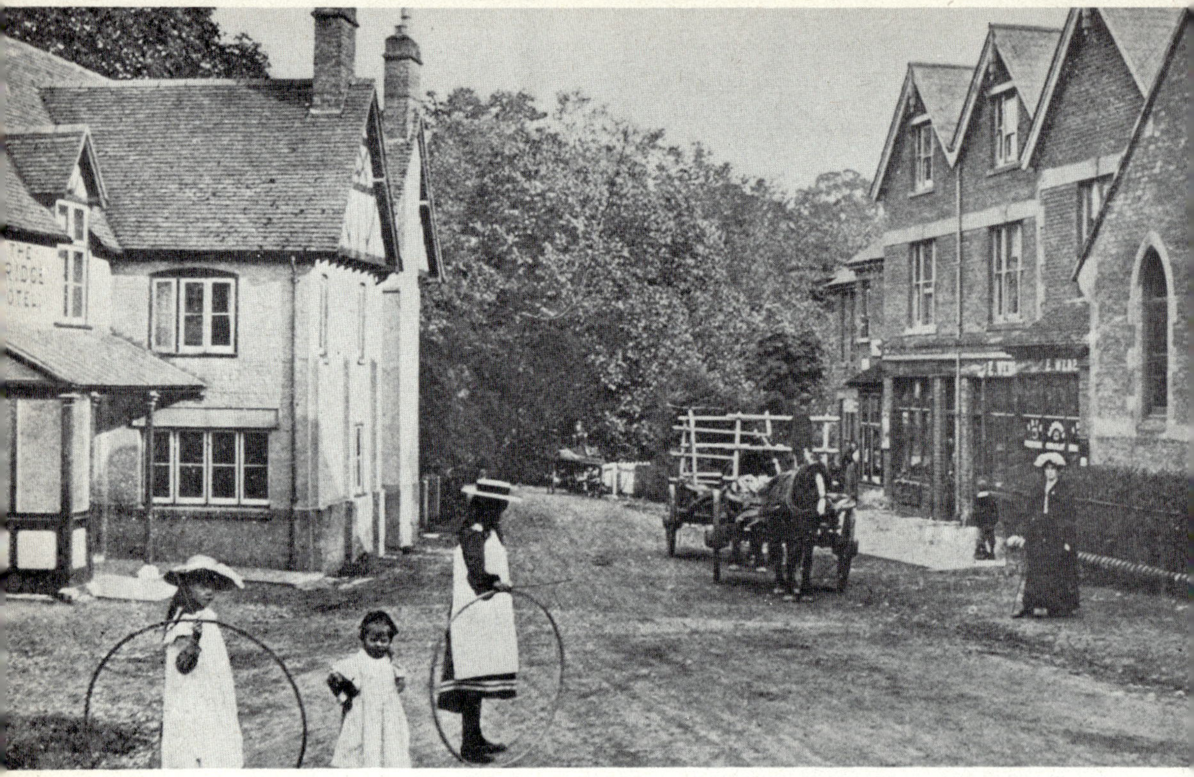

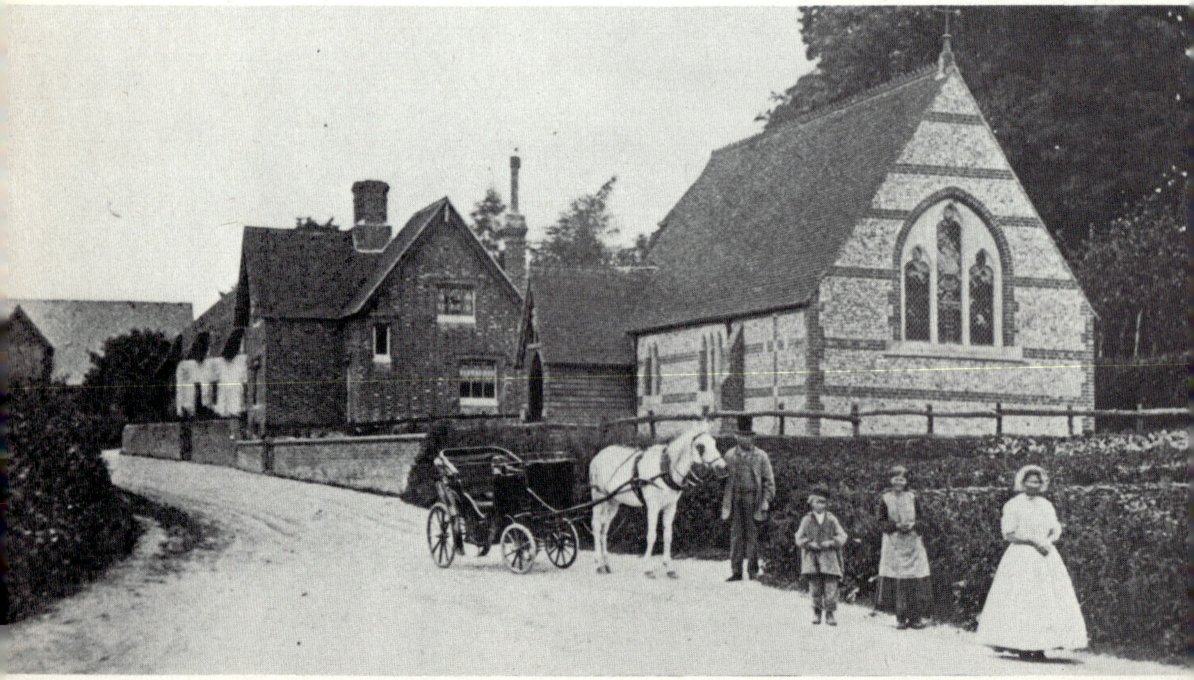

148 (Above left) Shawford. c 1905.

149 (Below left) Pitt School and chapel c 1870.

150 (Below) Charles Alderman, a carter at Newhouse Farm Botley, c 1900. Covered wagons were necessary when corn had to be carried to the mill in wet weather.

151 (Overleaf) Uplands Farm, Botley. c 1898. The man with the stick and the dog is John Alderman the farm bailiff and the little girl on the sack is his daughter Alice. Corn from the rick on the left is being threshed and the grain is being carted away in sacks on the right.

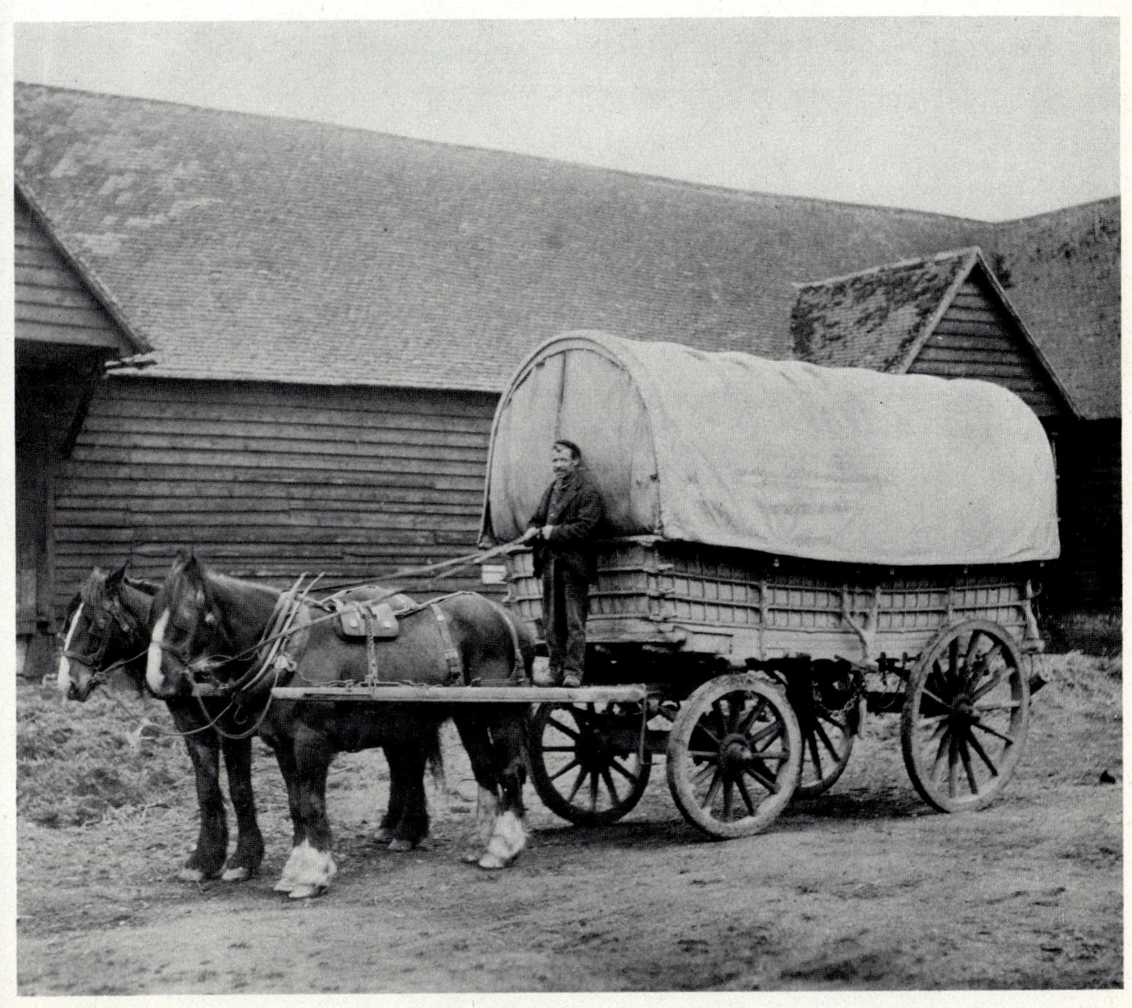

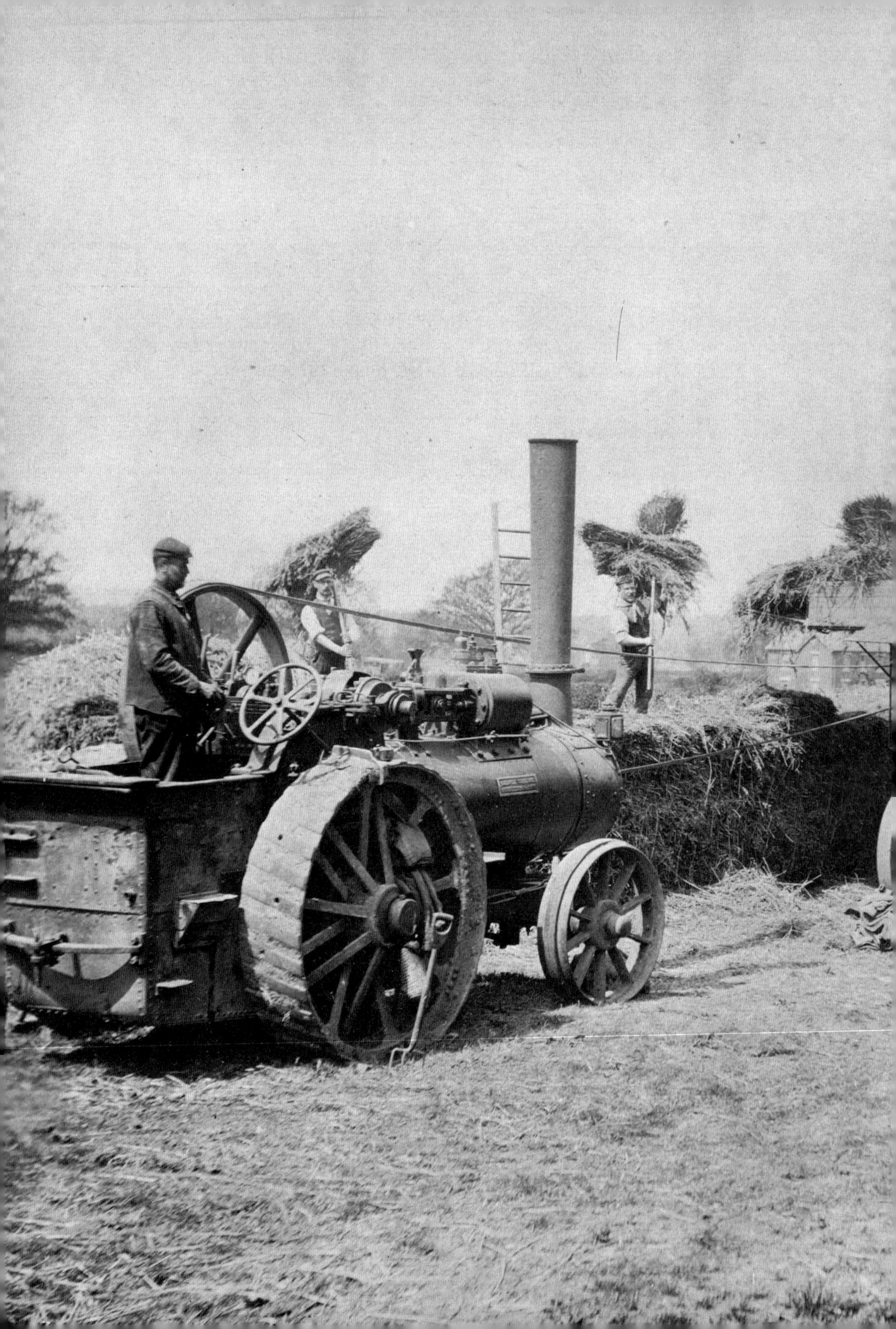

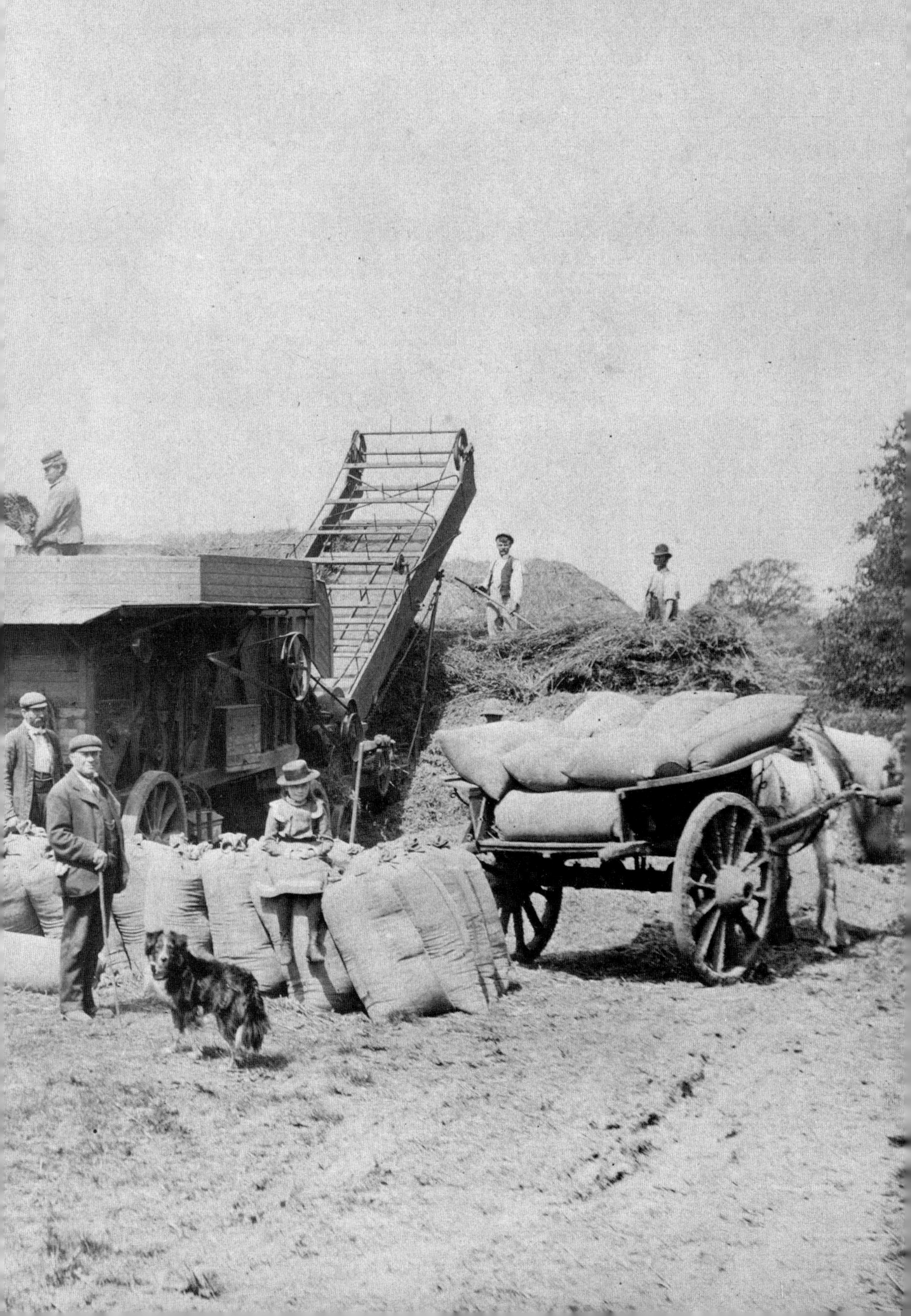